The Fourth Reich

THE FOURTH REICH

Brian Reading

WEIDENFELD AND NICOLSON
London

Weidenfeld & Nicolson
The Orion Publishing Group
Orion House
5 Upper Saint Martin's Lane
London WC2H 9EA

Printed in Great Britain by Butler & Tanner Ltd,
Frome and London.

A catalogue record for this book is available
from the British Library

ISBN 0 297 81453 2

CONTENTS

CONTENTS

CHARTS

TABLES

Preface

I cannot recall what I was doing on 22 November 1963, the day President Kennedy was shot. But I do remember 8 May 1945 vividly. Luneberg Heath means as much to me as Appomattox Court House must once have done to millions of Americans. It was there, fifty years ago, that Germany surrendered. It was VE Day, Victory in Europe, and I was a nine-year-old boarder at Scarborough College, evacuated to Marske Hall in north Yorkshire.

The first lesson of the morning had just begun when a senior boy rushed in shouting, 'The war's over, the war's over!' Work stopped and we all poured outside onto the lawn, banging together anything and everything to make a cacophony of noise. Church bells rang for the first time since 1940. Some could remember the last time they rang – an invasion false alarm. That afternoon we collected wood for a giant bonfire – something which had also been banned during the war. A local shopkeeper unearthed some old fireworks, doubtless his unsold 1939 stock. A feast was miraculously prepared. Dusk fell, the fire was lit, fireworks let off and the air was filled with the smell of woodsmoke and gunpowder.

How different it must have been for a nine-year-old German boy, starving amongst the debris of defeat, smelling the stench of smoking ruins and of unburied dead. Yet most young Germans had more reason to cheer than we had. We were celebrating our escape from falling into the clutches of a dictator; they could celebrate their release from his mailed fist. Some Germans, unfortunately, exchanged one dictator for another; East Germans had to wait a further forty-four years for their freedom.

This book starts with a summary of German history, just as my previous book *Japan: The Coming Collapse* (1992) also led off with an historical section. At the time, this earned me a rebuke from one reviewer, who observed: 'The injection of a superficial chapter covering Japan's history, from the beginning to 1945, does not help.' I think he was wrong. Few people know any history these days. A recent survey showed that three out of five French school-leavers know next-to-nothing of Germany's past; Britain's score was four out of five. Some knowledge of history, even superficial, is essential to an understanding of Germany's and Europe's future – particularly since too many people have not progressed beyond blaming Germans and Germany for two world wars. West Germany's exemplary post-war record, coupled with a longer view of the German people's past, shows that a reassessment is needed. German aggression was a brief aberration in the broad sweep of their history, occurring when power was grasped at the centre. Knowing why and how Bismarck unified Germany shows the way power, atypically, became concentrated in the hands of first a Kaiser and later a Führer. Apart from the Second Reich and Third Reich, Germans have had far more experience of federal government than most other Europeans. They are used to being governed by consensus and compromise, rather than by confrontation. This is what Europe now needs.

The focus of this book is an attempt to place the future of Germany and Europe in its longer historical and broader world setting. I believe that the current debate about how Europe should evolve is too briefly retrospective and too narrowly introspective. Many of the economic circumstances which led to protectionism and rival economic nationalism in the late nineteenth century, setting Germany and Europe on the road to disaster in the first half of the twentieth century, are now being replicated. The 1990s are more like the 1890s than the 1980s.

Europe needs a new vision to justify efforts both to deepen and widen our Community. It can no longer be driven by fears of German hegemony and efforts to prevent it. Great visions are spawned by great dangers and great opportunities. Europe, with its jobs and welfare crisis, faces both. The temptation to put up the shutters against change, hiding as the French would have us within 'Fortress Europe', must be resisted.

Germany must see to it that Europe remains open to trade and competition. Its natural partner in this is Great Britain. The Franco-German post-war marriage of convenience is falling apart. With luck it will end in a middle-aged divorce; 1996 will be a good year to celebrate this.

This book has been written in my spare time. My thanks therefore go to my wife, Candice, who has put up without complaint with her reclusive husband. I must also thank Benjamin Buchan of Weidenfeld & Nicolson for his suggestion that I write this book and for his encouragement at each stage. Missed deadlines were my fault. I must also thank once again Duncan McAra, who copy-edited and corrected the text. My assistant at Lombard Street Research, Jacey Allman, was ever helpful and my colleague, Gabriel Stein, read the whole book, offering many valuable suggestions. Finally I must thank Philip Armstrong, who again produced charts for my book.

BRIAN READING

London, 8 May 1995

Introduction

When Communism collapsed in 1989 and the Berlin wall came tumbling down, the ghosts of Marx, Lenin and Stalin were buried under the rubble. But immediately older ghosts of Bismarck, Kaiser Wilhelm and Hitler returned to haunt Europe. (Margaret Thatcher was credited with one of the first sightings.) The 'master race' had risen again, destined once more to dominate Europe. Thatcher, solidly and outspokenly as always, opposed unification. She said it should not come before the end of the century.

François Mitterrand was equally opposed, but more shrewdly he kept his worst fears to himself. He saw Gorbachev in Kiev in early December 1989 and then visited the East German Prime Minister Hans Modrow in East Berlin, hoping to persuade either or both to delay it. When he failed, he accepted the inevitable, making the most out of it for France. This meant gaining West German support for deepening economic relations within the Community before widening it to include new members. Mitterrand made French participation in the 'Two plus Four' negotiations (the two German states and the four former occupying powers, the United States, the Soviet Union, Britain and France) conditional upon Kohl's support for Maastricht. The French, anti-federalist almost to a man, did not regard European economic and monetary union (EMU) as involving any loss of sovereignty. Their commitment to the *franc fort* (pegging the franc to the Deutschmark at whatever the cost) had already handed responsibility for French monetary policy to the

Bundesbank. The establishment of a European central bank under EMU would, they hoped, get some of it back.

Thatcher's and Mitterand's fears were understandable, widely shared but mistaken. In December 1989 over 40% of French people and just under 50% of British were opposed to German unification. Yet in the five years following the wall's collapse, unification far from enhancing Germany's ascendancy seems to have brought more burdens than benefits. United Germany has remained reluctant to assert a more prominent international role. Hans-Dietrich Genscher, its former and long-serving foreign minister, tried to adopt such a posture over the Balkans and the result was a débâcle. Instead, as the door to Eastern Europe swung wide open, Germany snuggled up closer to France, afraid of going out on its own. Helmut Kohl, as an ardent Euro-federalist, seeks to submerge Germany's identity in a United States of Europe. The ghosts of Germany past still haunt Germans today.

Unified Germany's European hegemony remains a reality. It could not be otherwise. Germany's 80 million population far exceeds any other European country's. One in four Europeans are German. The German economy in the world's fourth largest – behind that of the United States, Japan and China. It is the world's second largest trading nation. Kohl's Germany in 1995 is industrially more powerful relative to its neighbours than was Kaiser Wilhelm's Second Reich in 1914 or Adolf Hitler's Third Reich in 1939. Russia and its former European satellites are considerably weaker than in those fateful pre-war years.

The threat of Communism has gone. Soviet troops have marched out of Berlin. British, American and French troops have also left the city. The United States is withdrawing from Europe. In July 1994, in imitation of John F. Kennedy thirty-one years earlier, President Bill Clinton spoke in Berlin of American support for Germany, pledging American loyalty to Germany 'now and for ever'. Both were deeply concerned and affected by developments in Eastern Europe, particularly in Russia. Indeed, said Clinton, they shared 'a more immediate concern with these interests than our friends in Europe'.[1] The reality behind Clinton's

---

[1] Politicians talking nonsense is nothing new. But this speech was unusually stupid. The French, British, other West Europeans and particularly former East European Soviet satellite countries manifestly have a far more immediate concern with events in Russia than Americans, thousands of miles away across the Atlantic.

words was that the US was pulling out of Europe and handling sole responsibility for Eastern Europe, including Russia, to Germany, the acknowledged *realpolitik* leader of the European Union. Clinton was saying, 'We'll love you and leave you.'

Thus was King Kohl crowned and Germany's Fourth Reich recognised. The symbolism did not end there. By chance the US dollar that day hit a new low against the D-Mark, while the German Constitutional Court gave the go-ahead for the deployment of Bundeswehr troops outside the NATO area on UN peace-keeping missions. In the same week, to add icing to the cake, elements of the 10th Panzers paraded in Paris down the Champs-Elysées on Bastille day.

Before the Germans can lead Europe into the future, they and we must come to terms with their past. Perhaps, after the celebrations of the fiftieth anniversary of VE day are over, memories of Hitler will finally fade. Nazi horrors should not be held against the grandchildren and great-grandchildren of those Germans who perpetrated or failed to prevent them; nor should they hold it against themselves. Germans may not want responsibility for Europe, but like it or not, they nonetheless have it.

German hegemony should be recognised and welcomed. Harping on its military past is unhelpful. The Germans have a right to be proud of their history. The Roman Empire was the original European political, economic and monetary union and, thanks to German support, it worked well for hundreds of years. The Germans inherited the western part when it collapsed. For seven centuries thereafter they protected Western European civilisation from barbarian assault from the east. The Germans repelled rather than launched invasions through most of their history.

The First Reich began when Charlemagne was crowned Holy Roman Emperor on Christmas Day 800. It was a federal state with powers diffused amongst princes and priests. Federalism, and with it the need for consensus and consultation rather that confrontation, has dominated German history. All German disasters have sprung from a concentration of power. The terrible sufferings of the German people in the Middle Ages, through the Reformation, Counter-Reformation and Thirty Years' War (which decimated the population), sprang from the conflict between state and authoritarian Roman Catholic Church. The eight-

3

eenth century was spent recovering from the seventeenth. It ended with Napoleon trampling all over the Germans. Then nineteenth-century German kings and princes clung so tenaciously to their sovereignty and absolutism that German nationalism could prevail only at the expense of liberalism and through Bismarck's 'blood and iron'. Power was consequently concentrated in the hands of Prussian Kaisers making Bismarck's Second Reich (1871–1918) a nation-state like France and Britain and arguably no worse. Unfortunately it arrived on the scene after the British and French had carved out global empires, enabling these countries to exploit less advanced races. The Germans felt ownership of an Empire was an essential attribute of nationhood. They wanted one. As Chancellor Bernhard von Bülow put it in 1897, 'We do not wish to put anyone in the shade, but we demand our place in the sun.' All the rival European nations were to blame for the First World War, even though technically Germany started it. The blot on German history (and there is no intention to minimise or excuse it) was the twelve-year life of Hitler's Third Reich (1933–45). But that has been followed by four-times-twelve years during which West Germany's democratic record has been exemplary.

The collapse of Communism and the spread of liberal free-market systems to developing countries has recreated the single world economy which last existed before 1914. Two-thirds of the world's population has been reintegrated into the market economy. More and bigger countries are industrialising than ever before. Moreover, the later a country industrialises, the faster it does so. The world faces its biggest boom ever. But for Europe this could be bad news. Advancing technology is destroying jobs based more on brawn than on brains. The relocation of industry in developing countries means that semi-literate and innumerate Europeans can no longer expect to enjoy European living standards doing jobs which well-educated workers in developing countries can do better and cheaper.

To date, Europe's job crisis has been caused by the repercussions of technological change. It owes almost nothing to competition from developing countries. The tidal wave of job losses from cheap imports has still to come – and it will. By the time the 1996 Inter-Governmental Conference (IGC) meets to discuss Europe's future, the EU's response to cheap foreign competition will have become a dominant issue. Europe will have to choose how to respond. The jobs crisis will place political pressure on all governments to resist change, protect old jobs and create a 'Fortress Europe'. A great battle will have to be fought between supporters of British free-trade liberalism and French protectionist mercantilism. If the free-traders lose, the result will be regional economic nationalism, coupled with European stagnation and decline. Germany will decide the outcome.

The first section of this book sets today's events in their long-term German historical context. The second section analyses West Germany's (and Europe's) post-war political and economic development. The third section discusses world problems and prospects. A final section suggests how Europe, under German leadership, should best develop.

PART I

GERMANY PAST

CHAPTER I

Romans and Barbarians

Germans have played a dominant and decisive role in European history for over 2000 years. But Germany, as a single nation state, did not exist before 1871 and disappeared again before the mid-twentieth century. The German people, on the other hand, share many and long histories. Their Bronze Age ancestors lived in southern Sweden and northern Germany. By the second century BC, they had fanned out all over Europe, driving Celts out of their way. Different tribes went in different ways. But nonetheless the Alemanni, Angles, Burgundians, Franks, Lombards, Ostrogoths, Saxons, Vandals and Visigoths (to name but a few) spoke roughly the same language and could understand one another. The Germans were a race centuries before they became a nation.

German barbarians first collided with Romans a century before Christ's birth. Until then Rome's expansion was at the expense of civilised people. Thereafter the Rhine and the Danube became the Empire's northern frontiers. Across these rivers, from the Netherlands to Budapest, Romans faced barbarian Germans, whom they could never subdue.

When Rome conquered Carthage and Greece it inherited organised political systems. It therefore allowed self-government in return for tribute. The conquered enjoyed the peace which the Romans brought in their wake and shared the resultant prosperity. The wealthy and worthy became Roman and were assimilated. Advancement was offered to the highest ranks in the Empire, regardless of race – except for the Germans. Barbarians they were and barbarians they remained.

THE ROMAN EMPIRE'S REBIRTH

The European Union is the rebirth of the Western Roman Empire. Maastricht plans political, monetary and economic union. The Roman Empire was all of these. It was a common currency area. It had a single tax system. It was a free trade area, in that goods could move 'freely' (i.e., without restriction) throughout the Empire, although harbour and customs duties were levied to raise revenues. People and capital could also move freely throughout the Empire. Good roads and seaways, safe from pirates, facilitated trade. There was even a welfare system: 'grain dole' was distributed to the unemployed. Ancient Rome had all the trappings of a modern state: a central authority, whose writ ran throughout the lands; justice under a rule of law, which high and low had to obey. *Libertas* meant freedom from arbitrary rule. There was freedom of speech and of belief, except where the state was threatened (e.g., by early Christianity in the pre-Christian Empire). There were elections. Private property was respected. Rome had armies to defend its frontiers and keep order within its boundaries. It had a civil service to administer and a tax system to finance the affairs of state, schools and universities, public buildings and works, and a postal system. Napoleon could not get a message from Brussels to Rome faster than the Emperor Augustus.

There were blemishes: slavery, cruelty, gladiatorial games and barbaric punishment, such as crucifixion. Romans were organised rather than civilised. But they gave West Europe peace, law, order and prosperity. Edward Gibbon, in his *Decline and Fall of the Roman Empire*, eulogised this period: 'If a man were called to fix the period in the history of the world during which the condition of the human race was most happy and prosperous, he would, without hesitation, name that which elapsed from the death of Domitian to the accession of Commodus (96–180).'

THE ECONOMICS OF EXPANSION

Unfortunately the Empire was dynamically unstable. When it ceased to expand it was under pressure to contract. The conquest of civilised and rich countries yielded plunder, land to be settled and a flow of tribute back to Rome. Expansion paid for itself. But by the end of the first century AD the Empire hit limits to further expansion. The Germans on the other side of the Rhine and Danube were disorganised tribes. They were herdsmen not farmers, owning little a conqueror might plunder and with no political organisation to be taken over. Capturing German lands yielded trouble not tribute. Winning wars against civilised people was profitable. Defending lengthy frontiers against impecunious neighbours was costly. When Rome reached the limits of expansion, it became ripe for plunder. In AD 85 German Dacians broke through the Danube frontier from Romania and the Emperor Domitian failed to force them out. He had to pay them to go away. Rome no longer exacted tribute, it paid it. Efforts to economise on defence expenditure was a major factor in Rome's downfall. The attractions of soldiering diminished when the army's main task became holding plundering barbarians at bay. Non-Romans had to be recruited to fill gaps the ranks. Originally they were enlisted individually and served far from their homes, until manpower shortages forced the Emperor Hadrian to recruit whole tribes and leave them protecting the areas where they were recruited. Most were Germans. Thereafter the Roman element in the army continuously declined, while the German element expanded.

Rome's inability to defend all its frontiers ultimately meant that it could defend none of them. The crisis came after Constantine split the Empire in two and the West was left to look after itself. In 406 Vandals fleeing the Huns poured over the frozen Rhine and occupied most of Gaul. In 410 Visigoths invaded Italy and sacked Rome. Despite these setback, some sort of order was restored by conferring federate status on the German tribes and setting them against other Germans. The Visigoths drove the Vandals out of France and into Spain, and settled themselves in south-west France. But the Vandals crossed into North Africa, overwhelmed Carthage in 435 and set up a hostile Vandal Kingdom, with the result that Rome lost its North African grain supplies.

Goths and Vandals were followed by the Huns. Attila attacked Gaul and unexpectedly suffered his one and only defeat in 451 at the hands of a combined Roman and Visigoth army. The Roman army was mostly German, so it was the Germans who saved Western civilisation. Vandals followed Huns in attacking Rome and finally, in 476, the Western Empire was carved up when a German, Odoacer, deposed the last Emperor, Romulus Augustulus, and proclaimed himself King of Italy.

ROME NEVER FELL

The Germans were blamed for destroying the Western Roman Empire. Yet by its end the Roman army was German in all but name. Germans had spent centuries defending Rome, and had also often fought each other in support of rival claimants to the Imperial throne. The claimants were not necessarily Italian. The aristocracy of other conquered races, such as Greeks and Gauls, were adopted into the Roman family and treated the same as its original Italian members. They could become Emperors and many did – but not the Germans, who remained barbarian however cultured and well educated they became. Whether pagan or Christian, they were always treated as unwelcomed lodgers. The family's growing poverty forced it to accept more and more of them. But they remained hated and despised.

Why so? Germans looked different. They were tall and muscular, light-skinned, fair-haired and blue-eyed. One theory has it that they were survivors of Neanderthal man. Blue eyes and blond hair are not found anywhere except among Northern Europeans. But Germans were hardly more different from Italians than Greeks, Gauls, Britons, Jews and Egyptians. The Germans were pagan, but so were most Romans. When they converted to Christianity they became Aryans. So did many Romans. The hatred of Germans *inside* the Empire was probably because Germans *outside* it were constantly raiding, plundering and pillaging. All Germans were thus condemned.

Rome's fall was like a hostile corporate take-over of a grossly mis-managed and over-extended conglomerate. German directors replaced Roman. The unwieldy company was split into manageable subsidiaries. The employees, customers and shareholders of Rome PLC, aided and abetted the take-over and break-up of the company. Rome collapsed when the Germans exercised for themselves the power they really held. But with the Imperial bag and baggage came the Roman Catholic Church. Indeed, as Rome weakened, the Church grew stronger, feeding off the declining Imperial power. The Catholic Church was a major factor sustaining division amongst the German people for centuries.

CHAPTER 2

Charlemagne's First Reich

The Germans inherited the Roman Empire and with it the Roman Catholic Church. Rome's fall left behind a handful of disunited German kingdoms. Instead of integrating into a single state, they disintegrated into a multiplicity of rival feudal kingdoms, princedoms and dukedoms. Germans were not to united for another 1470 years.

The Franks put together a Kingdom to rival old Rome in its extent. Their Merovingian and Carolingian dynasties dominated Europe for four centuries. Clovis I, who founded the Merovingian dynasty, converted to orthodox Christianity and attacked the heretical Aryan Goths. His campaigns were the first of the great religious wars which were to engulf Europe.

CHRISTMAS DAY 800

The Merovingian dynasty collapsed owing to problems of succession. The crown was seized by Pepin II who founded the Carolingian dynasty, famous for its greatest king, Charlemagne. The Carolingians were fine warriors, confronting and beating off all threats. By the end of the eighth century, the Frankish kingdom ran from the Ems to the Pyrenees and included most of the old European Roman Empire. It restored the link between state and Roman Church. But the Frankish kings indisputably held the reins. On Christmas day 800, Charlemagne was crowned Roman Emperor, and so began the First German Reich. (There is still some dispute over whether this was the beginning of the First Reich; a German was not always the Roman Emperor thereafter.) With the coronation of Charlemagne's son, Louis the Pious, the Imperial crown took religious form. The Emperor was God's temporal ruler; the Pope was God's spiritual leader, so they became earthly rivals. But as long as Christendom was under attack from Muslims and pagans, Frankish kings remained superior.

The problem of succession plagued the Franks. By 877 the Empire was divided into three: a west Frankish kingdom (which became France), an east Frankish one (which became Germany) and an Italian kingdom which stretched up through Alsace and Lorraine to the Netherlands and the North Sea. As Emperor, Charlemagne never dropped his lower titles, such as King of the Lombards. After the Frankish kingdom was divided, the Emperor's title continued, taking precedence in theory over lesser kings. Unfortunately this merely added a further layer of uncertainty and contention. Emperors struggled for power against kings and princes; kings and princes struggled against each other. All struggled for or against the Roman Church. Internal strife again left Christian Europe defenceless against external enemies and in the tenth century it was raided, invaded and devastated. The Vikings sailed from Norway and Denmark, raiding coastal towns and up rivers. Saracens attacked from North Africa, and Magyars from Hungary. The authority of the state collapsed and communities were forced back onto self-defence.

DECLINE INTO FEUDALISM

When the state no longer defended its boundaries, freemen everywhere placed themselves under the protection of local lords. Local lords sought protection from greater lords, who in turn paid allegiance to dukes, princes and kings. The populations of France and much of Germany was divided between nobles and serfs, with very few freemen in between. A feudal pyramid replaced the rule of law. Whenever the highest power was in doubt, this pyramid became unstable. Vassal lords could and did switch allegiances. Their feudal armies fought one another. Dukes, defending their lands without the king's help, declared their independence. Kingdoms fragmented. The Imperial crown became an empty title, passing from one Italian magnate to the next on the authority of the Pope (hence the view the first German Reich did not begin with Charlemagne).

The Church's authority waxed as the Emperor's waned. The hierarchical Church was not subject to the same instability. The rule of celibacy was a brilliant device – bishops and abbots could never hold hereditary offices, as none could have legitimate offspring. They merely enjoyed life-tenure of their earthly possessions. Younger sons from wealthy families went into the Church and when, as frequently happened, their elder brothers died without issue, the bishopric or abbey inherited the family fortune. The power of appointment became paramount; whoever held it, king or Pope, controlled the Church.

When the Carolingian dynasty collapsed in 911 a civil war seemed certain. But the Germans faced so much danger from outside that they united instead. Saxon, Frank, Swabian and Bavarian dukes chose a common leader. The principle of Imperial elections was established. In its way, Germany can claim to have invented federalism. The first elected Emperor was a Frank, but the second in 919 was a Saxon, Henry I. He was followed by Otto I who founded the Ottonian dynasty which created the medieval German Empire. Otto demanded the Imperial crown, becoming the first German Holy Roman Emperor in 962 (the other date at which the First Reich could be said to have begun).

Ottonian Emperors firmly controlled the Church. Otto and his successors established and lavishly endowed abbeys and bishoprics. But the lands and properties they gave ostensibly to the Church carried with them feudal obligations to the king. The king thus appointed abbots and bishops, who remained loyal to him rather than to Rome. Churchmen became subservient to the king in the same way as nobles similarly granted land. German Emperors deposed and elected Popes, and the Roman Church resented this. The result was a collision between Church and State, known as the Investiture Crisis, which tore the German Empire to pieces.

In 1073 Pope Gregory VII demanded that he regain the right to appoint (i.e. invest) bishops. The Emperor Henry IV refused. The Empire was plunged into a civil war lasting twenty years. German bishops supported Henry, their benefactor. So did Franconians, Swabians and Bavarians. But Saxon dukes and princes wanted to weaken the Emperor and supported the Pope. Many territorial magnates took no interest in the outcome but used the opportunity to grab Church or Crown lands. The war redistributed wealth and power to the princes and dukes at the expense of the two unifying forces, the Church and the Crown. It ended as a draw with the Concordat of Worms, which left neither Pope nor Emperor in control.

GO EAST, YOUNG MAN

The Ottonian dynasty was succeeded by the Hohenstaufens. Confrontation with the papacy continued and the Empire expanded. But as it did so, the Emperor's power in south Germany declined, while in the north and east it virtually ceased. Dukes, princes and abbots pushed Germany's frontiers into Brandenburg, over the Oder and down into Silesia, enlarging their own lands at the expense of Slavs. These lands were sparsely populated, mainly of forests and swamps, which nobody had previously wanted. But times were changing. The German population was rapidly expanding. Reclaimable agricultural land in the west had become scarce. With improved technology, the Germans were successful at draining swamps and clearing forests. They no longer raided for loot, but invaded for living room. The attractions of going east were considerable. The Teutonic Knights, a military-religious order founded in the 1190s, who had fought in the crusades and then in the civil war, could carve out their own domains. Serfs could obtain their freedom. People from all over the Empire flocked east. The German centre of gravity shifted north-east, culminating in the rise of Prussia.

When the Hohenstaufen dynasty ended with the death of Frederick II in 1250, a quarter of a century of disorder and confusion followed, until the process of choosing a new Emperor was regularised. Thereafter he was elected by three ecclesiastical and four lay princes (the Archbishops of Mainz, Cologne and Trier, the Count Palatine of the Rhine, the King of Bohemia, the Margrave of Brandenburg and the Duke of Saxony). Elections enhanced the political and economic powers of the Church and nobility against those of the Crown. Rival claimants had to bribe the Electors with gifts and favours, draining Imperial resources while augmenting the princes'. Once in office, Emperors could rebuild their wealth and power. The Electors therefore chose minor figures. In 1272 they elected Rudolf of Habsburg, a Swabian count whom they thought too weak to reclaim stolen Crown lands. They were wrong. Rudolf founded the Habsburg dynasty which lasted until 1918.

Elections often caused trouble. They were won by majority vote and the results were frequently disputed. Civil wars followed until Charles IV (elected 1355) devised a new constitution. Known as the 'golden bull' it took away so much of the Emperor's powers over the princes, that they no longer minded who got the job. The territories of the secular Electors were declared indivisible and to be passed down only through eldest sons. Princes could build castles, issue coins, levy tolls, dispense justice without appeal to any higher authority. They kept the peace within their own lands. Most trappings of central administration disappeared. Princes, however, could still be called upon to supply troops for defence of the Reich.

The clash between Church and State ensured a continued different development amongst the German races. The German Emperor lost control of the Church and then lost control of the princes with the golden bull. The Holy Roman Empire, as often observed, was thereafter no longer Holy, Roman or an Empire. The Imperial title was largely an empty one, although its holders remained powerful territorial princes in their own right. Germany was thus fatally partitioned into small and relatively unimportant states.

ELSEWHERE NATION STATES WERE EMERGING

In Spain, England and France, the foundations of modern nation states were laid. The Norman Conquest in 1066 established the English crown over its most powerful subjects. That power was frequently challenged, most notably by the barons against King John leading to the Magna Charta and again during Cromwell's Commonwealth. The English monarch gradually lost real power and became merely a figure-head. But, civil wars apart, there remained a single central authority in control of the nation. Power was wrested from the King by Parliament and later from the Lords by the Commons. But this led to greater integration, not disintegration. England evolved immensely slowly but remarkably peacefully into a democracy, whose unity was never seriously questioned. France similarly began emerging as a modern nation state in the thirteenth century, although it took longer before it became unified and its boundaries settled. By the fifteenth century both countries were recognisable modern nation states.

The motley collection of princedoms that comprised the Holy Roman Empire had the makings of a federal state, in which sovereignty is shared by different levels of government. This federal streak remains strong in the German make-up. The disasters of the Second and Third Reich resulted when control passed into an individual's hands, with no checks or balances on the use of power. Germans are better able to understand the give-and-take required to operate a federal European Union. Indeed it can be argued that the West Germans were willing to give too much to the French of the benefit of building a united Europe. United Germans should be more eager to go their own way.

CHAPTER 3

The Disunited States of Germany

Divided they fell. The Germans, who for seven centuries had been the most powerful of European races, were subsequently kicked around by almost every other race for the following five centuries. Their borders contracted. From the middle of the thirteenth century Germany was encircled by other powers eager to encroach. The princes rarely united to resist. The Holy Roman crown passed into, and then mostly remained in, the hands of the Habsburgs who had little interest in Germany *per se.* They concentrated on their own aggrandisement. They managed, mainly by astute marriage, to obtain far-flung empires, in Spain, on the Rhine and in Italy. An Austrian Empire was in the making which included an increasing number of non-Germanic subjects within its borders. It was not a unified empire on British or French lines. Its lands were dispersed geographically and administratively. By the mid-sixteenth century the Habsburgs controlled Austria and the Tyrol, Bohemia and Hungary, Spain, the Netherlands, Sicily, and parts of northern Italy. So varied were their possessions that the Habsburgs behaved more like landlords than rulers.

While the Habsburgs acquired a non-German empire, other German lands were lost. To the north, Poland recovered Prussia from the Teutonic Knights. In the centre, Bohemia broke away. The Netherlands and Switzerland became detached. France encroached upon the Rhinelands. This process of attrition left many Germanic people subject to foreign powers. German weakness produced a mingling of races inside and outside the old Empire.

WRECKED BY THE REFORMATION

The Reformation proved a setback to German reunification. It was originally a movement to reform the Catholic Church from within, rather than to supplant it with another Christian denomination. In the fifteenth century, the Pope and the Curia's powers were at their zenith. The autocratic Church imposed its dogma remorselessly throughout Christendom. The ground swell of concern was no longer confined to the status and behaviour of the Church, its doctrine and dogma were now being questioned. The charge was laid, the fuse set, all it needed was a spark to explode it. That spark required flint to strike steel.

The flint was Martin Luther, an Augustinian monk in the small German town of Wittenberg on the Elbe. The steel was new technology. The Catholic Church was always in financial crisis and employed many dubious means of raising funds. One was to sell indulgences, papal certificates promising the buyer remission of heavenly punishment from earthly sins. A Dominican salesman arrived in Wittenberg in 1517 and did a good trade. The sinful were plentiful. Luther was enraged. He believed such practices should be outlawed by the Church and, as was the custom, pinned a protest (from which the name Protestant comes) to the local church door. A copy was sent to the Archbishop of Mainz and thence to Rome. Rome banned him from preaching on this theme. That would have been the end of the matter, except for new technology.

The printing press had been invented, revolutionising communications. Luther's protest was translated into German, printed and widely circulated. News of it spread before he could be gagged. What was originally a protest against certain Church malpractices was made worse by efforts to suppress it. Encouraged by his fame and supported by his local prince, Frederick, Duke of Saxony, Luther challenged the Church's right to dictate dogma, claiming that the individual could save himself by personal faith. The Bible was the authority on which belief was to be based and not the categorical statements of the Church. Luther's translation into German of the New Testament was printed and circulated, thus providing literate Germans access to it. The Reformation became a Protestant revolution. In his *History of Religion and Philosophy in Germany*, Heinrich Heine was moved to assert that Luther was 'not merely the greatest but also the most German man in our history, so that in his character all the virtues and failings of the German were united in the most magnificent way'. The revolution spread like wildfire. Luther's religion appealed to many princes. Although he encouraged spiritual dissent from Rome, Luther demanded absolute obedience to secular authority on earth. German princes were delighted to establish Lutheran churches, particularly when they could lay their hands on Catholic wealth.

The Habsburgs, as Holy Roman Emperors, kept all their lands Catholic. Elsewhere the Catholic Church was largely ousted. By 1570 seven out of ten people in the Holy Roman Empire were Protestant. If a triangle is drawn with corners at Emden at the mouth of the Ems, Danzig on the Baltic and Nuremberg, the area enclosed was virtually all Protestant. Racial differences were now exacerbated by religious differences. What remained of German unity under the Holy Roman Emperor was destroyed and European Christendom was irredeemably split.

DESTROYED BY THIRTY YEARS OF WAR

The Reformation was met by the Counter-Reformation, a confrontation culminating in the disastrous Thirty Years' War which raged throughout Central Europe from 1618 to 1648. The war was fought over German lands, which were utterly devastated. No general succeeded in controlling his army before or after battles. Both sides were as bad. Cities, towns, villages were plundered and burnt not once, but time and again. The countryside was laid waste. The population was decimated. When, in 1631, a Habsburg army stormed Magdeburg on the Elbe 25,000 of its 30,000 population perished, many of the survivors being carried off as concubines or slaves. Berlin lost half and Chemnitz 80% of its population during the war. Bohemia's 3 million population dropped to 780,000, its 35,000 villages were reduced to 5000. Württemberg and the Palatinate lost between 80% and 90% of their population. The German population dropped from 21 million to 13 million. Devastation and deaths were on a vastly greater scale and extended over a more protracted period than in either of Germany's twentieth-century wars.

The Peace of Westphalia, which ended the war, sealed disunited Germany's fate. The combatants carved slices from German territories for themselves. Swedes, Danes and Dutch took every river mouth and the great city ports, thus depriving Germans of access to the sea. The Treaty confirmed the sovereignty of Germany's 300 states, legitimising and perpetuating its divisions. Each petty princedom and little town had a right under international law to exist and go its own way for ever. Secular princes could decide which religion their subjects were to follow. Ecclesiastic princes who had broken from Rome were allowed to remain Lutheran. The Thirty Years' War left most of northern Germany Lutheran, and most of the south Catholic.

The war was followed by half a century of relative peace in Central Europe. Germany slowly began to recover, although even a century later the damage was still discernible. The end of this respite coincided with the end of the seventeenth century. Throughout the eighteenth century, Europe was ravaged by a succession of dynastic and territorial conflicts.

THE RISE OF THE HOHENZOLLERNS

The German story during the eighteenth century is the rise of Prussia and the Hohenzollern dynasty and its rivalry with Austria and the Habsburgs. At the start of the century, Hohenzollern possessions were small and scattered. The main one was Brandenburg. Prussia, outside the Reich, was a Polish fiefdom. There were other territories on the Rhine and elsewhere, but none large. During the century, Prussia seized every opportunity to expand and join its lands. It acquired the southern half of west Pomerania from Sweden by joining in the Great Northern War after Russian victories had put its conclusion beyond doubt. Frederick the Great seized Silesia during the War of Austrian Succession, while Maria Theresa was busy fighting off Bavarian and French armies. But the biggest gains came when Poland was dismantled and its component parts shared out between Russia, Prussia and Austria between 1772 and 1795. The rape of Poland, which gave Prussia a bigger Slavic population than its Germanic one, was, however, rapidly overshadowed by the Napoleonic War.

The French Revolution was greeted at first with enthusiasm by ordinary Germans, but their princes were aghast. They were absolute despots of the kind overthrown by the French Republic. Three times German states joined coalitions against France and three times they were totally defeated. By 1806 Napoleon occupied or controlled all of Germany.

Napoleon brought political reorganisation and efficient civil administration in place of the rule of arbitrary despots and their functionaries. The rule of law finally returned to Germany after centuries of the rule of men. Municipalities obtained a say in their own affairs. Liberalisation created conditions for economic growth. Napoleon redrew the map of Germany, reducing the country's 300 territorial divisions to thirty-nine. He organised all bar Austria and Prussia into a Confederation of the Rhine, which seceded from the Holy Roman Empire. The Empire was disbanded, Habsburgs dropped the Imperial title and the First Reich came to an end.

The period reviewed in this chapter extended over five centuries, during which the concept of a united German nation-state reached its lowest ebb. What mark did German disunion leave behind it? The Reformation gave north Germany a Reformed Church, one that aligned itself with the absolute temporal power of the state, encouraging obedience to authority. The Thirty Years' War gave rise to an immense desire for stability and safety, reinforcing discipline to authority. Personal freedom was a luxury Germans could hardly afford. Strong government was essential, the citizens' only protection. Officials, however petty, must be obeyed, particularly when they were in uniform. The eighteenth-century wars, ending in defeat and occupation, heightened the German sense of racial insecurity so that, in consequence, they became profoundly conservative. Their political system stagnated, halting progress towards democracy.

Consider the contrast with England. In the seventeenth century, the English did not take part in the Thirty Years' War. They had their own troubles, the Civil War between King and Parliament starting in 1642, leading to Cromwell's Commonwealth which lasted until 1660. But this marked a milestone, not a millstone, on the road to democracy and the only one stained with blood. United with Scotland in 1707, Britain became a powerful nation state. Its trade expanded mightily, it gained great colonies in India and America and made massive strides economically, industrially and intellectually.

The Germans, by contrast, remained economically backward.

Huddled in their tiny towns and villages, in their tiny states and prin-
cipalities, cut off from the sea, they vegetated. They were not all bucolic
beer-swilling country bumpkins, but this national caricature is not
without substance. Their petty despotic rulers built for themselves fine
palaces from which their bloated bureaucracies misruled. What wealth
was created was devoted to the worthless end of inflating their own
dignity.

Germans, who had contributed so much to Europe in the 700 years
following Rome's collapse, contributed far less of value in the following
500 barren years. They created no Empires. They were responsible for
no great economic, financial or industrial breakthroughs. Germany will
always be remembered for Martin Luther. It had its philosophers, writers,
composers. There were oases in the great arid desert. The Germans
missed out on most of the progress other nations were making. Napoleon
dragged France screaming and kicking into modern world. He might
have done the same for Germany, had he not attacked Russia first. The
Germans entered the nineteenth century totally unprepared to deal with
the social and economic problems which the Industrial Revolution
brought in its train.

CHAPTER 4

The Rise of the Second Reich

After Napoleon's defeat at Waterloo in 1815, thanks to the Prussian Army, a great wave of patriotic fervour swept through the German people. Liberals hoped victory would lead to the creation of a national German state. German national liberalism must be understood in its early nineteenth-century context. Nationalists wanted Europe's frontiers sorted out along racial lines. In 1815 England and France were racially homogeneous nation states. Elsewhere state boundaries were drawn regardless of race (some still are, e.g. Belgium). Liberals challenged the divine right of kings, seeking instead constitutional monarchies, in which the people would be sovereign. Many thought that the German people, on being given democracy, would immediately unite as one nation. Instead the nineteenth-century struggle was between nationalism and liberalism, which liberalism lost. Squabbling princes were forcibly replaced by a single capricious, unstable, autocratic and arrogant monarch, the Prussian Kaiser. As a result, Germany developed violently and aggressively.

The liberals of 1815 were speedily disappointed. The Congress of Vienna was reactionary. Europe's monarchs fought France to restore old autocracies, not to create new democracies. They could not put back the clocks completely, leaving Napoleon's larger territorial divisions intact. But they did not put the clocks forward either. The Congress created a German Confederation including all the new states, as well as the parts of Prussia and Austria which had been in the old Empire. A Federal Council or Diet was established, but it represented sovereigns not their subjects. Its purpose was to protect rulers' rights and to organise mutual defence. The Federal Council saw no need to meddle in the domestic affairs of individual states. Kings and princes happily resumed their autocratic rule. There was nothing liberal about the new German Confederation.

German nationalism made mixed progress. Prussia, Austria and Russia stripped France of its conquests and shared them amongst themselves. They also horse-traded territories with one another. Prussia gave its Polish possessions to Russia in exchange for parts of Saxony and Rhineland-Westphalia. It lost Slavs and gained German subjects. (It also obtained the Ruhr coalfields, which turned out to be massively valuable.) Prussia became more German. Austria exchanged the Netherlands for Venice and areas on the Adriatic. It became less German. These frontier changes strengthened Prussia and strained Austria; they meant that a greater German state – one including Austrian and Habsburg possessions – would be so diluted by Slavs, Magyars, Italians and other non-Germanic races that most nationalists would not want it. A lesser German state – one which excluded Austria – would be racially purer but leave many Germans outside. It would be dominated by Prussia. The Prussian Hohenzollerns would not accept junior status in a large German state. The Austrians would not accept Prussian dominance of a small German state. No lesser prince wanted the Hohenzollerns to lord it over them. So German disunion remained an established European order.[1] It was perpetuated by the Congress.

When the Congress restored the old monarchies, it condemned Europe to bloodshed. As long as Hohenzollerns, Habsburgs and other kings and princes refused voluntarily to surrender absolute power, Germany could never be united peacefully. But German nationalism was too potent to be denied. It was bound to triumph in the end through Bismarck's 'blood and iron'. Either princes and kings would be over-thrown by popular revolutions creating a democratic Germany, or a superior king would unite Germany by conquest, creating an autocratic one.

---

[1] Even the Prussian delegate to the Congress of Vienna, Wilhelm von Humboldt, warned against unification. Percipiently he observed, 'No one could prevent Germany, as Germany, from becoming an aggressive state.' There are those who believe this to this day.

1848

Restoration Europe nonetheless enjoyed three decades of relative peace, not shattered until 1848. Industrial depression (the first affecting large numbers) was combined with failed harvests (the last that mattered, because of growing imports from all over the world) causing popular revolutions to sweep Europe. In France, King Louis Philippe was forced to abdicate and Louis Napoleon Bonaparte was elected President of a new French Republic. In Austria, Prince Clemens von Metternich fled Vienna and the imbecilic Emperor Ferdinand abdicated in favour of his nephew, Franz Josef. Rebellions occurred in Italy, Bohemia, Hungary, Denmark and Schleswig-Holstein. All German states were engulfed in uprisings. If the revolutionaries had succeeded in uniting Germany in 1848, Austria and France would have been too busy with their own problems to do anything about it. A democratic German nation state could have emerged.

The 1848 revolution failed because the German revolutionaries were intellectuals and bourgeoisie – and property-owners – who had no desire to overthrow the princes and kings. Many were bureaucrats, officials or university teachers in public employment, who feared a worker's revolution and were firm supporters of authority, law and order. They naïvely expected the princes to agree to the formation of a federal German state. When such an arrangement was not forthcoming, an all-German parliament, set up in Frankfurt, had no way of forcing the issue. It never obtained control over armies or any of the levers of power. When the princes got over the shock of the revolution, they used force to restore order. King Friedrich Wilhelm, however, gave Prussia a Constitution, albeit a loaded one; it had a directly elected lower house, the Landtag, but like the European Parliament it could not initiate legislation.

The failure of the 1848 revolution meant the baton of nationalism passed from liberal idealists to reactionary realists. Prussian Junkers took up the cause. They pursued nationalism at the expense of individual liberty. German unification, accomplished by wars, became synonymous with Prussian aggrandisement.

OTTO VON BISMARCK

The story of Germany now becomes that of Otto von Bismarck, the Junker appointed Minister-President of Prussia in 1862 and who resigned as Chancellor of the Second Reich twenty-eight years later in 1890. Bismarck was a gluttonous, corpulent, squeaky-voiced, neurotic, egotistical, brilliantly ruthless opportunist – a dedicated German nationalist megalomaniac, who never obtained absolute power. He remained subject to the King, the Landtag and the German Reichstag which followed it, and lacked authority over the army. Bismarck's success lay in playing off his opponents against each other. In this he was in no way inhibited by principles. He switched freely from being a reactionary monarchist to a liberal democrat, from free trader to protectionist, from anti-Austrian pro-French to pro-Austrian anti-French, as the occasion demanded. He understood power, and, aware of his own limitations, knew how to obtain it and use it. He did not hesitate to apply bribery, corruption and intimidation to members of the Landtag who opposed him. With the King he threw tantrums, cried, threatened to resign and even to commit suicide by hurling himself from an upstairs window.

Bismarck's appointment arose out of a row between King Wilhelm I and the Landtag. Wilhelm, who succeeded his brother Frederick Wilhelm in 1861, had a military background and sought to reform and strengthen the army. The Landtag was opposed to such expansion and refused to approve the expenditure. A constitutional crisis ensued which Bismarck was appointed to resolve. He simply ignored the Landtag, borrowed the money and went ahead with the reforms. The authority of the King as Commander-in-Chief was reasserted and with it that of the army and its Junker officer class.

THE WAR THAT DIVIDED GERMANY

When Bismarck disregarded the Landtag and the Constitution, Prussia became the enemy of democracy. From 1862 to 1866 Bismarck ruled without the Landtag. In 1866 he provoked the Austro-Prussian War, in effect a German civil war. Saxony, Hanover and Hesse-Cassel in the north and centre of the Confederation sided with Austria. So did several southern states. A long war was expected and the betting in Paris was four-to-one on an Austrian victory. Napoleon III reckoned France could sit on the fence until the rival German states exhausted one another. He then planned to step in and dictate a peace profitable to France. Instead, Prussia's reorganised armies decisively defeated the Austrian at the Battle of Sadowa. Bismarck offered Austria lenient peace terms and the war was over within seven weeks.

Far from uniting Germany, the Austro-Prussian War divided it. However loose the confederal relationship had been, Germans from the Baltic to the Austrian Tyrol had been linked together since the days of the Holy Roman Empire. Now northern and southern Germans (i.e. Austrians) were divided. They would only be united again briefly, from 1938 to 1945, in Hitler's Third Reich. Bismarck's foreign success broke the domestic deadlock. The Prussian Landtag absolved the Government of its constitutional improprieties. National liberals were torn in two. Bismarck's success had realised their nationalist aspirations by denying their liberal ones. When the arch-reactionary offered a liberal constitution for his new North German Confederation, most liberals swallowed it and became his supporters.

THE WAR THAT DESTROYED FRANCE

Bismarck did not plan the Franco-Prussian War of 1870–1. French hubris caused it. But when Bismarck saw the chance, he provoked hostilities and France suffered accordingly. The war was won by the Battle of Sedan, where the German army was brilliantly successful, thanks to Krupp's breech-loading guns. Victory over France cleared the way for Bismarck to unite Germans in a lesser German state. He threatened and bullied south German states into joining a new German Empire, or Second Reich, with Kaiser Wilhelm I its Emperor. Bismarck, as Prussian Minister-President, became the Imperial Chancellor. The German tribes, Austria excluded, were finally unified into a single nation state, but by Prussian conquest and against the wishes of many Germans.

The peace terms Prussia dictated to France were deliberately designed to cripple the country. Germany took back Alsace-Lorraine, industrially important for its iron and coal. Bismarck imposed a 5 billion gold franc indemnity, reverting to the old Roman custom that defeated nations paid for wars. The indemnity was around one-fifth of the French 1869

GDP. This may seem harsh, but it was calculated to be the same, on a per capita basis, as the indemnity imposed on Prussia by Napoleon I in 1807.

Prussia's victories over Austria in 1866 and France in 1870 were not simply the result of Bismarck's political or the elder Von Moltke's military brilliance. They were made possible by the rapid increase in Prussia's economic strength during the half-century following the Congress of Vienna. This altered the balance of power which had kept Germany disunited. As the nineteenth century progressed, military strength depended increasingly on industrial power. In its western acquisitions, Prussia obtained the Ruhr coal-fields, the basis upon which it rapidly industrialised. Even in 1809 the Ruhr, with its mines, steam engines and factories, had been likened to a little England. After 1815 the tempo of the Industrial Revolution greatly increased. Prussian policy positively encouraged rapid industrialisation. Old restrictions on economic activity were swept away – notably the Guild system which protected the skilled hand-workers. Trade within Prussia was freed from customs barriers. A customs union, Zollverein, established in 1819 with the tiny state of Schwarzburg-Sonderhausen, spread rapidly after 1834 to become an all-German customs union (but excluding Austria).

PRUSSIA'S GROWING INDUSTRIAL PROWESS

This history has finally reached the point at which some statistical evidence can be cited. Table 4.1 gives population estimates for the period from the Napoleonic Wars to the Franco-Prussian War. Between the defeats of Napoleons I and III, Prussia's population rose faster than any other nation's. On 1815 boundaries it almost doubled, while with territories annexed from Denmark in 1864 and after the Austro-Prussian War in 1866, Prussia's population rose almost two-and-a-half fold. From two-fifths of the German population it increased to five-eighths. The population of England, Wales and Scotland grew almost as fast as Prussia's. Infant mortality in Prussia was between two and three times the rate experienced in Britain. But Ireland's population, which climbed from 6.5 million in 1817 to 8.3 million by the mid 1840s collapsed to 5.5 million by 1869. French population growth was particularly slow, and the German population overtook the French between the two wars. Russia was and remained a giant.

Table 4.1 Population Changes, 1817–69 (millions)

	1817	1869	% change	% pa
Prussia	10.3	19.3*	86	1.3
		24.7†	40	1.6
Germany**	25.0	40.5	62	0.9
France	29.7	38.4	29	0.5
Britain	19.8	31.0	57	0.9
Britain ex Ireland	*13.4*	*25.5*	*91*	*1.2*
Russia	46.6	83.4	79	1.1

* On 1815 boundaries to 1864 before Prussia annexed Schleswig and Holstein from Denmark.
† On 1871 boundaries in 1871 after all annexations.
** 1913 boundaries.
The main source for this and the following tables is B. R. Mitchell, *International Historical Statistics: Europe 1750 to 1988.*

Despite the move from country to city, Prussia remained largely rural before the Franco-Prussian War. Its cities were far smaller than British cities (England's population at 22 million in 1869 was only slightly more than Prussia's). Prussian cities grew faster, but no faster than equally small British cities such as Bradford. All major Prussian cities were smaller in 1870 than the equivalent British cities had been in 1800. Dusseldorf, for example, was Germany's third largest city in 1870 with a population of 69,000. In 1800 London, Manchester, Liverpool, Glasgow and Birmingham were all larger, and Bristol and Leeds were not far behind.

Table 4.2 compares production and related data for Germany based on its 1913 boundaries (more or less those established in 1871) with those for France and Britain. No separate figures are available for Prussia. But much of German industrialisation took place in Prussia (notably in the Ruhr and Berlin). The figures are the earliest available after the end of the Napoleonic Wars in 1815 and for 1869, the eve of the Franco-Prussian War.

Britain was the only seriously industrialised country at the end of the Napoleonic Wars. German industry, starting from virtually nowhere in

Table 4.2 Production and Communications before 1869

	Germany	France	Britain
Coal output (m. tons)			
1817	1	1	22
1869	34	13	115
Pig iron (m. tons)			
1823	85	198	450
1869	1313	1381	5533
Crude steel (m. tons)			
1870	84	126	334
Beer (000 hl.)			
1818	10,200	na	1215
1869	23,900	7528	na
1881	*39,109*	*8625*	*44,955*
Cotton spindles (000s)			
1834	626	2500	10,000
1867	2000	6800	34,215
Merchant ships			
1815:			
Thousand tons	na	na	2485
1850:			
Sailing	3655	14,229	24,797
Steam	22	126	1187
1869:			
Sailing	4876	15,324	24,187
Steam	126	454	2972
Railway lines open (km)			
1825	0	0	43
1850	5856	2915	9797
1869	17,215	16,465	19,837*
% of 1913 network	27.1	40.4	60.8

* 1867.

1815, expanded faster than British to 1869, but on the eve of the Franco-Prussian War Britain was still producing about four times as much coal, iron ore, pig iron and steel. Britain took a massive lead in the communications revolution during the early nineteenth century. Its rail network was more than half completed by 1869. The Germans and French had by then built almost as many kilometres of track, but given the greater geographical size of both countries relative to Britain, their rail systems were much further from completion. Germany's went on to expand fourfold by 1913. At sea no continental country could compete with Britain's merchant fleet.

To sum up: by 1869 Germany was economically bigger than France, although Prussia may have been more or less the same size. Their populations were nearly the same. Germany produced marginally more coal, iron and steel (vastly more beer but much less wine) and had a smaller textile industry. Neither had much of a merchant fleet, but that hardly mattered in a competition between continental powers. Both had already constructed extensive rail systems. Neither could begin to compare with Great Britain. Rough estimates of gross domestic product are available for all three countries back to 1850 (French and British figures go back even further). In that year German GDP was equivalent to US $44 bn (at 1991 prices), compared with $33 bn for France and $60 bn for Britain. Thus German GDP was three-quarters of the British level, while French GDP was three-quarters of Germany's. All three countries grew at roughly the same rate between 1850 and 1869, with GDPs in that year of $66 bn, $49 bn and $90 bn respectively. Relative GDPs remained unchanged. Britain had a greater lead in productivity in 1869, 75% above Germany's and more than double the French level. Britain's lead in industrial production was also greater than its lead in GDP size, but Germany was catching up fast.

By the mid-1860s, Prussia had the economic strength to fight either Austria or France, both of whom opposed a united Germany. It did not have the strength to take both on together. It would have been even less able to face a coalition supported by Britain. But the British had withdrawn from continental affairs. They were more interested in Empire. Prussia was a natural friend, whereas France was Britain's traditional enemy. Bismarck was totally disinterested in French colonial possessions. He took nothing from them. The British could not then foresee that

Germany would become their industrial rival, and thus had no reason to resist the creation of Bismarck's Second Reich. The rival of Britain's rival was Britain's friend.

The creation of the Second Reich by force marked a major setback for democracy in Germany and a triumph for militant nationalism. Universal conscription bred obedience to authority. Military success encouraged arrogance and a belief in the superiority of German culture. From its birth the modern German nation was set on a course to disaster.

CHAPTER 5

The Second Reich, 1871–1918

The Second Reich was born of the sword and the gun.[1] Its existence was perpetually threatened by revolution at home and by war abroad. Five decades later it collapsed as the result of both. During the first two decades of the Second Reich Bismarck ruled and all went well. But he had set Germany on the path to disaster. To achieve his political ends, he whipped up fears of civil war and foreign wars. The former justified state repression at home; the latter bred jingoism and xenophobia, which later became uncontrollable.

The Second Reich was ruled by and for Junkers, paranoid about any threat to their privileges and wealth. They were east Prussian Lutheran landowners, the nation's nobility and squirearchy – descended from the Teutonic Knights. Some were very rich, but most were rather poor. Junkers monopolised top government, civil service and judicial jobs. The army officer class was overwhelmingly Junker. Most were ignorant and self-seeking, putting class interests above all else. They tenaciously resisted political and social progress. They were arrogant and acquisitive, full of a vainglorious sense of 'honour', yet lacking in morality. Junkers were responsible for the Second Reich's unhappy history.

Power in Bismarck's Reich was ill defined and diffused. The Constitution was vague and ambiguous. The Reich, in theory a loose federation, in practice became a unitary state controlled from Berlin.

[1] Four German kings, six grand-dukes, four dukes, eight princes and three self-governing cities were forced by Prussian armies to join Bismarck's Reich. Many Germans, particularly southern Catholics, did not want to. Prussian armies also forced France and Austria to accept the Second Reich.

The Second Reich's institutions were similar to the European Union's. The upper house, the Bundesrat, was an assembly of ambassadors representing states' governments. The EU's equivalent is the Council of Ministers. All legislation required Bundesrat consent. This could be denied by a blocking minority of fourteen out of fifty-eight votes. Prussia, with seventeen votes, could veto any legislation it did not like. Junkers, who controlled the Prussian Landtag, thereby controlled all of Germany.

A lower house, the Reichstag, was elected by universal male suffrage. But constituency boundaries, set in 1871, were never revised, so as the population became increasingly urban the working classes became massively under-represented. The Junkers could never command a Reichstag majority. Socialists and bourgeois centrists could have exerted such command if they had been able to agree on anything. The Reichstag could only veto legislation. Like the European Parliament, it was largely a talking shop.

Power was divided between the Kaiser, the Chancellor, the army, the Bundesrat and the Reichstag. The Bundesrat was the least important, except when Junkers used it to block liberal legislation, particularly the reform of taxation. The Reichstag, in turn, resisted conservative and reactionary measures, leading to political paralysis. The Kaiser had near autocratic power, but the ever-present fear of revolution forced him to heed the Reichstag. The Reich Chancellor's power lay in his ability to steer legislation through the Reichstag. He did not need its support to be appointed but he could not do his job without it. With support from the Reichstag the Chancellor could threaten the Kaiser with his resignation. With the Kaiser's support, he could threaten to dissolve the Reichstag and call new elections.

CREATING A MODERN STATE

In the 1870s Bismarck gave Germany the trappings of a modern unitary nation state. The Second Reich moved rapidly to full economic and monetary union with a single market. He established a single currency and coinage, adopting the gold standard in 1873, and two years later set up a central bank, the Reichsbank. The legal system was standardised and modernised; an Imperial appeals courts was established. Guild and craft restrictions on trade were reduced (but see comments below on industrial cartels).

In one crucial area Bismarck failed. The Second Reich never had an efficient system of federal taxation. The Government, like the European Commission, received revenues from tariffs and specified indirect taxes. The Bundesrat could vote it extra money 'matriculations' from the states' coffers, but control of taxation remained in the hands of the individual states. Ultimately this proved fatal. The Prussian junkers paid little if any taxation. They prevented, through their control of the Bundesrat, the introduction of a federal income tax. Consequently the tax system was both unfair and inefficient. The burden of taxation fell hardest on those least able to bear it. Increasingly government was financed by borrowing, ultimately culminating in hyper-inflation.

Abroad, Bismarck's Reich had no serious quarrels with most other Great Powers. The generous peace terms of 1866 left Austria as an ally. Russia was friendly because Germany was also a monarchy, it had no interests in the Balkans and supported the suppression of Polish nationalism. Great Britain was incredibly slow to see Germany as a rival or threat (Kaiser Wilhelm I's son, Friedrick, was married to Queen Victoria's eldest daughter). France was Germany's only real enemy and remained so until Sedan was avenged and Alsace-Lorraine recovered. Bismarck kept France isolated by remaining friendly with both Austria and Russia. This was tricky as Austria and Russia continually clashed in the Balkans over the carcass of the moribund Turkish Empire.

EARLY SUCCESS

The early years of the Second Reich were a success. The country was not a democracy, but was reasonably well governed until blown off course by the 1873–96 'Great Depression'. Between 1870 and 1873 industrial production rose by a third, but in 1874 production stopped rising and then stagnated for the rest of the decade. Meanwhile a flood of cheap food imports caused an agricultural recession.

Bismarck was a Junker and the agricultural recession attacked the Junkers' vital economic interests. German industrialists also came under intense competitive pressure in a battle for world markets. Prussia had been wedded to free trade. The Zollverein, or German customs union, was a stepping stone to the creation of a united Germany. But when the Junkers demanded protection, Bismarck abandoned free trade and introduced it. Ruhr industrialists, who favoured cheap food, were bought off. Industrial cartels were permitted, even encouraged. Defence spending provided fat profits. Import duties, favoured by the Junkers, also raised revenues for the federal government which helped to pay for mounting military expenditure.

Protectionism killed liberalism in the Second Reich. From 1871 to 1878 Bismarck relied on the free-trade National Liberals for his Reichstag majority. Following his switch to protectionism he gained centre-right support by inflaming fears of a red revolution. When an attempt was made to assassinate the Kaiser, he falsely blamed the Socialists and demanded coercive legislation against them. When the National Liberals opposed this he labelled them unpatriotic. This tactic brought large conservative gains in the 1878 general election. Bismarck's support rested thereafter on an alliance of industry and agriculture – steel and rye – made possible by the gross under-representation of the growing urban proletariat in the Reichstag. The economy from then on was run exclusively in the interests of Ruhr industrialists and Junker farmers.

Bismarck shared the fears of a red revolution which he exploited. It was not enough for the Government to repress Socialism. He also set about wooing workers with sanitised 'State Socialism'. He introduced compulsory accident and sickness insurance in 1881, gaining the credit for inventing the welfare state. But the Bundesrat forced employers and employees to foot the bill, rather than vote the Reich Government new powers of taxation – a problem a century later.

The red menace was exaggerated. The German worker was more responsible and amenable to discipline than his counterpart in other countries. For the most part, his real standard of living rose during the decades leading up to the First World War. Provided one did not mind 'State Socialism', Germany was not a bad place to live in – far better than Russia and probably better than Britain. It may be wrong to exaggerate the importance of the welfare state in providing the security of the dole, pensions and the like, as the prime factor restraining revolutionary forces in Germany. But the welfare sate and social contract does have roots which go back in the German psyche. Generous social welfare will not be lightly abandoned in the late twentieth century as a result of a repetition of the conditions which led to their introduction over 100 years ago.

Bismarck's power rested on his ability to manipulate the aged Kaiser Wilhelm I, who died aged ninety in 1888. His grandson, Kaiser Wilhelm II, was only twenty-nine when he came to the throne (Kaiser Freidrich III having died within three months of his father). He was a complex young man with many conflicting traits in his character. Bismarck expected to manipulate the young Kaiser but was mistaken. In 1890 Wilhelm proposed legislation to limit factory hours, regulate working conditions, ban child employment and restrict adult female employment and to set up industrial arbitration courts. Bismarck rejected the lot and in March 1890 he was dismissed.

AFTER BISMARCK

Within a week of Bismarck's downfall, the international balance of power he had struggled to maintain was destroyed. The Kaiser broke with Russia, which soon became allied with France. Germany tried to woo Britain into a triple alliance with Austria, but failed. Bismarck's Reich and Britain had been on good terms, largely because Bismarck entertained few colonial ambitions. He preferred to leave France and Britain to squabble over Africa. In the closing decade of the nineteenth century all this changed. Railways, steamships and telegraphs made the world seem a smaller place. As countries industrialised they became dependent on imports of raw materials and food and they needed expanding export markets. The prevailing mood in Germany was that if it did not acquire a colonial empire it could never become a world power.

Germany was a late starter. The grab for Africa was almost over. The best bits were already in British, French, Portuguese or Belgian hands. The US was building a Pacific empire. But the grab for China and elsewhere in Asia had only just begun (with Japan eagerly participating). The decaying Turkish empire also offered tempting opportunities nearer home. The German attitude to empire was summed up by Chancellor Bernhard von Bülow in 1897: 'We do not wish to put anyone in the shade but we demand our place in the sun.'

A great wave of public opinion supported Germany's *Weltpolitik* or world power politics. Although still a young nation, by 1890 Germans were thrilled by their country's success. In 1870 German and French industrial production were roughly the same though added together barely equalled Britain's. By 1890 Germany's industrial production had risen to 80% of Britain's (and by 1913 it was 20% greater). During the four decades preceding the First World War, German industrial production rose at double the British rate. Most Germans expected their Reich to play a world role commensurate with its growing economic and military might.

Being largely landlocked in Central Europe, the Germans had limited maritime experience. But they realised that they could not build a world empire without their own navy. To protect colonies and sea lanes, they needed long-range, and hence lightly armoured, cruisers. Unwisely they built heavy battleships with a limited range, which could be used only in the North Sea against the Royal Navy. By driving Britain in 1904 into the embrace of its traditional enemy, France, and to settle differences with Russia in 1907, Germany's arrogant and aggressive foreign policy proved counter-productive. Germans, facing this 'triple entente', felt encircled by unfriendly powers.

Count Alfred von Schlieffen, who became the army chief of staff in 1891, feared a war on two fronts. He concocted the infamous Schlieffen plan designed to win it. Russia was strong, but would be slow to mobilise. Schlieffen therefore proposed a massive pre-emptive strike through Belgium to knock out France, before turning to face Russia. Schlieffen's was a tactical plan, immoral (because it involved violating Belgian neutrality) and without strategic content. It was adopted by the Kaiser and army, without reference to the politicians.

The story of the outbreak of the First World War has often been told, but some aspects are worth stressing. Most Germans were *against* the policies which led to the war. In the 1912 Reichstag election, a majority voted for parties which opposed the naval build-up, militarism and colonial expansion. There were peace protests in Berlin at the start of the crisis. The Kaiser did not court conflict either. Had he wanted war he could have had one on more favourable terms during the 1905 Moroccan crisis.

The Austrians, on the other hand, were longing to slap down Serbia, which had been stirring up trouble amongst Serbs living in Bosnia-

Hercegovina. The assassination in Sarajevo of Archduke Franz Ferdinand, heir to the Habsburg throne, gave them their excuse. The Kaiser impulsively offered unlimited German support. Austria issued a harsh ultimatum, which Serbia partially rejected. The Kaiser was posturing or bluffing. When war threatened he furiously back-pedalled and the politicians finally got into the act. But the generals had already taken control over events. Acting without authority, they egged Austria on. The Junker generals wanted war.

Russia started to mobilise. Inflexible railway timetables meant Germany must immediately attack France, or the Schlieffen plan would have to be abandoned. The generals claimed that Germany would be the victim of combined Russian and French aggression unless it launched a pre-emptive strike. Germany declared war first, but the German people genuinely believed that France and Russia started it. They saw it as a war for national survival.

In August 1914 the army asserted its control of the country. After winning the battle of Tannenberg against the Russians in 1914, Generals Paul von Hindenburg and Erich Ludendorff became so popular that the Kaiser dared not dismiss them. From then until early November 1918 Germany was *de facto* a military dictatorship. The generals rarely informed and never consulted the Kaiser or politicians, but ran the country under martial law. The German people were fed a propaganda diet of untruths and half-truths – as were people in all other belligerent nations. They believed to the end that, although the war was horrendously costly, Germany would win it. Expecting victory, the German people clamoured out for spoils. They demanded a harsh peace, in which Germany would obtain major territorial gains and sufficient reparations to pay for the war. The Brest-Litovsk peace treaty with Russia, signed in March 1918 (by which Germany grabbed Poland, Courland, Livonia and Estonia and imposed massive reparations), showed how grasping Germany would have been if it had won in the west.

Defeat came as a bitter, unexpected blow. In late September, Hindenburg and Ludendorff told the Kaiser that the army was beaten and Germany would have to sue immediately for peace. Then in honourable Junker tradition, they abdicated from their unofficial dictatorship and handed the responsibility and odium for making peace back to the Kaiser and politicians. (Ludendorff fled to Sweden wearing sunglasses and false whiskers.) The Second Reich, created on 1 January 1871, ended on 9 November 1918. Kaiser Wilhelm II abdicated and fled to Holland. The majority Socialist leader, Friedrich Ebert, became Chancellor and Germany was declared a Republic. A red revolution began which threatened to become an all-out civil war.

CONCLUSIONS

This chapter describing the Second Reich has been lengthy because of the light it throws on the German character and on events today. The creation of the Second Reich out of the disparate states of disunited Germany, and the resulting institutions, bears a striking resemblance to the creation of the European Union and its institutions. The economic problems that Europe now faces are more directly comparable with those faced during 1871–1914 than with anything encountered during the following seven decades. The social problems thrown up by headlong structural change are similar. In the late nineteenth century there was a rapid outward movement of industrialisation from its core in Britain and Northern Europe, to the periphery in the new world. This brought enhanced competition from cheap foreign food and manufactures which prompted the German retreat from free trade.

Much of twentieth-century history can be explained by the social and political strains imposed by nineteenth-century industrialisation. Mass production pushed and pulled people from the countryside into the great new industrial cities, where they were crowded together, often in abject poverty. Industrialisation raised national income, though gains were inequitably shared, but lowered the living standards of a large part of the population. Where workers remained poor and income ill distributed, mass employment failed to generate mass markets for the products of mass production. An industrial society needs fair, efficient and relatively low taxes and an equitable distribution of income to operate successfully. Germany had none of these things.

Communists preached that there was a better way of organising production and sharing the rewards than free market capitalism. This was true where the rules of the capitalist system were overwhelmingly biased in favour of the wealthy factory owners and against factory workers. The rich and powerful countered communism with appeals to nationalism. They countered over-production and under-consumption, not with tax and social reforms to redistribute income, but by increasing public spending upon defence. Such expenditure was financed from borrowing. It planted the seeds which were to germinate and ultimately grow into the 1922–4 hyper-inflation which destroyed the entire German financial system.

If today, in response to competition from low-wage developing countries, we create a 'fortress Europe', we will destroy our prosperity once again. This is a ghost from Germany's past that could then return to haunt us.

THE SECOND REICH'S ECONOMIC SUCCESS

The Second Reich's disastrous political development was accompanied by notable economic success. The creation of the Second Reich in 1871 produced a new European power with a population of 41 million, taking the place of Prussia with a population of 24 million. As such Germany was a little larger than France (36 million) and a lot larger than Britain (31 million). Population growth in the Second Reich to 1913 was marginally faster than Britain's when Ireland is excluded (where the population continued to decline). But the French population stagnated, growing by only 10% from 1871 to 1913 against Germany's 63% and Britain's (excluding Ireland) 58%. Thus whereas there were six Germans for every ten Frenchmen and Britons in 1871, by 1913 there were eight. Faster population growth goes some way to explain the growing strength of Germany versus its West European neighbours. But compared with Russia, Germany lost ground. The Russian population doubled to 170 million by 1913.

All major Prussian cities were smaller in 1870 than the equivalent British cities had been in 1800. Over the following four decades the size of German towns increased more rapidly than their British equivalents, but on the eve of the First World War they remained smaller. Berlin's population passed 2 million, but London's passed 7 million (and Paris approached 3 million). Five British cities, but only two German, exceeded 700,000.

Table 5.2 compares production and related data for Germany, France and Britain from the end of the Franco-Prussian War to the eve of the

Table 5.1 Population Changes 1871–1913 (millions)

	1871	1913	% change	% pa
Germany	41.0	67.0	63	1.2
France	36.2	39.8	10	0.2
Britain	31.2	45.7	47	0.9
Britain ex Ireland	*26.2*	*41.3*	*58*	*1.1*
Russia	85.4	170.9	100	1.7

The main source for this and the following tables is B. R. Mitchell, *International Historical Statistics: 1750 to 1988.*

First World War. The speed with which Germany caught up and then overtook Britain in industrial production was impressive. But equally revealing is the way France trailed well behind. It was not simply the stagnant population which destroyed France's dominant position on the continent, it was also the country's failure to industrialise as fast as its neighbours. This can be explained partly by the loss of Alsace-Lorraine, which the French were understandably determined to recover. Germany's lead is more impressive in products introduced after 1870. The Germans had 1.4 million telephones by 1913, double the number in Britain and almost five times the French number. Germany generated nearly four times as much electricity as Britain and almost five times as much as France. But Germany was surprisingly backward in car ownership. While the French had 91,000 private cars in 1913 and the British 106,000, Germans owned only 61,000. Statistics for French commercial vehicles are not available, but against Germany's 10,000 the British had 103,000. Britain's merchant fleet also remained overwhelmingly dominant, although German cruise liners had made a dent in passenger transport. By 1913 Germany's GDP, at $243 bn, had overtaken Britain's, $217 bn, and both were far ahead of France whose GDP of $86 bn had still not reached Britain's 1869 level. British productivity was still a third higher than the German level, but British industrial production was a sixth lower.

Table 5.2 Production and Communications 1872–1913

	Germany	France	Britain
Coal output (m. tons)			
1872	42	16	125
1913	277	41	292
Iron ore (m. tons)			
1872	4742	2782	16,089
1913	28,608	21,918	16,254
Pig iron (m. tons)			
1872	1828	1218	6850
1913	16,761	5207	10,425
Crude steel (m. tons)			
1872	189	130	417
1913	17,609	4687	7787
Cotton spindles (000s)			
1877	4700	5000	44,207
1913	11,186	7400	55,653
Merchant ships			
1872:			
Sailing	4311	15,062	22,103
Steam	216	512	3673
Thousand tons	941	1089	5751
1913:			
Sailing	2765	15,824	8510
Steam	2170	1895	12,382
Thousand tons	3320	1582	11,895
Railway lines open (km)			
1872	22,426	17,438	22,097
1913	63,378	40,770	32,623

CHAPTER 6

The Weimar Republic, 1919–33

The lies and illusions of the Wilhelmine Reich survived to poison the Weimar Republic and prepare the way for Hitler. The Socialists became the legitimate Government after the Kaiser abdicated, but in reality President Ebert had no control over any of the levers of power. Nonetheless, General Wilhelm Groener (Ludendorff's successor as Quartermaster-General) volunteered the army's support. The 1918–20 red revolution consequently failed. But when *freikorps* troops (freelance ex-army units) helped the Socialists to put down the Communist Spartakus rebellion in Berlin in January 1919, they brutally murdered the Communist leaders, Karl Liebknecht and Rosa Luxemburg, driving a wedge between Socialists and Marxists which widened over the years until the left was unwilling to unite even to resist Hitler.

The 1918 victors left the Germans to sort out their own domestic problems. They neither occupied Germany nor disarmed or disbanded its army (which was, however, renamed the Reichswehr and reduced in size). The Junker officer corps remained in control. When Ebert used freikorps to suppress the red revolution, he put the Weimar Republic in hock to the old regime. Had the Social Democrats led their own moderate revolution, the army and establishment would have been forced to come to terms with them, instead of the other way round.

Industrialists eagerly came to terms with their workers and unions. On 15 November 1918, four days after the Armistice, unions and employers signed an agreement proclaiming that cooperation between capital and industry should form the basis of industrial relations in future.

(Neither side kept their bargain, but that was understandable in the difficult economic times that lay ahead.) Employers accepted collective bargaining without reservation, an eight-hour working day and works councils to help regulate wages and shop-floor conditions. Workers agreed to submit disputes to independent tribunals before contemplating strikes. The Weimar Government later made works councils mandatory in firms employing twenty or more workers. The foundation was thus laid for the distinctive German system of industrial co-determination. The 1920s works councils were precursors to worker representation on supervisory boards in the 1950s.

The Weimar Republic failed to destroy the power of the Junkers. Top army officers, civil servants, clergy, judges, university professors and schoolmasters all kept their jobs. Students were taught by anti-Weimar reactionaries. Judges, appointed for life, handed down harsh sentences on Communists, while imposing the mildest on monarchists. Kapp and Hitler were rapped gently over the knuckles for their putsches. Landowners and industrialists retained their possessions. There was no cleaning the stables to root out those to blame for the war. The privileged elite, which had led Germany to disaster, retained their positions of power, albeit behind the scenes. They had no liking for Weimar democracy, but while there was dirty work to be done clearing up the mess they had made, the reactionaries were willing to leave Socialist politicians to do it.

A freely elected National Assembly, meeting out of harm's way in Weimar, devised the ill-fated Republic's Constitution. It has been blamed for Weimar's failure. It could have worked if there had been the will to make it work. It established a Reich President as head of state, elected by popular vote every seven years. He appointed the Reich Chancellor and, on the Chancellor's advice, all ministers, officers and top civil servants. The Chancellor and Government were, however, answerable to the Reichstag (the lower house of the German federal parliament) and, while ministers need not be members, the Government had to command a Reichstag majority to remain in office. The Reichstag itself was elected at least every four years by proportional representation and adult suffrage. The maldistribution of seats under the Second Reich was eliminated and women given the vote. An upper house, the Reichsrat, replaced the old Bundesrat, appointed by the governments of the seventeen new Länder or states. Although seats in the Reichsrat were allocated according to the size of each Land, Prussia's dominant position was eliminated. (Within Prussia, the class-based three-tier franchise was abolished, so that the Junkers lost control and the Social Democrats took over. Germany's lurch into Nazi dictatorship was led not by Prussians but by Bavarians.) The Reichsrat could only delay legislation, although on some issues it required a two-thirds Reichstag majority to overturn its veto.

While proportional representation allowed all shades of opinion to be fully represented, it was at the expense of creating a multiplicity of parties. Moreover members were elected from party lists drawn up by their leaders, who could thus impose strict party discipline. Rival party leaders were mainly interested in personal power, indifferent to the public damage which ineffective Government inflicted. There was always a large minority, Communists to the left and conservatives to the right, who were opposed to the Weimar Republic and willing to paralyse democratic government in an effort (ultimately successful) to bring it down. Governments were unstable coalitions, rarely able to take tough action or, when they did, not lasting long afterwards.

Power evolved upwards to the popularly elected President. Under Article 48 of the Constitution he could declare an emergency whenever he believed that 'public order or safety to be seriously disturbed or threatened'. The Chancellor, at the President's whim, then governed by decree. But decrees subsequently had to be ratified by the Reichstag. If the Reichstag threw them out, the President had a choice: he could dismiss the Chancellor and attempt to find another who could command a majority; or he could dissolve the Reichstag, hoping that new elections would produce majority support for the existing Chancellor.

The Weimar Republic was destroyed by big lies and hard times. The biggest lie was that the army had never been defeated. Monarchists and reactionaries claimed it had been stabbed in the back by the 'November traitors' – the sailors who mutinied in Keil and civilian revolutionaries, particularly Jews. Hindenburg and Ludenorff fostered this lie by conveniently forgetting that they had begged the Kaiser to sue for peace before either the mutiny or revolution began. The Germans were also astonished by the 'war-guilt' clause in the 1919 Versailles Peace Treaty, which labelled them the sole aggressors. They firmly believed the half-lie that they had been forced into a defensive war by foreign aggression. The clause had immense practical importance. It was the peg on which reparations were hung.

HYPER-INFLATION

All Germans hated the Versailles Treaty. Having got rid of the Kaiser, they expected to be let off lightly. But the peace terms were harsh and, to German frustration, their leaders were forced to accept them. Had they refused, the armistice would have ended and hostilities would have been resumed. The victors penalised all Germans collectively, instead of punishing guilty Germans individually. The nation as a whole was saddled with war guilt – not the Kaiser, the generals or the Junker officer corps. There was never a hope that the Versailles Treaty would be willingly observed.

The Versailles Treaty imposed arms limitations on Germany. All Germans thenceforth supported rearmament. Germany lost an area of 27,000 square miles which included 6 million people. All Germans thenceforth supported re-expansion. Alsace-Lorraine was returned to France. A new Polish state was carved out in the east, with the Danzig corridor to the sea dividing once again east and west Prussia. These adjustments meant that in these racially mixed regions, Germans had to live in lands governed by the French or the Poles, where in 1914 French and Poles had lived in lands governed by Germans. Compared with their harsh treatment of Russia in the Brest-Litovsk Treaty, the Germans got off lightly. The Second Reich could easily have been dismembered. A quarter of a century later, during the Second World War, the Allies seriously considered this possibility.

The peace terms contributed to but did not cause hyper-inflation in the 1920s. The Allies took until 21 May 1921 to decide their total reparations demands: 130 bn gold marks. According to Carl-Ludwig Holtfrerich, author of *The German Inflation 1914–1923*, German national income averaged 60 bn gold marks a year in 1919–23. On this basis, reparations equalled two years' national income, ten times larger than the reparations (one-fifth of a year's national income) which Prussia imposed on France in 1871.

The bill Germany paid was very much smaller. For a short while it met its obligations, but from the end of 1921 it defaulted. Acting unilaterally, France marched into the Ruhr in January 1923 to extract payment. But the Germans refused to work and the occupation led to a débâcle. Meanwhile Germany's hyper-inflation reached its peak. The currency was stabilised after September 1923 and under the 1924 Dawes Plan (named after the American General Charles Dawes who chaired the committee which produced it), Germany's annual payments were temporarily reduced to levels compatible with her ability to pay. From 1925 to 1928 Germany met its Dawes Plan obligations and in early 1929 the country seemed prosperous enough for an agreement to be negotiated to normalise the situation. This was the Young Plan (named after the American banker, Owen Young) which cut the total amount due to 37 bn gold marks and spread repayment out until 1988. But no sooner was the Young Plan agreed than Wall Street crashed, signalling the start of the 1930s depression. Germany defaulted once more and in June 1931 payment obligations were suspended for a year by President Herbet Hoover under the *Hoover moratorium*. Finally payment was *de facto* terminated by the Lausanne Agreement of July 1932. In all, Germany probably paid cash reparations of about the same one-fifth of a year's national income as France paid after the Franco-Prussian War. But German payments were spread over eleven years, whereas French payments were made within twenty-seven months.

Germany borrowed to finance reparation payments. Capital inflows from abroad, mainly the US, averaged 3.5% of each year's national income during 1925–30, around 1% more than paid out in reparations. Germany defaulted when foreign capital inflows became outflows after the 1929 Wall Street crash. If account is taken of the fact that those who lent Germany money between 1925 and 1930 lost most of it, net reparation payments were negligible.

There would still have been hyper-inflation even if the Allies' reparations demands had been more modest or if the French had not marched into the Ruhr. Hyper-inflation stemmed from wartime finance. The Germans expected to win and then receive reparations to defray their war costs; instead they lost and were expected to pay their enemies' costs. There was about 30 bn gold marks' worth of public sector bonds already outstanding when the First World War began. During the war around 110 bn marks' worth of war loan stock was issued, taking public sector debts to 140 bn marks or 200% of national income. Interest at 5% per annum on this debt would have cost 10% of national income. This could not have been met without heavier taxation. But the Government dared not impose heavy taxes on the rich for fear of an army coup, or on the poor, for fear of revolution. Inflation was the solution, not the problem. It wiped out Government debt.

The 1923 currency stabilisation is regarded as a notable achievement, credited to Gustav Stresemann (Chancellor from August to November 1923) and to the banker, Hjalmar Schacht. On 23 September, Stresemann bravely called off German passive resistance in the Ruhr (prompting Hitler's abortive 9 November Munich beer-hall *putsch*). Three days later he established the new Rentenbank which issued the Rentenmark and appointed Schacht as currency commissioner. The Rentenmark commanded respect because it was backed by mortgages on industrial assets and agricultural land – real things that kept their value. Its supply was strictly limited. It was given the same fixed gold value as the old Reichmark (but was not convertible to gold) and psychologically it became a store of value. It also provided a stable unit of account for financial transactions.

Exchanging one paper money for another would not have worked without successful measures to put public finances on a sound footing. An extremely reprehensible method was used to raise revenues. The Government decreed that debtors must pay 15% of the original gold value of their Reichmark debts, whether these debts had already been settled in depreciated currency or remained outstanding. Private debtors were thus deprived of some part of their inflationary gains. The State was the biggest debtor, but the Government did not apply the rule to itself. The Government kept all its own inflationary gains and, adding insult to injury, demanded a share in private debtor's gains. Creditors got virtually no recompense for their inflation losses because most of the debtors' payments went to the Government in special taxes. This embittered the German middle classes against the Weimar Republic possibly more than hyper-inflation itself.

Once prices were stabilised, the six years from 1924 to 1929 proved a period of recovery and growing prosperity for most Germans. In 1919

German industrial production was not quite 40% of what it had been in 1913. By 1929 it was slightly above where it had been before the war. By comparison, French industrial production (including Alsace-Lorraine) was nearly a quarter above its pre-war level. So was British industrial production, despite sterling's return to the gold standard at a grossly overvalued level in 1925. The Weimar Republic continued another old Bismarckian tradition – it tried to gain workers' support with generous welfare provisions. These included improved sickness benefits and an unemployment relief scheme which was introduced in 1927.

Chart 6.1 Seats in the Weimar Reichstag

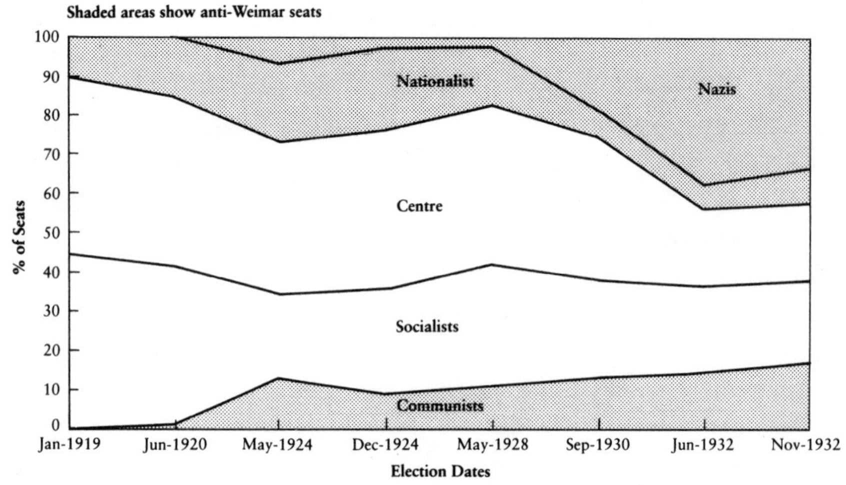

Shaded areas show anti-Weimar seats

Despite Weimar's successes in the later 1920s, left- and right-wing extremists never became reconciled to it. At its high point, the 1928 election, one in four Germans still voted for parties which opposed the Republic. (See Chart 6.1.) But popular support for the extremes (shaded areas in Chart 6.1) declined and there was the beginnings of a flowering of liberal democracy in Germany. The Nazi party had thirty-two Reichstag members in 1924 and twelve in 1928 when they pulled only 810,000 votes. They were a lunatic fringe. The Weimar Republic was, however, too weakly an infant to survive world depression, heralded by the October 1929 Wall Street crash.

MASS UNEMPLOYMENT

When Britain went off the gold standard in 1931, a gold block remained, dominated by the US and France. Germany elected to be part of it. In March 1930 Heinrich Brüning had been appointed Chancellor. Mounting unemployment was already causing tax receipts to fall and expenditure on unemployment benefits to rise. The unemployment benefit scheme had been designed to support a maximum of 800,000 workless; there were soon twice this number entitled to benefits and the scheme would have been rapidly bankrupt but for government subventions. The budget moved into deficit which rapidly worsened. Fears of hyperinflation remained rampant and Brüning both clung obstinately to gold and responded to recession by attempting to balance the budget.

Brüning cut public sector pay, welfare benefits and raised taxes. But the more he endeavoured to reduce the budget deficit, the deeper the economy sank into recession and the higher unemployment rose. This only prompted further retrenchment. Central Government spending was cut by more than a quarter between 1928 and 1932 (whereas Britain's went up), but tax revenues also fell by a quarter (and again Britain's rose). Unemployment in 1930 was 3.1 million or 15% and this number rose to 5.6 bn by 1932 or 30%. The rate of unemployment amongst trade union members soared to 44% and the total number out of work was around 6.5 million.

The comparison between German, French and British experience during the 1929–32 slide into depression is enlightening. German GDP fell by a fifth, French by sixth and British by a twentieth. German industrial production fell three-fifths, French by a quarter and British by a tenth. The collapse in trade was a half or more, but again Britain fared best and Germany worst. German unemployment rose to nearly three times the British rate.

The Reichsbank President, Hans Luther, later entitled a chapter of his memoirs, 'Brüning's Policy: There was No Alternative'. Britain's departure from the gold standard and subsequent recovery indicates that this was far from the truth. The determination to stick to gold and retrench massively increased the severity of the German slide into depression. The alternative, abandoning gold and reflating through higher public spending, was rejected as dangerously inflationary. The

1922–4 hyper-inflation was still an extremely fresh memory. Brüning persisted with his suicidal course because he truly believed that there was no alternative. He sacrificed German democracy due to his paranoid fear of inflation.

Parliamentary Government effectively ceased on 28 March 1930, the day Brüning became Chancellor, because the Reichstag would not vote for retrenchment. Presidential Government followed in which Brüning, subservient to the wishes of the reactionary 83-year-old Hindenburg, ruled by emergency decree. Brüning was ditched in May 1932 and replaced by the conservative Franz von Papen. Nonetheless Government remained paralysed until, on 30 January 1933, Adolf Hitler was appointed Reich Chancellor.

Hitler came to power constitutionally, though hardly democratically. Hindenburg had abandoned democratic government. But if at any time before 31 July 1932 the centre parties had united to keep Hitler out, they had the Reichstag majority to do so. With Hindenburg's support, the Army could have put down the SA and SS and restored order. Instead between 1930 and 1933 hundreds of Hitler's opponents were killed in street battles or murdered by Nazi assassins. Hindenburg went even further to establish the precedent for Hitler's usurpation of power. In 1932 von Papen attempted to compete with the Nationalists for popular support. On 20 July he declared a state of emergency in Prussia, appointed himself Reichkommissar, and dismissed the Socialist ministers on the grounds that they had failed to prevent street violence (for which he was to blame for lifting the ban on the SS and SA). This *coup d'état*, which went unresisted, was followed by a purge of the Prussian civil service to get rid of Socialist supporters. Thus was Germany's most populous and industrial state deprived of democratic government even before Hitler became Chancellor.

CHAPTER 7

The Third Reich, 1934–45

Hindenburg died on 1 August 1934 and the very next day the Third Reich was born. Hitler amalgamated the offices of Reich Chancellor and President and assumed them himself under the title of Führer. The Generals even agreed that officers should swear an oath of allegiance to him, which through their corrupt and hypocritical sense of honour they took extremely seriously. This oath excused many in their own minds from any guilt associated with committing atrocities on the orders of their superiors. It became more honourable to gas a Jew than to disobey the order to do so. It was also much safer. Hitler slowly and cautiously brought the Army under his personal control, while embarking on the policies which led, in 1939, to world war.

Hitler's bully boys cannot have forced millions of Germans to vote in secret ballots for the Nazi party. More likely they deterred support. Hitler's powerful oratory and evil political genius captured the enthusiastic support of a nation, which deeply wished for strong leadership. The Germans had been exhausted in a single generation by catastrophic war casualties, unexpected defeat and a punitive peace treaty, red revolution, hyper-inflation and finally bloody street violence and unemployment on an unimagined scale. The Germans yearned for law, order and security. Today there are 2.5 million west Germans without jobs out of a labour force of 28.5 million. To equal the 1932 unemployment rate there would have to be 11.5 million on the dole. Even east Germany's much higher jobless rate would have to double. Hitler gave Germany strong government with a vengeance. He made the nation 'great' again in an incredibly short space of time. Instead of being kicked around, the Third Reich did all the kicking. Soon Germans were wallowing in national pride. But Hitler did what he did by creating a totalitarian police state in which, ultimately, every aspect of people's lives was controlled. The Nazi reign of terror began spasmodically and was disorganised until after 1934, when it was rationalised and systematised to become an instrument of repressive government. Even so, by the end of 1933 when the Nazis had been in power for only eleven months, there were already fifty concentration camps.

The economy was run in detail by the state, highly effectively compared with France and Britain. German real net national product rose by 90% between 1932 to 1938, a growth rate of 11% a year. It was then 50% above its 1913 level, despite the loss of Alsace-Lorraine. German industrial production more than doubled. By comparison, French industrial production was no higher in 1938 than it had been in 1932, having fallen in the meantime. French GDP rose only 13% or 2% a year to 36% above its 1913 level. Britain's industrial production rose by half and GDP grew by a quarter to 29% above its 1913 level. The Nazis quickly gave everyone jobs and money to go with them. In 1934 unemployment fell by 2 million. In 1936 it was lower than in 1929 and by 1938 it was under 500,000. There were still 1.75 million Britons out of work in 1938, down one million from 1932. German jobs were created by public spending, which rose 40% between 1932 and 1934 (the last year for which there are figures). Tax revenues, which rose from Rm 5 bn in 1932 to Rm 18 bn in 1938, give a further indication of the expansion of the state into the economy.

The steps by which Hitler consolidated his dictatorship over the German state need only be sketched out here. Individuals unsympathetic to Hitler were quickly rounded up and confined in concentration camps or murdered. Within months all political parties except the Nazis had been abolished and one-party rule had been established. Formal opposition was quickly suppressed. There was virtually no organised resistance to the Nazi take-over and in a plebiscite in November 1933, nine out of ten Germans supported Hitler. The Civil Service was purged. Taking control of the Army was another matter. Hitler did not attempt to do so. Instead he kept the Generals happy by rearming and by removing the challenge to the Army from private armies, the SS and SA. This was done on the 'night of the long knives', 30 June 1934. With the Army's connivance, the SS rounded up several hundred people and executed them without trial. The Army supplied transport and the barrack's yard in Berlin where many were shot. The victims included Hitler's Nazi party rivals, notably Ernst Röhm, leader of the SA, together with former politicians such as General von Schleicher, who had replaced von Papen in December 1932 as the last Chancellor before Hitler. All opposition to Hitler within the Nazi party was eliminated. The Army and Generals were the only organisation in Germany which could have removed Hitler, but they sold the pass when they succumbed to his blandishments and condoned his murders.

At least in 1939 there was no question who started the war. Nor later, when Germany had been occupied and reduced to rubble, was there any question about who lost it. When Hitler started it, his Generals were alarmed and the German people were aghast. They only became elated in 1940, after the blitzkrieg defeated France and Germany seemed to have won. Total defeat in 1945 ended the Third Reich and Germany's past.

The fifty years which have passed since Germany's defeat can be considered Germany's present, although arguably the future began when the Berlin wall came tumbling down in 1989. Germany's present has been totally different from Germany's past. This raises crucial questions on which Germany's and Europe's future depend. Are Germans different from all the rest of us? Were they collectively to blame for their nation's unhappy history during the seventy-four years from unification in Bismarck's Second Reich to the destruction of Hitler's Third Reich? Or was their history so different and unique that circumstances were to blame?

Blaming the Germans is tempting. The vast majority did support Hitler. He was immensely popular, at least until the war started to go against Germany. Even then, many Germans believed in him to the end. Resistance to the Nazis was feeble in the extreme. David Clay Large, in his book *Contending with Hitler: Varieties of Resistance in the Third Reich* (1992), maintains that 'There was very little resistance deserving the name that was not soon discovered.' Such opposition that survived was little more than non-conformity.

To maintain that the average German had no idea what was going on is a nonsense. Hitler set out more or less what he planned to do in *Mein Kampf* (1924), a copy of which almost all Germans found it prudent to own. News of the Holocaust leaked out of Germany long before the war ended. In 1943 the US *Daily Tribune* carried reports of the massacre of the Jews. People could not have been unaware of neighbours disappearing. Knowing or suspecting is one thing; caring and daring enough to oppose it is another. To protest was futile and it carried the death penalty. Collectively there was nothing the German people could do. No organisation existed that was capable of orchestrating collective action. Communists and Socialists did covertly and courageously resist Hitler, but having failed to prevent his rise there was little they could do to bring about his downfall.

The view taken here is that it is wrong to blame the Germans as a nation for the crimes committed by Hitler. Circumstances, not the German character were to blame. In the Third Reich everyone looked first and foremost to personal survival. Who is to say that most of us would not have behaved the same way in similar circumstances? French collaborators in Vichy France were just as bad as the Germans.

But it is right to blame the German Army and officer corps. As this history has shown, it was the Generals who accepted without qualms the Schlieffen plan with its invasion of neutral Belgium and started the First World War. It was the army and General Hindenburg which destroyed the Weimar Republic and put Hitler in power. After Hindenburg's death in 1934, only the Army and the Generals had the power to depose Hitler in a successful *coup d'état*; they failed to do so even though aware of the full extent of Nazi atrocities. The abortive bomb plot on 20 July 1944 stands out as a rare event – but it was the work of conservative Army officers, convinced that the war was lost and wanting to avoid the total disaster to which the mad dictator was leading the nation.

Hundreds of thousands of German soldiers died needlessly because their Generals dared not disobey Hitler. The refusal to withdraw from Stalingrad was one example. When one looks at the German regular officer corps, with its Prussian Junker antecedents, one comes closer to what was most rotten in Germany. The corps was an élite which had always looked solely to its own interests. If we could wipe out from 2000 years of German history considered in this first section of this book the twelve years of the Third Reich, it is doubtful whether anything else in Germany's past would today cause us concern for the future. But remember the conditions which culminated in Hitler's rise to power.

PART II

GERMANY PRESENT

CHAPTER 8

Divided They Stood

The present in Germany began on 8 May 1945, called VE (Victory in Europe) Day in Britain and *Stunde Null* (Hour Zero) in Germany, when the enormity of the disaster struck home to the German people: the totality of their defeat; industry and homes reduced to rubble; three million servicemen killed, one million prisoners in the Soviet Union, most never to return; half a million civilians dead from the bombing; a country occupied, shrunken and subsequently divided. Doubtless the German people were dazed, felt hopeless and helpless at the catastrophe that had befallen them. But this catalogue of negatives serves mainly to emphasise the positive of their – the West Germans, that is – miraculous post-war recovery.

The recovery was meretricious not miraculous. Advanced and educated nations inevitably pull themselves up from defeat and disaster with alacrity – mostly because they are determined to regain self-esteem. The Japanese recovered even more rapidly. Chart 8.1 puts Germany's performance into its historical perspective. Real GDP rose on average by 2.75% a year from 1850 to 1913. (Prior to 1871 the figures relate to the area which became Bismarck's Second Reich in that year.) Had this rate of growth continued, Germany's GDP would now be almost double what it is. But it could never have continued. During the second half of the nineteenth century Germany was catching up with Britain. Laggards can always grow fast exploiting the technical breakthroughs of the leaders. When they themselves become leaders, the pace of expansion invariably slows. The German performance is remarkable in that after 1949 the chart relates to West Germany. No allowance has been made for losses of land, capital and labour due to defeat and division. When the 2.25% a year real growth trend from 1850 to 1938 is extrapolated, it can be seen that Germany's 'miraculous' 1950s and 1960s recovery was mainly making good lost ground. Once that had been achieved, German growth slowed to a more leisurely pace (as did Japanese).

Chart 8.1 German Growth, 1850–1995

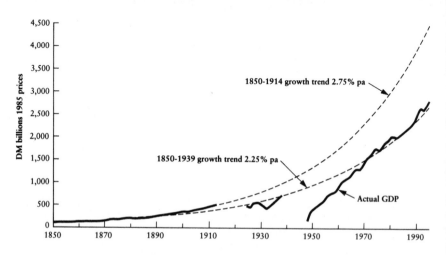

In 1945 West Germany's political economy had more things going for it than people realised (and East Germany had more going against it). In the West conditions were established enabling a sound democracy to take root. Occupation by three out of four victors was a blessing, and while Soviet occupation was a curse to East Germany, it could be regarded as a blessing to the West Germans. In contrast to 1918, when Germany was squeezed until the pips squeaked, with disastrous results, from 1945 occupation conferred responsibility on the Americans, British and French for running and subsequently reorganising and rescuing West Germany.

Allied occupation, as with the US occupation in Japan, relieved German politicians of the odium of making the painful decisions needed to rebuild German institutions. In the tough three years after the war, the blame for muddle, confusion and failure could be pinned on the occupying powers. There was no German State and no German Government to blame. That being so, the Third Reich's debts could not be honoured. But unlike the First World War, the Second World War was financed largely by short-term borrowing from banks, instead of through the sale of long-term Government bonds to the public. It was paid for by printing money and inflation, which left less of a legacy of debt. Germany, as a single political and economic unit, had ceased to exist. However, this was only temporary. Once the Federal Republic of Germany (FRG) was set up, it regarded itself as the legal successor not only to the Third Reich, but to earlier German states as well. This was implicit in the name of the state. The East German Government claimed that there were now two equal German states – the German Democratic Republic (GDR) and what they called the 'German Federal Republic' neither of which was the legal successor to preceding German states. Not so, said the West German Government: 'We the Federal Republic of Germany are the legal successor to all earlier Germanys, while you are the Soviet Occupation Zone.' In consequence, West Germany assumed responsibility for the German national debt (and continues to pay interest on outstanding bonds). It also accepted responsibility for the acts of the Third Reich and continues to pay reparation to victims of the Nazis – in stark contrast with Japan, which still does not admit war guilt.

OCCUPATION-DIVIDED GERMANY

There was no German Peace Treaty to compare with Versailles, and there was no German Government forced to sign one. Unlike 1918, Russia was one of the victors. In retrospect it is obvious that there was little possibility Joseph Stalin and the West would agree on how to treat the defeated Germans. As a result, the whole process by which Germany's future was decided fell apart. Some things had been agreed before the war ended. The most important were those decided by Stalin, Roosevelt and Churchill at their Yalta summit starting on 17 July 1944 – the day the first atomic bomb was successfully tested in the deserts of New Mexico. Germany would be divided into four occupation zones with boundaries set down in advance. (Anglo-American forces had to be pulled back 50–150 miles to the agreed frontier after the war ended.) Berlin, in the Soviet zone, would be occupied by all four powers and divided into sectors. There would be reparations, in kind not in cash, and Russia would get half, but the amount was never agreed. Germany was to be maintained as a single economic unit – each occupying power providing the apparatus of administration in its own area. It was envisaged that the victors would get together after the war to decide the nation's political future. Meanwhile the country was to be run from Berlin by an Allied Control Council consisting of the four commanders-in-chief. Decisions were to be unanimous. Nothing was said of what would happen when agreement could not be reached. The country was to be demilitarised and denazified. That was about as far as the Allies got at Yalta. When the war ended there was a delay of two months before Stalin, the new American President, Harry Truman, and the new British Prime Minister, Clement Attlee, met in Potsdam in July 1945. The Potsdam conference decided virtually nothing, other than to establish the Nürnberg Tribunal to try leading Nazis for war crimes. Thereafter Germany's fate was determined not by conferences and compromise, but by confrontation.

Germany's eastern boundaries were established by *fait accompli*. Stalin's aim, understandably, was to push the Germans as far west of Moscow as possible. Russia seized east Prussia from Poland and compensated the Poles at Germany's expense. The Polish-German boundary became the line of Oder and Neisse rivers. Poland now controlled both west Prussia and, thanks to the continuation of its border south along the Neisse river, Silesia. Old Prussia, the home of the Hohenzollerns, was lost to Germany. Sudentenland, with its 3 million German inhabitants, seized by Hitler at Munich in 1938, was returned to Czechoslovakia. These boundary changes were imposed by the Soviets on the Western Allies, who merely maintained that the question of where boundaries were to be set should remain open until the expected Peace Conference.

DIASPORA 'CURED' BY RACIAL DISCRIMINATION

Poles, Magyars and Czechs did not wait for confirmation of their post-war frontiers before expelling their German inhabitants. This process was ultimately beneficial. Germany's diaspora was reduced as its national and racial frontiers became more nearly the same. One of Hitler's objectives was thereby achieved, but at the expense of another. The Germans, who set out in 1938 to grab *Lebensraum* at the expense of the

Slavs and other east European neighbours, ended up losing it instead. Some 10 million ethnic Germans were forced back, or fled back, inside the country's new boundaries. Many kept going until they reached Western zones of occupation. Racially this prepared the way for the creation of a single German State, with most Germans inside it and few left outside. But that had to wait for another forty-five years.

The removal of the ethnic Germans from most of Central and Eastern Europe (a few remained in Russia, which would not let them out, more remained in Romania which had sided with Germany during the war) closed a historical chapter. In the Middle Ages, Germans had been invited by (mainly) Czech and Polish rulers to come and form a middle class. These countries at this time were divided into aristocracy and peasantry. The ruling classes did not want a middle class developing among their own subjects, as this could become a threat to their own position. Instead, they invited foreign groups which, it was thought, would never strike roots in the country. An earlier wave of foreigners had been Jewish. But from the mid-fourteenth century onwards, they tended to be Germans. With the 'ethnic cleansing' after the Second World War, this centuries-old German Diaspora almost completely disappeared.

Even the division of Germany had beneficial effects for West Germans. The Russian Zone, which became the German Democratic Republic, included five Länder – Mecklenburg, Brandenburg, Saxony, Saxony-Anhalt and Thuringia. Almost all of Prussia's 1815 eastern possessions were lost. The western lands which the Hohenzollerns had acquired – Westphalia and the Rhinelands – remained in Western hands. The Junker and Prussian influence was virtually wiped out. Unconditional surrender, occupation and disarmament finally eliminated what remained of the officer corps' power. In 1918 Prussian militarism was left alive and kicking; in 1945 it was dead and buried.

This division of Germany had major political effects on the West. The centre of gravity moved from the Prussian Protestant north towards the Bavarian Catholic south. Catholics accounted for 30% of the population of the Third Reich, but 45% of the Federal Republic's. West Germany also lost predominantly socialist areas. Prussia had been a Social Democrat stronghold pre-war. But most important, the division on the left between Marxist Socialists and Social Democrats was diminished. The crude way in which the Soviet Union imposed its puppet Communist regime on the east, the manner in which it treated the population in its zone and the mass migration from it, the cold war, the Berlin blockade and later the Berlin wall, served to eliminate virtually all electoral support for Communism in the west. Politics are discussed in more detail below. It is sufficient to note here that three main parties emerged in West Germany: the Christian Democrats and its sister party from Bavaria, the Christian Social Union (CDU-CSU); the Social Democrats (SPD); and the Free Democrats (FDP). The CDU-CSU was a combination of the old Catholic Centre party with Protestants from the National Liberal party. (The CDU does not seek election in Bavaria or the CSU outside it.) The FDP was the old Democratic party, which sought middle-class anti-clerical support. The SPD was a direct continuation from Weimar.

West Germany was shaped by the manner in which the different zones developed. Having conceded that the Anglo-American troops would retreat to their agreed zonal frontiers, the Russians in June 1945 allowed the three Western Powers to move into Berlin. But sector frontiers, access arrangements, supply lines, etc., had not been agreed at Yalta and the Potsdam meeting was not held for another month. The Western Generals had to haggle as best they could with the Russian General Zhukov for their rights and got the worst of the bargain – only one out of Berlin's three airports for example. Western sectors of Berlin also had to be supplied and fed from West Germany because the Russians refused to supply them from their zone. West Berlin, however, obtained its water from the Russian zone, which was never turned off. The failure to get agreement on almost anything at Potsdam, of which Berlin was an example, meant the Occupying Powers were each left to do their own things in their own zones. The American and British zones were combined in a single administrative unit in July 1946 called Bizonia. Only some 5% of Bizonian industrial plant was dismantled – probably doing the Germans a favour by relieving them of obsolete equipment they might not otherwise have scrapped. It made sense to stop undermining Germany's ability to recover. The longer they were too poor to pay for food imports, the longer the Allies faced the bill themselves.

REPARATIONS IN REVERSE

Germans suffered much hardship during the early post-war years. When the war ended there was mass migration and population movements at a time when the transport system was in ruins. Up to 10 million Germans displaced from East Europe, including 3 million from Sudetenland, had to be absorbed. There were 7 million German ex-servicemen making their way home, while forced labour and Allied prisoners had to be moved out of Germany. West Germany, while much reduced in size compared with Hitler's Third Reich, was much less reduced in population (from 68 million in 1937 to 47 million in 1947). There was no fuel, little housing and very little food. Indeed it was the British and Americans who fed the Germans in their zones and did so at their own taxpayers' expense – reverse reparations well in excess of any payment in kind received from Germany. The British and Americans stopped dismantling German plant in May 1946 for their own use, although they continued slowly dismantling some for the Soviets. Admittedly food rations were inadequate (a similar number of calories as in Buchenwald concentration camp) and although deaths from starvation were rare, malnutrition contributed to deaths from other causes. Everyone was short of food and British rations, although larger than German rations, were less than they had been during the war. The British taxpayer paid for Germans to eat food taken out of their own mouths. This would have been unthinkable in 1919. It was widely criticised at the time. But while more British went hungry (and many consequently remained healthy), fewer Germans starved to death.

The winter of 1946–7 in Europe was one of the coldest on record. Canals and waterways in Germany froze, coal stocks froze, the transport system was paralysed. It was the same in Britain, but the suffering was less. By the summer of 1947, the issue of economic recovery was in doubt throughout Europe. The problem was simple. Industrialised European economies were dependent upon imports of food, raw materials and fuels. With industries crippled they could not export. Without exports they could not afford the fuel and raw material imports needed to rebuild their crippled industries. They were too far below levels of self-sufficiency to pull themselves up by their own bootstraps. Moreover each nation's inability to import correspondingly reduced the

ability of others to export. A spiralling collapse in international trade for
lack of bank credit caused the interwar depression. After the war, many
people feared a return to depression and in 1947 one seemed to be in
the making. In Germany coal was in desperately short supply. Without
it no steel could be made; without steel the railroads and mines could
not be repaired. Without mines and railways no more coal could be
produced.

MARSHALL PLAN

In one of the greatest acts of generosity in history, US General George
Marshall announced on 5 June 1947 that America was prepared to
finance European reconstruction provided the Europeans produced a
co-ordinated strategy to ensure that the money was well spent. Aid was
also conditional on the recipients pursuing liberal trade policies. The
Soviet Union, Eastern Europe and all Germany were included in the
offer, known subsequently as the Marshall Plan. The Soviet Union
refused and forced Easter European countries to follow suit. This refusal
was followed by the failure of a further conference in London in
December 1947 to make any progress in running Germany jointly. The
US was finally forced to recognise that the West would have to go it
alone in its own half of the country.

Western European nations got together to form the Organisation for
European Economic Co-operation (OEEC) to administer the Marshall
Plan aid programme, which passed Congress in the summer of 1948. (In
1960 the US and Canada joined the OEEC which was reborn as the
Organisation for Economic Co-operation and Development – OECD.)
Marshall Plan aid was far more than the economic catalyst which put
Western Europe back on its feet. It precipitated the political change
which produced the two rival German states. The US forced a reluctant
France to merge its zone with Bizonia. A crucial step to West German
economic rehabilitation could now be taken: the reform and stabilisation
of the currency. For over three years the old Reichsbank had been
struggling to keep going while the Reichsmark had become virtually
worthless. Despite no vindictive peace treaty (à la Versailles) or major
reparation demands, Germany suffered hyper-inflation for the second
time in a generation. Savings were once more wiped out. Cigarettes

became the medium of exchange and, given the continuation of Nazi German price controls, food and most other goods disappeared from the shops. They were obtainable only at exorbitant prices on the black market. The West allowed this state of affairs to continue as long as a unified German state and economy remained possible. But when General Zhukov marched out of the Allied Control Commission in March 1948, this possibility finally vanished.

CURRENCY REFORMS

On Sunday 20 June 1948 the old Reichsmark was declared worthless. A new bank was established called the Bank deutscher Länder and a new currency, the Deutsche Mark or D-Mark as it is often called. Germans were allowed to swap RM 40 for DM 40. After that all savings were converted at a rate of RM 100 = DM 6.5. The saver was obliged to provide a statement of his financial wealth before exchanging Reichs-marks for D-Marks (not popular amongst tax-evading black-marketeers). Debts, however, had to be repaid at a rate of RM 100 = DM 10, which helped out creditors. The Bank deutscher Länder, owned by the Länder central banks, could not be a central bank for all Germany. That is why it was so named. (In 1957 it became the Bundesbank.) The day the currency reforms were revealed, the German Director of the Economic Administration Office for Bizonia, Professor Ludwig Erhard, ignited a bonfire of controls covering wages, prices and supplies. Suddenly money was scarce and valuable again. The black market disappeared and goods returned to shop shelves. The West German economic miracle had at last begun, three years after the war's end.

BLOCKADE – AND AIRLIFT

There was no problem in D-Marks circulating freely in the three Western zones. The Soviet Union naturally blocked the currency's circulation in its zone of Germany (ironically the D-Mark now circulates in Russia). The Soviets said they would be happy to accept the D-Mark, provided they were given some of the plates to print it. The Allies refused and went ahead on their own. This did not matter for separate zones, but the D-Mark had to be introduced in Berlin, which was still a single economic unit. Here the Soviet Union faced the problem of establishing and maintaining an exchange rate between the old currency and the D-Mark, which would reveal the Soviet zone's inferior performance. Averse to do so, it embarked on action designed to evict the Western Powers. It blockaded all land movement between the western zones and Berlin. As nothing had been formally agreed concerning access, the Soviet Union could not be accused of breaking any obligations. The West's answer was the Berlin airlift, a tricky operation as aircraft needed to land one every two minutes in West Berlin's only airport. Nonetheless the task was achieved and Berlin saved. The West had shown its determination to stand up to Moscow and Stalin's provocative gesture had been premature. The Soviet Union needed a few more months before it would have the atomic bomb. Until then, brinkmanship could be extremely dangerous. B29s, which were stationed in Britain at the start of the crisis, were capable of dropping nuclear bombs on Soviet cities.

BASIC LAW

The cold war which started with the Berlin blockade was crucial to West Germany's future. The West Germans ran to the arms of Western Europe and the United States to escape a Communist bear hug. In July 1948, following the currency reforms, the Allies called on the Minister-Presidents of the western Länder (local government had already been returned to German hands) to establish a Constituent Assembly to draw up a new Constitution for West Germany. Loath to abandon hope of unification, they refused. A Constitution might imply the permanency of the division. In their view a German Constitution could not be adopted until a peace treaty had been negotiated and signed. Legally Germany's frontiers remained in a time warp, those of 1937. Instead of appointing a Constituent Assembly they compromised upon an elected Parliamentary Council which was given the job of producing a document described as the *Basic Law*. This established the Federal Republic of Germany, not the German Federal Republic. There is an important difference in this seemingly irrelevant semantic. As mentioned above, West Germany saw itself as the legal successor to the earlier German state and assumed all the rights and obligations this entailed. East Germany, on the other hand, by calling itself the German Democratic Republic, disclaimed all connection with the Third Reich and earlier German states. Berlin continued to be administered by the four Occupying Powers. The Western sectors were not included in the Federal Republic. Elections to the Parliamentary Council returned twenty-seven CDU-CSU representatives and the same number of SPD representatives; five FDP representatives were elected, together with two each for the Centre party and the Communists. Konrad Adenauer was voted the Council's Chairman.

Germany's Basic Law aimed to avoid the shortcomings of the Weimar Constitution. It drew heavily on the 1848 Paulskirche Constitution. The Basic Law's authority was stated to rest on the will of the inhabitants of the western Länder, acting on behalf of all Germans. The task of designing a Constitution was postponed until Germany might be reunited. But at least they were allowed to construct their own Constitution, unlike the Japanese who had an American one imposed on them. Moreover this first act of German post-war democracy was supported by all major German political parties, unlike the Weimar Constitution. This might not have been the case if, like Weimar, the Basic Law had been promulgated in the immediate aftermath of defeat. Coming four years later it had a much better chance. (In 1948 over 40% of Germans told opinion pollsters that they believed Nazism was a good thing badly carried out.)

The Basic Law sets out human rights, which a Constitutional Court was established to uphold. It created a decentralised Federal Government, in which power was to be shared between the centre and the Länder. A Federal Assembly, the Bundestag, was established, elected every four years by universal suffrage. Half the Bundestag seats are allotted to single member constituencies and the other half are chosen by proportional representation from party lists. Voters have two votes, one for their local constituency member, the other for a party. To prevent proportional representation leading to a multiplicity of tiny parties, a national 5% threshold of the popular vote must be exceeded (or three single member seats won) to obtain a share of the PR seats. The 5% rule was applied separately to the old and new Länder in the first all-German elections in December 1990. It helped some reformed communist members of the Party of Democratic Socialists (PDS) to obtain PR seats. But in the 1994 election the 5% rule was applied across all Germany. This system has worked satisfactorily. After the first two elections, all Bundestag seats were won by the major parties until 1983, when the Greens overcame the 5% hurdle. In the first all-German election in 1990 the Greens fell short of 5% in the old Länder but passed it in the new. The PDS, former Communists or 'Red Socks', by passing the 5% threshold in the new Länder, obtained a total of seventeen seats to the Greens' eight.

In the 1994 election the Greens and the Free Democrats both got more than 5% of the all-German vote, while the 'Red Socks' won four constituency seats allowing their 4.4% share of the vote to be included in the PR share-out. Although Helmut Kohl's CDU-CSU, FDP coalition won a narrow ten-seat majority, it should remain stable. When a Bundestag delegate dies there is no by-election. His place is filled by the next on his party's PR list.

An upper house, the Bundesrat, is appointed by Länder Governments. It reflects their political composition and represents their interest. Representatives from a Land vote as a block. Representatives change whenever Länder Governments change. Legislation is divided into three kinds:

- 'Exclusive' measures which are solely in the Federal domain, such as police, justice, foreign affairs and defence. (Länder are often responsible for the local administration of Federal measures, such as justice and police.) The Bundesrat considers exclusive measures and can veto them. But such vetoes can be overruled by the Bundestag. A measure rejected by a simple majority in the Bundesrat can be negated by a simple majority in the Bundestag (but of all members, not simply a majority of those voting), but one rejected by a two-thirds majority needs a two-thirds majority to be overruled. The SPD and its allies are now close to a two-thirds majority in the Bundesrat.
- 'Concurrent' measures are ones where the Federal Government and Länder have shared interests and responsibilities, such as taxation. The Federal Government is normally the collecting agent (as for VAT), but the proceeds are shared with the Länder. More will be said of this arrangement in Chapter 13 dealing with the costs of unification. Like US Congressional legislation, concurrent measures must be passed by both chambers, each having a veto. Since the Bundesrat is often, as now, controlled by the opposition, this requires a high degree of consensus government.

• All remaining measures covering matters for which each Länder Government is solely responsible inside its own Land are determined by the Länder alone. They include education and cultural affairs.

The Government is made up of a Chancellor and ministers, who need not be members of the Bundestag, but can choose to attend its sessions and may be forced to do so by the Bundestag. The Government must command a majority in the Bundestag and the Chancellor is chosen by it. The process is slightly complicated. Before a Chancellor can be voted out on a no-confidence vote, forty-eight hours' notice must be given and his successor must be named. The old cannot be discarded unless the new has been selected. This is called a 'constructive' vote of no-confidence and it prevents the political paralysis which occurs when two extremes, with no common candidate, unite in opposing the centre. Helmut Schmidt was ousted in this manner in October 1982 by Helmut Kohl. The Chancellor can also demand a vote of confidence in himself. If he loses, the Bundestag has three weeks in which to agree on a successor. If it fails to do so, the Chancellor has the right to request new elections. Kohl, for example, deliberately lost a confidence vote to engineer an early election in March 1983.

A President is elected by the Bundestag and an equal number of representatives chosen by the Länder. His job is largely ceremonial. When a Chancellor loses a confidence vote and the Bundestag cannot agree on a successor, he is not forced to ask for fresh elections. The President may, with the approval of the Bundesrat, declare laws passed by emergency decree. This procedure may be used for one six-month period during a Chancellor's tenure. If deadlock continues thereafter, fresh elections must be called.

The Basic Law can be changed by a two-thirds majority of the Bundestag and Bundesrat. But its Federal character cannot be altered. Members of the Constitutional Court, which stands as the guardian of the Basic Law – importantly deciding on boundary disputes between the Federal Government and Länder – are chosen in turn by the Bundestag and Bundesrat.

The Basic Law is undoubtedly an improvement on the Weimar Constitution. It avoids rivalry between a popularly elected President and a popularly elected parliament, the multiplicity of small parties, political irresponsibility by opposing extremes and the abuse of emergency powers. But it has worked only because there has been a willingness to make it work. Power is shared between the Federal Government and the Länder in a way which could easily lead to political paralysis. If there were large numbers of Germans wishing to bring down the system, they could create a crisis in which power would pass into other hands. The major difference between 1918–33 and 1949–89 has been the lack of extremists. This is understandable. The Nazis were discredited. The Communists, thanks to Russia's behaviour in East Europe, never had a chance in the West. The old interest groups and the establishment lost power during the Third Reich, the war and the occupation. Collectively they might have made a comeback in 1945, restoring some form of autocratic government, if Germany had never been occupied. They had little hope of doing so by 1949 when, after a shaky beginning, the Western Allies gave the German economy a flying start. Adenauer's authoritarian behaviour as Chancellor satisfied the German desire for firm government. He allowed individual members of the old establishment to regain their former standing. Denazification was never carried far or applied fairly in the American and British zones. Too many Germans had been involved to some degree in working for the Third Reich. Even so, Adenauer put the clock back as far as he could.[1] A measure introduced in 1953 wiped the slate clean on former Nazis who, while never being tried for war crimes, had suffered civil disabilities and lost their pensions. Pensions and jobs were restored, some at the expense of non-Nazis who then held them. Unfair maybe, but in this manner democracy came to be accepted by the overwhelming majority of West Germans.

The Parliamentary Council passed the Basic Law on 8 May 1949, four years after VE Day. On the same day the Soviets lifted the Berlin blockade. They had gone ahead to establish the German Democratic Republic, creating a Stalinist Communist state in East Germany. The first elections to the Federal Bundestag were held on 14 August 1949.

[1] David Marsh shows in his book *The Bundesbank: The Bank That Rules Europe* (1992) that between 1948 and 1980 nearly 40% of all council, directorate and Land board members of the Bank deutscher Länder and Bundesbank were former Nazi party members. Karl Blessing, the first President of the Bundesbank, was a former Nazi. This was not exceptional. In 1952 the majority of top Foreign Office officials were former Nazis. Adenauer included former Nazis in his cabinets, notably Gerhard Schroder, Interior Minister, in 1953 and Theodor Oberlander, a former SS member, as Minister for Refugees.

To general surprise, the CDU–CSU won more seats than the SPD and were able to form a government with FDP support. Konrad Adenauer, then aged seventy-two, became Chancellor. It says a lot for the stability of the new system and his own vitality that he remained Chancellor for fourteen years to 1963.

The cold war, a stable constitution, Marshall Plan aid and a favourable international economic environment gave West Germany the growth and prosperity needed for the success of democracy. German hard work is often stressed. The Germans probably did work a bit harder than other people, but they certainly don't now. They were better educated and organised than most and more highly motivated. A Japanese friend observed recently that at the end of the war most ordinary Germans and Japanese felt lucky to be alive. They owed a duty to their fallen comrades to rebuild their countries. The victors felt differently. The British had made great sacrifices. They did not expect to have to go on struggling. They believed that they deserved to be rewarded. The winners thought their countries owed them a living, the losers believed they owed their lives to their countries.

CHAPTER 9

Enemies, Friends and Neighbours

Chapter 8 described the post-war division of Germany and the creation of the Federal Republic, which was overwhelmingly the work of the Americans and British. This chapter outlines political development in the Federal Republic up to 1957, when the European Economic Community was formed. This is a story of waning Anglo-Saxon influence and growing French. Neighbours, whose battles the British and Americans twice intervened to settle, finally made up and became friends, or so it seems. But what brought this about? The Germans and French remain very different people and lasting harmony between them seems too much to hope for, particularly if it is at the expense of discord with Germany's eastern neighbours. This is one of the questions whose answer will determine Europe's fate.

The French role in Germany's disastrous history has to be explored. Although the Germans usually started wars, the French always helped to provoke them. Admittedly Bismarck trapped the French into starting the 1870 Franco-Prussian war. But the French people and Napoleon III were looking for a fight, having failed to appreciate Prussia's growing industrial might. Until 1870 the French entertained delusions of grandeur, seeking European hegemony. Sedan destroyed French delusions. Thereafter France endeavoured to gain through diplomacy what she could no longer win single-handedly on the battlefield. The French wanted revenge for Sedan and the return of Alsace-Lorraine. They formed an alliance with Russia to keep Germany in its place. As the Wilhelmine Reich increasingly threatened and alienated Britain, another old French enemy became a friend. Germany and Austria were isolated in 1914. They were not the only countries armed to the hilt and with mobilisation plans prepared in the utmost detail. The whole of Europe was an armed camp ready for war.

The First World War cannot be blamed on Germany alone. Every major power had a hand in causing it. Similarly the punitive Treaty of Versailles cannot be blamed on France alone. In the immediate aftermath of war no democratically elected politician could have let Germany off lightly. Public opinion amongst the victors was baying for blood. A vindictive peace settlement was inevitable. But long after Britain and American opinion had turned in favour of more lenient treatment for Germany, the French remained vindictive. In 1922 they prevented agreement on easing the burden of reparations. Their unilateral occupation of the Ruhr in 1923 helped to fuel hyper-inflation and almost brought down the Weimar Republic. French refusal to make concessions to Stresemann's policy of fulfilment during the later 1920s contributed to its failure. If fulfilment had been well rewarded (as Adenauer's co-operation with the Americans was to be thirty years later), the Weimar's opponents would have been weakened. The Republic might have withstood the depression – although this is doubtful given the crass stupidity of Chancellor Brüning's deflationary policies. Yet had reparations gold payment obligations been less, perhaps Germany would have followed Britain in 1931 off the gold standard. What is clear is that the French behaviour towards Germany in the 1920s and early 1930s was a significant factor in helping Hitler's rise to power.

In 1945 the French attitude towards the Germans was almost as vindictive as it had been in 1918. They had, it seems, learnt nothing from their inter-war mistakes. It was fortunate, therefore, that France had far less say in Germany's post-war treatment. They did not deserve much. The nation's role during the war had been ambivalent, to say the least. Yet the crimes of Vichy France were swept under the carpet. France was given a small zone of occupation almost as an afterthought. It was carved out of the American and British zones, since the Soviet Union would not give anything up. This grace-and-favour gesture carried with it membership of the four-power Allied Control Commission, giving France a veto over policy towards Germany. With singular ingratitude, the French systematically obstructed the Americans and British. French national pride had been affronted by exclusion from Yalta and Potsdam. So they sided with the Soviets against the creation of the central agencies needed to run Germany as a single economic unit (which had been agreed at Potsdam). Sir Alec Cairncross in *The Price Of War* (1986) describes the French attitude to Germany at that time:

> First, the French made it clear that they did not accept this provision of an Agreement to which they were not themselves a party. They wanted to ensure that Germany was sufficiently weakened through the detachment and military occupation of the Ruhr and the Rhineland, and the annexation of the Saar. Before setting up central agencies they also sought to secure for themselves continuing access to German coal supplies on favourable terms, intended to build in France the heavy industries denied to Germany.

France wanted to do everything in its power to prevent Germany from reindustrialising and regaining any part of its former economic strength. The French refused to join Bizonia in 1946, and opposed Marshall Plan aid for Germany in 1947. They objected to any rebuilding of German industry. The French obstructed German recovery in every way they could. But the tide of events was against them. The cold war made a changed attitude imperative – so too did the French need for dollars. Instead of denying Germany a share of Marshall Plan aid, the French almost lost their own, being forced to merge their zone into Bizonia before receiving their share. Finally the centime dropped: if the German beast could not be prevented from getting back on its feet, perhaps it could be trained to obey French masters.

STABLE GOVERNMENT

When the war ended the Social Democrats were the most popular party in Germany and the Communists also scored well in opinion polls. The centre and right were compromised and in retreat. Had there been immediate elections, as after the First World War, a left-wing government would have been formed and would have embarked on a policy of nationalisation. The Socialists supported public ownership of the means of production. But like their counterparts in Britain, they hoped to achieve their social aims through the ballot box. The Communists blamed the war on capitalism by their assertion that big industrialists, who profited from rearmament, were to blame for Hitler's rise to power. But by the time the first Federal election was held, on 14 August 1949, the political pendulum had swung away from the left. The Communists, discredited by Soviet behaviour in the GDR, polled only 5.7% of the popular vote to win fifteen Bundestag seats. The Socialist SPD became the largest single party with 131 seats. The CDU won 115 but its Bavarian sister party, the CSU, won another twenty-four to give a CDU-CSU total of 139 seats. The FDP took fifty-two seats. As a free-market laissez-faire party, opposed to nationalisation, the FDP supported the CDU-CSU. But together their 191 seats fell eleven short of a majority. These were secured from amongst the eight smaller parties which shared eighty seats, but only just; Konrad Adenauer was elected Chancellor by a single vote.

Politically the Federal Republic was very stable. During the forty years from 1949 to 1989 there were only six Chancellors, compared with ten British Prime Ministers. Adenauer lasted over fourteen years, Helmut Schmidt six years and if Helmut Kohl runs his full term he will have served sixteen years before going in 1998. The stability of the parties was equally impressive. Expressed as percentages of their combined Bundestag seats, the CDU-CSU share ranged from a low of 43% to a high of 56%, the SPD from 34% to 46% and the FDP from 8% to 12%. This stability conferred on the FDP a pivotal position. For most of the time it straddled the 50% line, able thereby to put into office either Christian Democrats or Social Democrats. A Christian Democrat-Free Democrat coalition held office for the first seventeen years of the Federal Republic's four-decade life. In 1966 the FDP split, Chancellor Ludwig Erhard was ditched and the Socialists joined the Christian Democrats in a great 'Black-Red' coalition with the CDU's Kurt-Georg Kiesinger (a Nazi party member as early as 1933, when membership was still mainly voluntary) as Chancellor. Surprisingly it lasted nearly three years. The FDP returned to government in 1969 and kept the Social Democrats in power for nearly fourteen years under the Chancellorships of Willy Brandt and Helmut Schmidt. Finally it switched its support back to the Conservatives in 1982, to put Kohl into office.

The CDU and CSU were not entirely right-wing parties, rather an amalgam of Protestants and Catholics, originally thrown together by opposition to Hitler. The Catholics from the old Centre party leaned to the left and had the support of Catholic trades unionists, who opposed the Social Democrat party because of its anti-clericalism. The result was that the CDU–CSU helped develop the social market economy which so differentiates Germany from both the Anglo-American free-market model and the French centralised dirigiste regime. The CSU–CDU introduced the 1951 Co-determination Law which gave unions parity on the supervisory boards of Iron, Steel and Coal companies, coupled with one-third membership of the boards of large companies in other sectors. They also supported Helmut Schmidt's 1976 measure to extend parity of supervisory board membership to all large companies. Indeed CDU economic policy under Ludwig Erhard, its astute Finance Minister, seemed as hostile to capitalists as to labour. Erhard campaigned long and hard against cartelisation, in the teeth of opposition from employers' organisations.

If the Conservative parties were tinged pink in fine Bismarckian tradition, the Socialists turned somewhat blue. They dropped many left-wing policies at their Bad Godesberg conference in 1959, including nationalism and their opposition to NATO, the European Iron & Steel Community and the European Economic Community. They moved from being an anti-clerical working-class party to one aiming at a broad appeal to attract the growing middle classes. The key slogan was coined by Karl Schiller: 'Competition as far as possible – planning as far as necessary.' The result was that the main parties held very similar views over a wide range of policies, giving consensus government (which the differing composition of Bundestag and Bundesrat made necessary) the chance to work. The Bad Godesberg U-turn was designed to bring the SPD in from the political cold and it succeeded. The same move is only now being made by the Japanese Socialists and for the same reason. Britain's Labour Party, under its young leader, Tony Blair, agreed thirty-six years later to scrap Clause 4 in its manifesto which calls for national-isation.

THE GERMAN PREDICAMENT

The Social Democrats' shift towards the middle ground on domestic issues pushed foreign affairs to centre stage. The issues here bear a close resemblance to those of today. West Germans shared a great desire for reunification and a strong aversion to Communism. The desire for the former argued for a policy of appeasement towards the Soviet Union which would involve West Germany in distancing itself from its European neighbours and the United States. The Soviet Union would have willingly considered reunification if West Germany were neutral and disarmed. On the other hand, the cold war and threat of a Communist take-over argued powerfully for West German rearmament and the closest possible links with its Western Allies. This apparently ruled out any possibility that the Soviet Union would agree to reunification. A choice had to be made between east and west. Reunification and Communism were a package deal. Later, a second choice had to be made between Anglo-Saxons and French, of which more below. Today similar choices face Germany. It seeks a deeper relationship with its existing European Union partners in the West, together with a wider and freer relationship with its neighbours to the East. It will be shown later that, if Germany continues to pursue the development of the EU along the lines mapped out in the Maastricht Treaty, its relations with East Europe must remain distant. But if the Maastricht approach is ditched, Germany must fall out with France. So it is important to see why the two fell in together in the first place.

Adenauer was a crafty politician and an autocratic Chancellor (as is Kohl). His suspicion and hatred of Stalin and Soviet Communism was immense. He saw no possibility of Soviet agreement to reunification which did not involve, sooner or later, a Communist take-over. He was a hard-liner, supporting confrontation and rejecting compromise completely. He therefore endeavoured to bind the Federal Republic as closely as possible into the Western Alliance. This had the added attraction of promoting West German sovereignty and winning acceptance back into the community of nations in the shortest possible time. Initially it meant pursuing a strongly pro-American policy. But later, after Stalin's death in March 1953 and the end of the Korean War a month later, the cold war started to thaw a little. The United States and the Soviet Union renewed their search for an agreed solution to the German question. Adenauer's response was to tie the German economy so closely to France that communism could never take root in a united Germany. He wanted at all costs to avoid Soviet hegemony in Europe. (The French are now trying to tie united Germany more closely into the EU, to prevent German hegemony of Europe.)

When France lost the battle to deny Marshall Plan aid to Germany and to keep its zone separate, it realised it could not prevent German economic and military recovery against American and British wishes. It became necessary therefore to lock Germany into the Western European community so that its growing strength might be controlled. When France could no longer hope to rule Europe alone, at least she could share the hegemony of Europe with Germany. War guilt would prevent the Germans from pursuing too independent a role and French diplomacy would ensure the Franco-German axis moved Europe in the direction France wanted it to go. This policy of containment has been pursued by France ever since, and with increased vigour following unification, as shown by the rush to negotiate the Maastricht Treaty.

The French made their first move in a letter from the Foreign Minister, Robert Schuman, to Chancellor Adenauer on 8 May 1950, proposing the formation of a European Coal & Steel Community. This exemplified the French dirigiste approach to competition. Tariffs and quotas between member countries, initially France and Germany but expanded to the Benelux and Italy, would be scrapped. But trade would not be free. Coal and steel resources would be pooled and allocated by a High Authority. Britain was invited to join but declined. The Treaty establishing the ECSC was signed in April 1951 in Paris. The European Atomic Energy Community (Euratom) followed. The long march towards European political, monetary and economic union had begun. It was to be given a powerful thrust by dramatic events unfolding on the opposite side of the world.

COLD WAR TENSIONS

The creation of the Federal and Democratic Republics came on the eve of the Korean War. The cold war had intensified with the Communist take-over of Czechoslovakia in February 1948 and the 1948–9 Berlin blockade. It froze solid with the outbreak of the Korean War in 1950. This taught many lessons. Germany, divided in two like Korea, feared a Communist invasion. If the Soviets pushed the Americans out of Berlin, would their tanks be sent rolling over the Rhine? What was to stop them? In the summer of 1950 the Soviets had 175 divisions in East Germany or nearby. Only twelve divisions faced them in Western Europe. The US sensibly refused to use nuclear weapons in Korea, which underlined Western Europe's exposure to conventional attack. Europe had been put under America's nuclear umbrella by the establishment of NATO in 1949 and B29s with nuclear weapons were already based in Britain. But if the balance of conventional forces was to be tilted less against the Western Alliance, the Federal Republic had to make its contribution and rearm.

German rearmament would deepen divisions within Europe. For those who still hoped that unification of a neutral Germany could be negotiated with the Soviet Union, rearmament was anathema. For people remembering German militarism it was truly alarming (i.e., to neighbouring Europeans and also many Germans). The new armies would be run by officers from the old. The army's 1930s involvement in Weimar politics, and the help it gave Hitler in his climb to power, still caused widespread concern. Yet nationalist extremists opposed rearming almost as much as Socialists and Communists. They attached the greatest importance to unification, which they believed would be totally ruled out.

Adenauer, as we have seen, took a different view. Perhaps as a Catholic Rhinelander he was less enamoured of sacrifices to reunite Germany. Nonetheless he openly espoused the view that sticking up to the Russians held out the best, even the only, prospect for German reunification. And how this view was mocked! The American historian, Gordan A. Craig, observed in *The Germans* (1982) that Adenauer was 'injudicious in his repeated insistence that a policy of strength, based upon German rearmament and adhesion to the Western Alliance, would force the Soviet Government, in due course, to permit reunification. The best that can be said for this argument is that the British and particularly the Americans believed in it even more fervently than the Chancellor.' While William Carr, in a revised fourth edition of *A History of Germany 1815–1990*, published in 1991, expressed similar thoughts: 'Adenauer beat the anti-communist drum loudly, insisting that an unarmed Germany would only encourage Russian aggression; far from postponing re-unification, the armed might of the west, augmented by German divisions, would eventually force Russia to negotiate, a dangerous illusion – if Adenauer ever believed it – which he shared with the American Secretary of State John Foster Dulles.'

These quotes are not intended to deride their authors' lack of foresight. Their views were widely shared and both books are superb. It was nonetheless through confrontation and an arms race that the Soviet Communist system was finally forced to collapse, opening the way to reunification. But it took rather a long time and no one can know whether a less bellicose approach might have worked sooner and at less of a cost. The Soviets, after all, had good reason to fear for their safety in view of the aggression shown to them in the past.

A storm of protest greeted the news that Adenauer was willing to see Germany rearmed. But rearmament locked Germany into the Western Alliance. On 24 October 1950 the French Prime Minister, René Pleven, offered the rearmed Germans a place within a proposed European Defence Community, in which Germany's forces would be a part of an integrated European Army. Adenauer agreed to the proposal with alacrity, believing that membership of such an organisation on equal terms with other members would enhance Germany's international status. Already Adenauer's pro-West policy was paying dividends. Following the formation of the first post-war Federal German Government in September 1949, the Allied High Commissioners had granted Germany an 'Occupation Statute', setting out the rights and obligations of the Occupying Powers with regard to the new Republic. No peace treaty had been signed but at least Germany's surrender was no longer unconditional. The Americans had defined limits to their power.

EUROPEAN DEFENCE COMMUNITY

When Adenauer agreed to rearm, the Federal Republic was allowed to negotiate the European Defence Community Treaty in its own right. The six European Governments involved took almost two years to agree the Treaty of Paris setting up the EDC. It was signed in May 1952 by all six. Britain was not amongst them. It was one of two treaties. The other, the Treaty of Bonn, cancelled the Occupation Statute, wound up the High Commission and bestowed full sovereignty on the Federal Republic. The Treaty of Bonn was to come into effect when the Treaty of Paris had been ratified. At this stage, however, the French had second thoughts.

The loss of sovereignty involved in having the French army part of the EDC was not popular and the Treaty seemed unlikely to be ratified by the National Assembly. Indeed, the Government feared to put it to the test. Bundestag ratification came on 19 March 1953. But when finally placed before the French National Assembly in August 1954, the Treaty was rejected. Britain was blamed for her refusal to take part. Germany was then invited to join NATO. Full sovereignty was granted on 5 May 1955, just under ten years after VE Day, and the Federal Republic became a NATO member four days later. Paradoxically Germany's return to the community of nations was completed at the same time as the Federal Republic undertook to raise a 500,000-strong national army.

Adenauer's belief that a hard line against the Soviet Union would pay off received some confirmation. When Stalin died in March 1953 and the Korean War ended a month later, the cold war began to thaw a little. The Soviets were willing to negotiate over the status of a united Germany and the Americans agreed. The Soviet objective appears to have been to block the formation of the EDC and prevent Germany from rearming. As success would have involved concessions to the Soviet Union, Adenauer's response was to move Germany closer to France. The negotiations, however, were protracted and unsuccessful. Meanwhile, the failure to create a defence community gave France and Germany a push towards creating an economic community. Less than a month after obtaining its sovereignty, the Federal Republic plunged into the negotiation which led to the Treaty of Rome, signed on 25 March 1957 by the six members of the ECSC. The European Economic Community (EEC) was born.

TREATY OF ROME

A thought must be given to Germans and French motives at that time. The idea of a peaceful and co-operative European community of nations was not new. It had always been seen as an antidote to nationalism, particularly German nationalism. It had been mooted after the First World War by the British Prime Minister, David Lloyd George, amongst others. Winston Churchill proposed it during the Second World War. Many people in all countries shared the dream of a peaceful and united Europe. Moreover it is hardly surprising that Europe's post-war leaders should espouse it. Political leaders such as Robert Schuman, Adenauer and the Italian Alcide de Gasperi all came from border areas ravaged by war and were Catholic. Moreover, having had a national army forced upon Germany, Adenauer was keener than ever to bind the Federal Republic economically into the West. There is no doubt of the deep desire amongst Europeans, looking to the past, for some means to prevent a repetition of catastrophic European wars in the future. But looking to the future, politicians on all sides had ideas about how they wanted European integration to develop and what national advantages they hoped to get out of it.

An economic deal between Germany and France was at the heart of the EEC from the beginning. Germany already had a large and advanced industrial sector. France had a large and relatively backward agricultural sector. West Germany had been cut off from its natural food supplies by the loss of Prussia and Silesia and by the division of the country. A deal was therefore struck under which the French bought cheap German manufactures and in return the Germans bought dear French food. The former was accomplished by the removal of tariff barriers within the EEC and the imposition of a common external tariff against imports from outside it. The latter required the invention of the notorious Common Agricultural Policy (CAP). This deal clearly favoured producers over consumers. It had added attractions for German industrialists in that competition policy was raised from the national to the community level. Large German combines could retain a monopoly of their domestic markets provided they faced competition from other EEC countries.

The Treaty of Rome, setting up the EEC, was signed on 24 March 1957 by Germany, France, Italy, Belgium, the Netherlands and Luxemburg. At the political level, France gained leverage in so far as Germany could be led in the direction that the French wanted to go. While the Germans, constrained by war guilt from overtly playing a world role appropriate to their economic weight, were able covertly to do so. Membership of the EEC imposed a further barrier to German unification other than on terms of a free-market, capitalistic model. The German Democratic Republic was meanwhile moving further towards the Stalinist Communist economic model. As the two systems became increasingly dissimilar, integration could no longer be envisaged simply through the expedient of neutrality and all-German elections. One or other system would have to be abandoned before Germany could be reunited.

CHAPTER 10

The Road to Reunification

The year 1957 was full of great events. The birth of the EEC in March was one. In August the Soviets launched a missile with an atomic warhead and in October shot the world's first satellite, Sputnik, into orbit. In December NATO decided to authorise the use of tactical nuclear weapons in Central Europe. The result was a chain reaction which led ultimately to Communism's collapse and German reunification – but it was hard to see this at the time.

The Germans did not simply rely on closer economic relations with their neighbours to contain the risks rearming involved. The new Bundeswehr was a far cry from the old Wehrmacht. Its soldiers were 'citizens in uniform' enjoying considerable civil rights, including the right to belong to a trades union and to have access to an Ombudsman. The Bundeswehr was placed firmly under civil political control and operationally was under NATO command. A 500,000-strong army never did materialise. By the end of 1957 the Bundeswehr was around 120,000 strong against its original 370,000 target. In a booming economy, meeting the original target would have placed too great a demand on industrial manpower. For this reason Germany's 1950s industrialists resisted rearmament. But with other countries equally reluctant to release manpower for armies, it became apparent that Western Europe was never likely to build up conventional forces to a sufficient level to resist a Soviet attack. Hence NATO's decision in December 1957 to authorise the use of tactical nuclear weapons in response to any conventional attack.

When the Soviet Union launched Sputnik 1 the world changed. The

Soviets had taken a lead in space and had the power to direct inter-continental ballistic missiles onto American cities. The American mon-opoly of the nuclear deterrent ended as the use of tactical nuclear weapons in Europe was authorised. It was doubtful whether the Americans would press the nuclear button to defend Europe once the Soviet Union could retaliate by wiping out Washington DC. But equally the Soviets would hesitate to launch a conventional invasion into Western Europe if the result might be a nuclear war. The world was thus confronted by the possibility of Armageddon. The Soviets endeavoured to capitalise on the missile lead they had gained. In November 1958 Nikita Khrushchev demanded that Berlin be demilitarised and that agreement be reached within six months on its status as a free city under four-Power guarantee. If not, the Soviets would transfer control over access to the German Democratic Republic which would, in all likelihood, resume the block-ade. The GDR might call America's bluff by forcibly stopping supplies reaching the city by air. The Allies instead called Russia's bluff, firmly indicating that they would respond to any such action with force. As neither side wanted a nuclear confrontation, Khrushchev backed down and broader talks were initiated on Germany's future.

It may seem strange that Berlin was always so great an issue. To the Western Alliance it was symbolic. The Soviets must never be allowed to impose solutions on the West. For the Soviet Union and the GDR Berlin posed a more pragmatic problem. It was the interface between the economies of the Federal Republic and the Democratic Republic. In Berlin the success of a capitalist free-market system was on display and could be contrasted with the failure of the Communist command economy. East Germans were also able to vote with their feet by emi-grating, via Berlin, to West Germany. The West German economy was steaming ahead. By the late 1950s West German GDP was 50% higher than pre-war, East German GDP had just about regained its 1938 level. A higher proportion of West German output was consumer goods, which East Germans lacked. West Germany also offered freedom. West Berlin was the shop window and gateway to the West. During the 1950s an average of 600 East Germans a day made their choice and crossed over. The GDR was not merely losing labour at an intolerable rate, but losing young, skilled and enterprising labour. Those who did not leave still knew how well the West Germans were doing. The Communists pretended the East German economy was also doing quite well – an illusion accepted by both sides and not dispelled until after unification. The reality was that the GDR faced a deepening economic crisis. The Soviets had to do something about Berlin. It was a thorn in their side and one being pushed deeper by the day.

Talks on Germany's future as usual got nowhere. Khrushchev broke off a summit meeting with Eisenhower in Paris in May 1960 after an American U2 spy-plane was shot down over Russia. When the young John F. Kennedy became President, Khrushchev renewed his threats and time limits, but was again met by firmness. A simple and pragmatic solution was finally applied. On 13 August 1961 a barbed wire fence began to be erected around West Berlin, which was soon replaced by a concrete wall. Henceforth East Germans were shut out of the West and physically prevented from emigrating. The Berlin Wall did not cause a crisis, it temporarily solved one. The Allies raised no serious objections. A year later the Americans and Russians clashed in earnest during the October 1962 Cuban missile crisis. Khrushchev had miscalculated. Neither side was prepared to start a nuclear war and the Russians were forced to back down (although, as a face-saver for Khrushchev, Kennedy reduced US missiles based in Turkey). This crisis eliminated any remaining possibility of Germany being reunited by force from either side. The Soviet hold on East Germany was as unbreakable as the Alliance hold on West Germany. Each half of the country was henceforth regarded an integral part of its respective block. Germany could be reunited only if one rival system failed. In the meantime both sides had to learn to live with this state of affairs.

Kennedy's famous Berlin speech, made in 1963, must be seen in the historical context. 'Ich bin ein Berliner'[1] he proclaimed in bad German ('ein Berliner' means a jam doughnut, just as 'ein Frankfurter' means a sausage and 'ein Hamburger' a Big Mac). But the mis-translation did not matter. Kennedy's speech was a pledge to use the might of the United States to defend the freedom of Berliners and West Germans. Having won the Cuban showdown, it was, to beleaguered Berliners, a promise worth having.

When the Berlin Wall was built, Adenauer's long reign was almost

[1] He should have said simply 'Ich bin Berliner.'

over. The Bundestag election on 17 September 1961 went badly and the CDU–CSU lost its overall majority. The FDP, with some reluctance, kept Adenauer in office, but only on the promise that he would retire in 1963. Adenauer was deeply disappointed at the Anglo-American willingness to accept the status quo in Germany. The hawkish nature of the CDU–CSU attitude to the division of Germany was typified by the Hallstein Doctrine (named after a Foreign Office official), in force since the establishment of the GDR in 1955. Not merely did the Federal Republic refuse to admit the GDR's existence (which to the legalistic German mind would confer legitimacy on the East German regime) but it promised to break off diplomatic relations with any state – excepting the Soviet Union and East Bloc countries – which did recognise the GDR. This was, of course, a ludicrous policy which could achieve nothing of merit. Nonetheless the fact that the British and Americans were prepared to negotiate with the Soviet Union on a basis which effectively assumed that the division of Germany was permanent, pushed Adenauer still closer to France.

General de Gaulle was also an autocrat and strongly opposed to American influence in continental Europe. France still aimed to play the role of a big power and hoped to broker a settlement between the Russians and Americans. But it needed a strong European partner for support. Britain's pro-American stance ruled her out (de Gaulle anyway disliked the British, feeling he had never been treated with the respect due to himself and France during the war). France therefore turned to Germany. In January 1963 Adenauer and de Gaulle signed a Franco-German Treaty of Friendship. It was more symbolic than substantive, but it firmly established the Franco-German axis at the heart of Europe. Part of the deal was to allow de Gaulle to veto Britain's application to join the EEC, which he promptly did. Yet arguably de Gaulle made the wrong choice of European partners. His views on Europe were closer to those, later, expressed by Margaret Thatcher for instance, than French views today; de Gaulle was as jealous of French national sovereignty as Thatcher was of British. The original European body, the ECSC, was run by a supranational High Authority, but the EEC played down the importance of those elements in its make-up (the Commission and the European Parliament) and enhanced the power of councils of ministers. De Gaulle favoured a Europe of nations acting in concert, rather than a federal system with a further tier of government above the national level. Germany, on the other hand, had long experience of shared sovereignty in a federal system. Whereas Adenauer saw the Franco-German partnership as the rock on which European unity was founded, and was willing to compromise to promote it (as over the French veto of British EEC membership), de Gaulle was not. In 1965 he took France out of the NATO command structure and brought EEC development to a halt over the issue of majority voting.

Adenauer resigned the Chancellorship in October 1963 aged eighty-seven. He departed under a cloud owing to his handling of the 'Spiegel Affair' the previous year.[1] In consequence he was unable to prevent Ludwig Erhard from succeeding him. Adenauer did not have a high opinion of Erhard's leadership abilities and in this he was proved right. Erhard had neither the strength to pursue Adenauer's hawkish foreign policy nor the courage to amend it. There followed three years of drift, during which the post-war recovery period ended and the Federal Republic suffered its first mild economic crisis. Inflation accelerated and both the balance of payments and budget moved into deficit. Erhard, father of the German miracle in 1949 was, by 1966, fated to be presiding over Germany's collapse. As related above, the Free Democrats finally split and a constructive vote of no confidence placed Kurt Kiesinger in the Chancellorship heading a grand coalition of CDU-CSU with the SPD. The next three years were spent clearing up the economic mess.

OSTPOLITIK

The political story of Germany's development over the remaining two decades to the collapse of the Berlin Wall in 1989 does not require detailed description. The Socialists finally came to power with Free Democrat support after the September 1969 Bundestag election. The new Chancellor, Willy Brandt, launched his Ostpolitik, reflecting the view that German reunification was highly unlikely in the near future and the best that the West Germans could do was to try, in small ways, to make life easier for the East Germans. Ostpolitik meant appeasement

---

[1] *Der Spiegel* was an investigative newspaper which revealed scandals about ministers and leaked sensitive army information. In late 1962 Adenauer had its offices raided and its editor locked up. His Defence Minister, Franz Josef Strauss, was forced to resign after lying to the Bundestag about the matter.

and ultimately recognition of the GDR. It was a policy of realism as well. Abandoning the Hallstein Doctrine, Brandt set out to negotiate non-aggression treaties with the Soviet Union, Poland and the GDR. The Kremlin was keen, desiring access to German capital, skills and products. The GDR under Walter Ulbricht was less enthusiastic. Hard-line opposition from the CDU–CSU hawks had enabled him to portray West Germans as revengeful and vindictive. Agreements were reached, however, with the Soviet Union and Poland, each of which recognised existing frontiers as 'inviolate', meaning that the Federal Republic accepted the Oder-Neisse line. Ulbricht was replaced by Erich Honecker, who turned out to be not much of an improvement on his Stalinist predecessor, but at least an agreement was reached with the GDR which put relations between the two Germanys on a more normal basis.

ENLARGEMENT OF THE COMMUNITY

General de Gaulle's resignation in April 1969 cleared the way for British entry into the European Community in 1973, along with Ireland and Denmark. The six became nine, to be increased to twelve with the later admission of Spain, Portugal and Greece. France initially welcomed British membership as providing a counter-weight to the growing economic strength of West Germany and, in Edward Heath, they faced a man who shared French goals for Europe. In the event, Heath was soon gone and ever since Britain has remained an awkward European partner.

In the 1970s and 1980s German politics became increasingly bound up in the evolving world economic and political scene. On the economic side, the Bretton Woods system crumbled in the early 1970s and finally collapsed in the spring of 1973 when the D-Mark was floated. This was shortly followed by the introduction of the European 'snake' – precursor to the European exchange rate mechanism (ERM), which tied EC currencies more formally together from 1979 onwards. The currency upheavals of the early 1970s were followed by rising inflation, the first oil price shock of 1973–4 and the 1974–5 world recession. Germany recovered slowly and excessive fiscal stimulation unbalanced the budget. The second oil shock of 1979–80 and the 1980–1 recession followed. Politically a second cold war freeze began in 1977 when the Soviet

Union installed SS20 medium-range missiles in Eastern Europe for which NATO had no response. The result was NATO's twin-track policy of building up its nuclear capabilities in Europe while, at the same time, offering to stop if the Soviets reduced theirs as well. After Soviet intervention in Afghanistan in 1979 and Ronald Reagan's election to the US Presidency, the stick of the twin-track policy received more attention than the carrot. Through his projected 'Star Wars' programme and substantial military spending Reagan began an arms race which the so-called 'Evil Empire's ailing economy could not hope to win. By March 1985, when Mikhail Gorbachev took control in the Soviet Union, the game was already up. The collapse of Communism, which opened the way to German reunification, had begun. In the end, Adenauer was right. Western strength finally forced the Soviet Union to give up East Germany.

Against this background, Willy Brandt's Chancellorship lasted until 7 May 1974, when he resigned to take the blame for the discovery that one of his aides was an East German spy. He was replaced by Helmut Schmidt, who saw the German economy through the collapse of Bretton Woods and two oil shocks. Deserted by the Free Democrats in 1982, the Socialists fell from power and were replaced by Helmut Kohl at the head of the CDU-CSU. Kohl's period in office began with the Eurosclerosis of the early 1980s. West Germany endured a protracted period of fiscal consolidation in the mid-1980s to correct the budgetary excesses of Schmidt's Socialists. Other European countries, notably France, experienced similar difficulties with slow growth and rising unemployment. A solution was sought through the 1986 Single European Act, which was to establish a single market by the end of 1992. This then was the political state of affair in 1989, when the Berlin Wall came tumbling down.

Three Decades of Success

In 1938 Germany's gross domestic product was one-quarter larger than Britain's; in 1948 West Germany's was a quarter of Britain's. The loss of land and people was partly to blame. A quarter of the Third Reich's 470,000 sq km went to the Soviet Union, Poland and France. East Germany, accounted for another quarter. West Germany was only about half the area (246,000 sq km) that all Germany had been before Hitler's war. The population also shrank, but not as much. It fell 30% from 70 million to 50 million. West Germany's recovery was dramatic, as Chart 11.1 shows, and by 1960 its GDP again equalled Britain's. This recovery was regarded as miraculous, the result of German hard work, discipline and efficiency. None of these factors can be denied – but frequently they have been exaggerated.

The West German recovery was more fortunate than miraculous. It owed as much to the Americans and British as to the Germans. The war victors created a world in which all could prosper. Germany possessed a wealth of human capital in education and skills. It had plentiful managerial ability in its demobilised officers and Third Reich bureaucrats, many of whom kept their jobs. Physically it retained far more industrial capacity than was generally supposed. But city centres were devastated by Allied bombing: much commercial property was flattened; one-fifth of all houses and flats were destroyed and a further 30% severely damaged. The 17 million housing stock was halved, while 10 million refugees flooded in from the east seeking somewhere to live. Roads, railways, bridges and inland waterways had been systematically destroyed. Com-

Chart 11.1 Germany's GDP relative to Britain's, 1850–1993

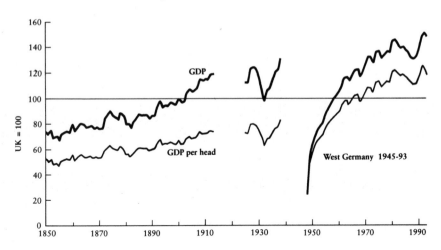

munications and power systems were in ruins. But factories, on the outskirts of cities, were far less damaged and most machinery remained intact or could be easily repaired. German wartime production did not collapse until 1945, when the country ran out of fuel. Some 10% to 20% of industrial equipment was destroyed by bombing and, since capacity had increased at least 20% during the war, the industrial capital stock in 1945 was probably larger than it had been in 1938.

The Allies originally intended to dismantle and cart away as reparations all plant in excess of the bare minimum which they calculated the Germans needed for survival. But the Americans and British soon realised that this was a mistake. If the Germans could not produce a surplus to export, they could not import the food to feed themselves. The Allies would then have to feed them, or watch while thousands starved to death. The cost of feeding Germans was greater than the value of the plant and equipment taken as reparations. In May 1946 the Americans, closely followed by the British and the French, stopped dismantling German factories – except those to which the Soviet Union was entitled, since its share exceeded what could be removed from its zone.

German industry suffered from disorganisation rather than destruction. If power and raw materials were available, industry could still produce. If transport were available, it could export. But as these things were lacking after the war, industrial production collapsed. The contrast with east Germany following unification is striking. Industrial production there had also collapsed, again not for want of capital or labour. But the east German legacy is a plethora of obsolete plant and over-expensive labour – east German industry has been economically destroyed.

West Germany's stalled economy needed a jump-start: money to buy raw materials; fuels to power plant and equipment; trucks to take away the products; and markets in which they could be sold. For three years all (bar increasingly worthless money) remained scarce and production stagnated. Real GDP fell from the equivalent of DM 568 bn measured at 1980 prices in 1938 to DM 129 bn in 1948, a drop of almost three-quarters. Over a quarter could be blamed on the fall in the population. Given a jump-start, recovery was dramatic. West German real GDP trebled in eight years so that in 1956 it equalled all German GDP in 1938. Sound money was a main factor, resulting from Erhard's June 1948 currency reforms. He also scrapped 90% of the wage and price controls imposed by the Nazis in 1936 and continued by the Allies after 1945.

Marshall Plan aid was decisive, not only for Germany but also for Western Europe, in preventing a relapse back into depression. Between 1948 and 1951 West Germany received $1389 m, one-tenth of Marshall Plan aid. This may not sound much today, but between 1948 and 1950 it paid for a quarter of Germany's imports, providing fuel and raw materials vital for industrial output, and also contributed to public finances. The D-Mark proceeds from the sale of imports purchased with American aid accrued to the German Government. In the second half of 1948, after the currency reforms, West German industrial production rose by 50%, and by a further 25% the following year. In 1948 exports totalled $540 m and imports $950m. Three years later both had climbed to $3.5 bn and German trade was in balance. By 1953 West German living standards had recovered to their 1938 level.

GENERAL AGREEMENT ON TARIFFS & TRADE (GATT)

Germany's recovery, like Japan's, was significantly aided by the boost which rearmament gave to world demand following the outbreak in

1950 of the Korean War. But it also occurred at a time when, thanks to the United States, the international trading environment was unusually open and benign. The institutional framework established at Bretton Woods in 1944 is mostly still extant, although the International Monetary Fund and World Bank look somewhat battered and bruised after over half a century's hard wear. The fixed exchange rate system collapsed in the early 1970s, but by then its main work had been done. It gave Germany and Japan the benefit of two decades of competitively undervalued currencies, allowing them to develop massive export industries partly at the expense of American and British manufacturers. The General Agreement on Tariffs & Trade (GATT), established in 1947, led through six rounds of multinational negotiations, starting in Torquay in 1950–1 and ending with the Uruguay Round in 1988–93, to a progressive reduction of tariff barriers throughout the world. The victors created a world fit for the vanquished.

The pattern of German post-war growth falls neatly into the four decades leading up to unification in 1989. Conveniently, the last year in each decade was at or near a cyclical peak, so that average growth rates over each are not seriously distorted by the business cycle. The 1950s were years of post-war reconstruction. West Germany achieved dramatically fast growth, but from such a low base that it was hardly surprising. By the end of the decade, real GDP had risen to equal Britain's and GDP per head was only a little lower.

In the 1960s technological advances were exploited to sustain historically rapid growth of 5% or more. Germany pulled ahead of Britain, but performed no better than the average of OECD countries. The 1970s by contrast, were problem years for everyone. This inflationary decade began with the collapse of the Bretton Woods fixed exchange rate system and continued with the two oil price shocks. Growth slowed down and, although Germany continued to outperform Britain, it again broadly matched the OECD average. Finally the 1980s were years of adjustment after the 1970s excesses. West Germany underperformed the OECD average and even did worse than Britain, significantly so in terms of productivity.

The poor showing of the West German economy in the last decade before unification was significant. Like Japan, the machine which had

Table 11.1 West German and British Growth Rates 1950–89 (% pa)

	1950–9	1960–9	1970–9	1980–9
Real GDP				
Germany	7.9	5.6	3.9	1.8
Britain	2.9	3.7	2.5	2.4
Population				
Germany	1.2	1.0	0.2	0.1
Britain	0.4	0.6	0.1	0.2
GDP per head				
Germany	6.5	4.5	3.6	1.7
Britain	2.4	3.1	2.3	2.2
Employment				
Germany	3.6	1.1	0.2	0.4
Britain	0.5	0.5	0.5	0.6
Productivity, whole economy				
Germany	13.8	4.5	4.0	1.4
Britain	2.4	3.2	2.2	1.8

produced such an outstanding performance through most of the post-war years seemed finally to be failing. When the Berlin Wall fell in 1989, the late 1980s boom was fading. It had failed to lift German 1980s growth from the foot of the international league table – twentieth out of twenty-two OECD member countries. From 1980 to 1987 GDP grew on average by less than 2% a year. In the boom of 1988–9 it spurted, but did not reach 4%. Unemployment had remained high and a West German 1991–2 recession would have driven it higher. Germany was relying on other countries' growth and a growing balance of payments surplus to pull it along. It could not have gone on doing so for much longer. Unification, in other words, came just in time to rescue the increasingly ossified West German economy.

The following sections examine German economic performance in each decade in more detail. They explain the circumstances which contributed to the economy's fine performance in the 1950s to 1970s and show how they had changed by the 1980s. Chart 11.2 on pages

104–5 provides a bird's eye view of the West German economy's progress over the post-war period as a whole.

THE 1950S: YEARS OF RECONSTRUCTION

The Bretton Woods fixed exchange rate system, while it lasted, had a particularly benign impact on Germany and Japan. In the late 1940s, when their currencies were stabilised, nobody wanted D-Mark or yen. Neither country had much to sell. Everyone wanted dollars and, as a second best, pounds sterling. Exchange rates were established (after the pound was devalued in 1949) which, at the time, may have reasonably valued the reserve currencies against those of the defeated nations. The D-Mark was fixed at DM 4.2 to the US dollar throughout the 1950s, the yen at ¥360. But both Germany and Japan were certain to outperform Britain and the United States as they repaired wartime devastation. They each had large underemployed or unemployed labour reserves, which helped to promote wage moderation. Migration from East Germany continually boosted the West German labour force. German unemployment, which exceeded 10% at the start of the decade, fell to 2.6% by its end. The German system of national wage determination also contributed to moderation (see Chapter 13). Both Germany and Japan achieved rapid productivity growth, thanks to heavy investment in reconstruction. Gross fixed capital formation accounted for more than a quarter of West German GDP during the 1950s. A high level of investment ensured an up-to-date capital stock. A virtuous circle resulted from fast growth, in which rapid productivity gains held down costs and increased competitiveness and profits. Thanks to Bretton Woods fixed exchange rates, the D-Mark became increasingly undervalued against the US dollar and pound sterling, giving Germany export-led growth. Export earnings surged by nearly 20% a year during the 1950s, providing more than enough foreign exchange to finance increased imports, particularly of raw materials, food and capital goods.

Rapid productivity growth provided workers with large nominal wage increases without leading to inflation. Between 1950 and 1959 hourly earnings rose by 7.4% a year against 1.9% rise in consumer prices, whereas in slow-growth Britain monthly earnings rose a modest

3.7% a year and yet retail prices rose by 3% a year. Apart from a surge at the beginning of the decade, associated with the world commodity price explosion which followed the outbreak of the Korean War, German consumer prices rose by marginally less than the OECD average.

WELFARE BURDEN KEPT DOWN BY FAST GROWTH

Throughout the 1950s, the share of GDP taken by public spending remained low in Germany, under a third, keeping tax costs down. But public spending nonetheless rose rapidly, thanks to the fast GDP growth. The new FRG took on the debts of the Third Reich. It paid compensation to the victims of Nazi crimes. At the same time, however, all public servants who had lost their jobs during the Allied denazification process but had not been imprisoned for war crimes, got them back, or, if over retirement age, received full pensions. An Equalisation of Burdens law was passed in 1952. It helped those who had lost everything (particularly refugees from the east) at the expense of those who had retained land and businesses in the west. Taxes of 50% were levied on all property, but payment was spread over twenty-seven years to make this tolerable. These measures, together with the 1948 currency stabilisation which had limited the one-for-one exchange to RM 40 per head, were regarded as socially just and equitable. Ordinary Germans, however, who had not been Nazi victims, public servants or refugees, felt cheated, particularly pensioners. Social security benefits were therefore greatly improved, notably through the introduction in 1957 of a 'dynamic' scheme by which pensions were indexed to the cost of living. Employers and employees bore the cost in social security contributions. But under the 'pay-as-you-go' system, the burden was light as long as the labour force was large and pensioners few. A fully funded system from the start would have shown the true and much heavier costs. The 'social budget', a concept developed for planning purposes in the 1970s, endeavoured to capture all kinds of public social spending including tax allowances. It was estimated to have been 17.1% of GNP in 1950, rising only modestly to 20.7% by 1960. But as nominal GNP trebled over this period, social spending in Germany more than trebled.

EUROPE'S POST-WAR SOCIAL COMPACT

Social justice was the rock upon which post-war democracy in Germany was founded (a far cry from the inequitable system of taxation during the Second Reich and in the Weimar Republic). There was, in effect, a social compact between governments and citizens in all Western countries after the war aimed at preventing the misery, suffering and injustice which fed nationalism, Facism and Communism in the 1930s depression. It had international and domestic dimensions. Under American and British leadership, a multilateral free trade system was founded, based upon a system of fixed exchange rates. It was designed to prevent a repetition of the trade wars and competitive depreciation which impoverished the world before the war, and in this it was successful. Rapid GDP growth in the 1950s was accompanied by an even more rapid growth in the volume of world trade. Exports in general rose twice as fast as GDP. As nations prospered, social security systems were designed fairly to share increasing affluence. They could afford to be generous and were.[1] Pension schemes take many years to mature and are cheap when the average age of the population is low. Unemployment fell rapidly after the war to extraordinarily low levels – less than 1% in many countries. Health care was comparatively simple and cheap. Nobody in the 1950s and 1960s foresaw a return to double digit unemployment, the problem of ageing populations or the cost of modern medicine. But this is a story to which we shall return later.

Rapidly rising real incomes in West Germany after 1948 provided increasing room for savings after the necessities of life had been obtained. Personal saving rose from 3% of disposable income in 1950 to 8% in 1960. The country as a whole saved. National savings were high. There were large budget surpluses. The corporate and income tax system was tilted against dividend payment, causing companies to finance the greater part of investment out of retained profits. Indeed high savings caused the current account to move into surplus in 1951 and remain there. Over the decade as a whole, the West German surplus exceeded $6 bn, averaging about 2% of GDP. The proceeds went entirely to rebuilding

---

[1] One problem today is that the baby-boomer generation, as voters, has promised itself too affluent a future in retirement than its too few sons and daughters may willingly finance. This, unthought-of in the 1950s and 1960s, will become one of the great structural problems of the 2000s and 2010s. The old are bound to be disappointed.

Chart 11.2. A Bird's Eye View of the German Economy, 1950–94

GDP
% change

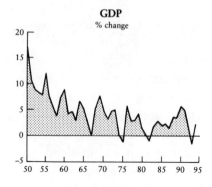

Consumer prices
% change

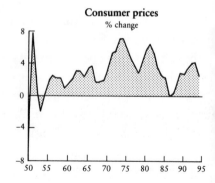

Real hourly earnings
% change

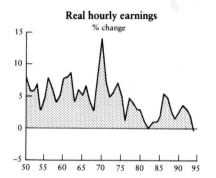

Unemployment
Percent

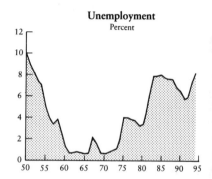

Balance of Payments [1]
% of GDP

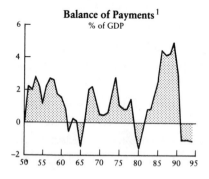

Capital investment
% of GDP

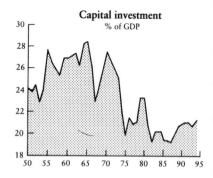

1. Current account; all-Germany from 1991

Household savings
% of disposable income

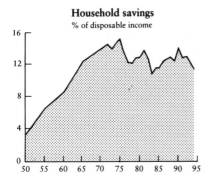

Public spending [1]
% of GDP

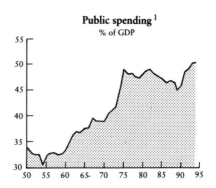

Government deficit [1,2]
% of GDP

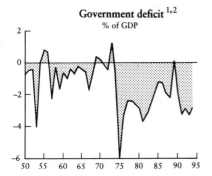

D-Mark exchange rate
DM/$, end December

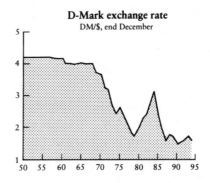

Industrial share price index
% change

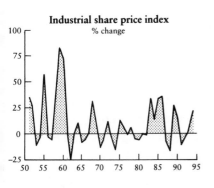

Interest rates
Percent

Bond yield, period average

Discount rate, end Dec

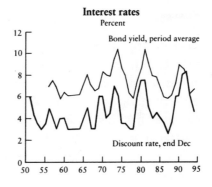

1. All-Germany from 1991
2. Federal government deficit to 1969, general government deficit thereafter

Germany's foreign currency reserves. Although long-term capital outflows were resumed in the second half of the 1950s, short-term capital
inflows swamped them, contributing a net $1 bn to Germany's foreign
currency reserves.

THE 1960S: YEARS OF WINE AND ROSES

The Germans and other nations spent the decade to the mid-1950s
repairing their economies from the ravages of the Second World War.
The decade to the mid-1960s was spent modernising them by exploiting
nearly three decades of technological advance. In these years the mass
consumer society was created, in which every family expected to own a
car, a washing machine, a fridge and a black-and-white TV set. In
Britain this new consumerdom was encapsulated in 1959 when the
Prime Minister, Harold Macmillan, commented, 'You have never had it
so good.' The 1960s were the first 'normal' years since the 1900s. They
were years of continued fast growth and low (but gently rising) inflation
and unemployment. Like the British, the West Germans had never had
it so good. They little realised in the 1960s how much this was due
to good fortune. They attributed it entirely to their own efforts and
intelligence. They seemed to have invented a wondrous growth machine
which could never falter or stop. They were mistaken.

GERMAN SUCCESS BECOMES A NUISANCE

Germany's first brush with the currency stability problem came in 1961.
The strength of its payments balance in the 1950s was undoubtedly
impressive, but largely at the expense of the British and French, who
were struggling with perennial deficits. The D-Mark was clearly undervalued and markets correctly believed it would have to go up. Speculative
short-term inflows, substantial over 1955–9, became a flood. Despite a
booming economy, the Bundesbank cut interest rates and expanded
credit (an inflationary solution). It regarded the D-Mark's fixed parity as
sacrosanct, just as the British establishment regarded talk of devaluation
as 'spitting on the flag'. (After Harold Wilson became Prime Minister in
1964 he even banned the use of the word 'devaluation' throughout

Whitehall.) Against Bundesbank opposition, Erhard persuaded Adenauer to order a 5% revaluation in March 1961.

Britain's position, the weaker of the two reserve currency countries, was invidious. Nobody wanted to hold pounds rather than dollars. The only way to protect the pound from devaluation was to deflate. Slower growth curbed imports and temporarily 'cured' payments deficits. But persistent deflation weakened the economy by inhibiting investment. The medium-term damage to the supply side of the economy made it more difficult to control inflation. In 1967 Britain was forced to devalue the pound from $2.8 to $2.4, a 16.7% cut. The Bretton Woods fixed rate system was fatally weakened and over the following years it slowly collapsed. Germany was forced to revalue again by 8.5% in October 1969, after Willy Brandt's Social Democrats (with Free Democrat support) broke away from Kiesinger's Grand Coalition. Next came the 'Nixon shock' in August 1971 when President Nixon suspended dollar/gold convertibility. Currencies floated until December when, at the Smithsonian Institution in Washington, DC, agreement was reached to fix them again with new parities. It did not work. The pound broke ranks in June 1972, the French franc followed and, in March 1973, when the D-Mark floated, the Bretton Woods fixed exchange rate system expired.

LIFE WITH FLOATING CURRENCIES

The German economic system, like the Japanese, had been reconstructed after the war and naturally contained significant bias designed to encourage the high level of savings needed to finance post-war reconstruction. When that task was complete and there was less need for a high level of investment, bias nonetheless remained. High savings continued and indeed became excessive. This became a problem in the early 1960s. By resisting the D-mark's appreciation, the Bundesbank allowed the economy first to overheat, then to over-react. Growth slowed abruptly as the Bundesbank tightened aggressively. In the 1950s, fiscal policy played no part in demand management. The Basic Law required the budget to be balanced. Revenue forecasts were conservative and surpluses resulted. The proceeds were frozen in central bank deposits which became known as the 'Julius Tower', after the fortress at Spandau where Prussian kings kept their war treasure. The result of aggressive tightening

was a 'growth recession' in 1963, when the rise in real GDP fell below
3%. Unemployment remained low for a simple reason. The Berlin Wall,
built in 1961, reduced immigration from the east to a trickle. Labour
force growth was sharply checked. Fewer new jobs were on offer, but
fewer new workers were looking for work. Unemployment remained
incredibly low at under 1% of the labour force. The end of immigration
from the east was, however, followed by a sharp rise in the arrival
of *Gastarbeiter* (guest-workers) from southern Europe, notably Italians,
Yugoslavs, Greeks and Turks. They did not, however, have the same level
of skills and education and their arrival did little to reduce upward
pressure on wages.

ERHARD'S MISMANAGEMENT

Germany's current account surplus virtually disappeared in the first half
of the 1960s. There were small deficits in 1962 and 1965. Compared
with the 1950s, the growth in the value and volume of exports was
halved. After the 1957 Treaty of Rome, the creation of the common
market led to a diversion of trade to EEC partners. Between 1950 and
1961, Germany's share in world exports rose from 3.5% to 10.5%. In
1965 it was no higher than in 1961. Between 1958 and 1963 the share of
exports to the EEC in total German exports rose from 30% to 45%. The
share of other countries fell from 40% to 35% and the developing
countries' share dropped from 20% to 10%. These were unusually large
changes in relative shares, the fall in sales to developing countries illus-
trating the failure of the international trade and payments system to
return to its pre-1914 pattern. Germany's current account balance was
also hit by rising invisible payments. As Germans became wealthier, they
took more foreign holidays (bagging the best deck chairs early each
morning). The inflow of guest workers produced a return stream of
payments to the families back at home. German foreign transfers also
rose, notably through EEC contributions.

The deterioration in Germany's trade performance in the early 1960s
contributed to the growth recession. Export-led growth was over, at
least for the time being. After Erhard finally became Chancellor in
October 1963, there was a feeling of drift in the management of the
economy. The recovery in 1964–5 was weak and short-lived. Fiscal

policy began to be used deliberately to bolster demand. Rising public sector deficits replaced current account surpluses to mop up excess private savings. Public expenditure continued to rise strongly after economic growth slowed down. It increased from 32.4% of GDP in 1959 to 38.8% in 1969. This 6% point rise was less than the 7% rise in France and 9% in Britain, and German public spending remained on the low side compared with European neighbours. But the increases put public spending in Europe substantially above the levels in the US and Japan.

Table 11.2 Public Spending: An International Comparison, 1950–69 (% of GDP)

	US	Japan	Germany	France	Britain
1950	21.3	28.7	33.6	33.9	34.5
1954	26.2	24.1	30.4	34.9	33.6
1959	26.6	20.3	32.4	34.6	32.2
1964	27.4	23.2	36.8	33.9	33.9
1969	30.1	21.5	38.8	41.5	41.5
Change 59–69					
%	3.5	1.2	6.3	6.9	9.3

The increase in German public spending was politically motivated. The CDU-CSU under the ageing Adenauer, having lost its absolute majority in the 1961 general election, was keen to regain it four years later. Erhard was too easygoing and weak to control spending ministers. Pensions were raised substantially, reaching 60% of final salary in many cases. (In Britain the state pension is still only 20% of average earnings.) The Berlin economy had to be bailed out and kept going after the Wall went up. Uneconomic industries, such as coal-mining, textiles, steel and shipbuilding were subsidised, often at local level. The Federal Government had little control over the Länder, which received the greater part of tax revenues and were responsible for more public spending than the Federal Government. It had no control over the Federal Labour Office, a self-governing body incorporated under Federal Law, which controlled unemployment relief and family allowances. The Federal Labour Office ran large surpluses in those full employment years and so raised benefits substantially.

The rise in public spending was not matched by increased taxation. By 1965 the Federal budget moved into record deficit. The current account was also in deficit to the tune of DM 6.5 bn. With labour scarce, unions became more aggressive in demanding and receiving large wage increases. The rate of inflation accelerated to over 3%. Erhard's CDU-CSU just about held its own in the 1965 election. The SPD did not make too much of the Government's problems, as that would have meant advocating large tax increases or painful public spending cuts. The FDP was the main loser, but retained the balance of power in the Bundestag. Reluctantly, it confirmed Erhard in office, allowing drift to continue through 1966. Eventually, in November of that year, it withdrew its support, leading to the Grand Coalition under the former Nazi, Kurt-Georg Kiesinger.

CLEARING UP THE MESS

The year 1966 was climactic for Germany. It marked the end of post-war reconstruction and recovery. As the year closed, the economy dived into its worse post-war recession. (Germany was also beaten by England in the World Cup soccer final in extra time at Wembley, although in fairness one of the decisive English goals was a bit dubious.) Fighting against fiscal profligacy the independent Bundesbank pushed interest rates too high for too long, causing the sharpest post-war collapse in capital investment. The world economy was also weak. The new Government had to restore confidence. It set about controlling the budget by cutting spending and raising taxes. It also brought in an Act to Promote Economic Stability and Growth, which increased Federal authority over taxation and Länder spending. It increased the role of economic planning and shifted fiscal policy decisively away from balanced budgets and towards Keynesian counter-cyclical demand management. The severity of the German 1967 recession, in which real GDP fell despite 4% OECD growth, and unemployment jumped despite the repatriation of guest-workers, led rapidly to fiscal easing through a special capital expenditure programme. It also led to union wage moderation and inflation dropped back to around 1%. The current account balance turned round dramatically, moving from a record deficit of 1.5% of GDP in 1965 to a 2% surplus in 1967–8. Upward pressure on the D-Mark was resumed, which encouraged the Bundesbank to move swiftly to ease monetary policy. The recession, although sharp, was exceedingly short, giving way to the usual end-of-decade boom.

The 1960s, for all their problems, were a decade of wine and roses. Growth was less rapid and more volatile than in the 1950s, but vigorously fast in historical terms. Inflation, although creeping up, remained low. Unemployment was amazingly low, the spike to 2% in 1967 was regarded as shocking! The balance of payments was in surplus. The currency was strong. Democracy took root, although the bland Grand Coalition pushed opposition onto the streets, as witnessed by the rise of the Baader-Meinhof gang. Violence has remained a footnote to German development ever since. It is always there, nasty and shocking, but relatively insignificant. The outbreak following unification has been particularly unpleasant, notably the assassination by the Red Army Faction of the head of Treuhand, Detlev Rohwedder, in April 1991 and the murders of two Turkish women and their three daughters by skinhead arsonists in December 1992. Nevertheless Germans had every reason to believe that their social market model was as good as any economic system in the world. The end of the decade ushered in a Social Democratic Government, set to build on its success. One of its very first acts was to revalue the D-Mark from DM4=$1 to DM3.65.

CHAPTER 12

An End to the Miracle

During the days of the Bretton Woods system, countries with current account deficits experienced downward pressure on their currencies, while those with surpluses suffered upward pressure. If these were temporary, they could be resisted by exchange market intervention. Countries trying to prevent their currencies rising had fewer problems. They had, or could print, an unlimited quantity of their own money with which to buy foreign currencies. The only danger was that this would increase domestic money and credit growth, leading to overheating and inflation. Countries whose currencies were under attack, however, had limited reserves of foreign currencies with which to intervene; if they needed more, they had to borrow. The International Monetary Fund (IMF) and other countries provided loans, but on such onerous conditions that, if the borrowers met them, it would have no need for the loans. While changes in exchange rates were banned, downward pressure on a currency could be relieved only by deflation. If surplus countries would not speed up growth, deficit countries had to slow down, accepting higher unemployment. While world growth was rapid, the United States and Britain could tolerate the relatively slow growth rates they suffered to protect the Bretton Woods fixed exchange rate system. Once world growth slowed down, neither was willing to tolerate stagnation to this end – hence the collapse of fixed rates.

THE FIRST OIL SHOCK

The collapse of Bretton Woods seemingly removed the balance of payments constraint on growth. Floating rates would automatically look after payments imbalances. Governments could concentrate on managing demand to secure fast growth and full employment. Following two decades of relative price stability, few politicians worried about the inflationary consequences of going for growth. Inflation could always be held in check by prices and incomes policies. German moderation was much admired. People thought that deals could be done between governments, unions and employers to prevent wages rising too fast despite strong demand. Unfortunately no producer in a free-market economy would reject the chance to raise prices in a sellers' market. Wage moderation thus meant more profit rather than less inflation.

In the early 1970s, everyone expanded demand simultaneously, causing a synchronised world boom. The 1972–3 boom was not exceptional in any individual country, but because all were marching in step it caused an unusually large world boom. Commodity and oil prices had been falling ever since the Korean War stockpiling boom. Between 1951 and 1968 *The Economist*'s all-items index fell by a fifth, while OECD consumer prices rose by half. Real commodity prices were halved. Then in 1968 commodity prices started to rise and in 1972–3 they increased sharply. Between 1968 and 1973 *The Economist*'s index rose 90% and OECD consumer prices rose 30%, giving a real commodity price rise of 45%. Next came the October 1973 Yom Kippur War between Israel and Egypt. Egypt started it but Israel finished it. Irate Arab oil producers embargoed oil sales to the industrial countries which had supported Israel. The embargo was a failure, so instead they combined to quadruple prices.

The 1972–4 commodity and oil price hikes were cost-inflationary and demand deflationary. Industrial economies initially responded by fiscal and monetary restraint in order to combat increased inflationary pressures. The world in 1974–5 lurched into slumpflation.[1] The response in 1975 was to counter the recession by powerful fiscal stimulation, while

---

[1] The author believes he coined the word in an article entitled 'The word is Slumpflation' in *The Economist* (30 March 1974).

trying to prevent inflation with prices and incomes controls. Controls generally proved ineffective and the inflationary surge was validated rather than negated. All major countries suffered both rising inflation and rising unemployment.

The German economy performed better than most. Fiscal profligacy during the 1960s had created a structural deficit of nearly 3% of GDP. 'Structural' means what the budget would be if the economy were neither overheating nor stagnating. Technically this is when real GDP equals its 'potential' level. The structural budget balance has to be estimated since GDP rarely equals its potential level for very long. The calculation allows for the effect of booms in boosting tax revenues and cutting public spending on unemployment, which reduce the budget deficit, and of recessions which raise spending and cut revenue to increase deficits. The difference between the actual and structural budget deficits is the cyclical component. In 1970 the German economy was strong and consequently the actual budget balance showed a small surplus, i.e. the cyclical effect of the strength of the economy improved the budget balance by more than the structural 3% deficit.

Like everyone else, the Germans tried to ward off recession by fiscal reflation. Between 1973 and 1975 the structural budget deficit widened from 1.6% of GDP to 5.3%. With the lurch into recession eliminating the favourable cyclical component, the actual balance deteriorated from a surplus of 1.2% to a deficit of 5.7%. The Germans, more fearful of inflation than most other nations, moved swiftly in 1976–7 to curb this deficit. Public spending had risen from 39% of GDP in 1969 – when Willy Brandt took over from Kiesinger's Grand Coalition – to 49% in 1975 during Schmidt's first full year as Chancellor. It was cut back to 47% by 1979. German unemployment rose to 3.6% in 1975, a little less than British and French unemployment. Thanks to union moderation, German inflation peaked far lower than other countries. Over 1973–6 it averaged less than 6% a year when nearly everywhere else inflation went into double figures. The German current account, despite heavy oil dependency, remained in surplus. Money growth was well controlled, with the result that interest rates generally remained lower than elsewhere and the currency appreciated. It was a fine performance, although Germany sacrificed growth to achieve it. Only Britain fared worse on this score.

The German current account surplus in 1974, despite the oil price hike, exceeded 2% of German GDP and totalled $11.6 bn. By pursuing less stimulative policies than other countries following the 1974–5 recession, and thanks to German unions' wage moderation, German growth was aided by other countries' measures to expand. This was not generally acceptable and at economic summits in the late 1970s Germany (and Japan) was bullied into fiscal reflation. The improvement in the structural budget deficit was halted in 1978 and sharply reversed in 1979 when, following the Bonn summit, Germany undertook to add 1% to GDP growth through fiscal stimulation. The German current account surplus also plunged into deficit in that year, thanks to rising oil prices and the strong D-Mark.

THE 1980S: EUROSCLEROSIS

Most industrial economies dealt with the second oil shock better than the first. This is apparent when the two tables measuring international performance are compared. Except in Japan, the 1980–2 recession was deeper than in 1974–5. Policy was tougher with a sharper correction to structural budget deficits, higher interest rates and generally slower money supply growth. Inflation was negated rather than validated, as it had been following the first oil shock. It was lower in the US, Japan and Britain, no different in Germany, but worse in France. The French Socialist Government, under the newly elected President Mitterrand, went for growth and suffered not only more inflation but also from a seriously weak currency, which had to be devalued against the D-Mark in the European exchange rate mechanism (ERM), established in 1979. It was this experience which led to the Socialists' dramatic U-turn in 1983 when the '*franc fort*' or strong currency policy was adopted, since when France has made preserving the franc's parity with the D-Mark its top policy priority. When it failed in August 1993 and the ERM margins had to be widened from 2.5% to 15%, France refused to cut interest rates despite recession and high and rising unemployment. In consequence the franc gradually climbed back to above its old narrow-margin floor.

The German economy again performed better than most, but not so well as it had done in the mid-1970s. The German recession of

1980–2 was as bad as in other countries, but inflation was more moderate. Unemployment, however, which had risen to 3.6% in the second half of the 1970s, climbed to 7.7% in 1983. Despite this flaw, the social market model was reckoned to have equalled any other in these difficult times. There was little feeling that German industry needed protection. But with Schmidt's departure from the Chancellorship in 1982 and the return of the conservative CDU-CSU under Helmut Kohl, it was clear that some changes were needed. In particular the level of public spending, which had now climbed to almost 50% of GDP, had to be tackled – as did the structural budget deficit which had increased to over 4% of GDP. Public sector debt, which had been relatively stable at about 20% of GDP in the 1950s and 1960s, had doubled in the decade to 1982 to reach 40%. A period of fiscal retrenchment was needed.

REAGAN TO THE RESCUE

Kohl has always been lucky. Reversing the fiscal profligacy of the late 1970s, which had helped keep the economy growing despite excessive private savings, was bound to depress growth. Matters would have been far worse had not the United States, under President Ronald Reagan, embarked upon structural supply-side reforms. The 1982 US tax reforms sharply reduced the cost of borrowing and thereby increased the demand for credit relative to the supply of savings. They stimulated investments and attracted capital inflows from Europe and Japan. These inflows drove up the dollar exchange rate. (So did the relatively tough monetary stance which the Volcker Fed adopted as the US budget deficit widened.) By 1985 the dollar had become grossly overvalued. It had climbed from DM 1.7 at end-1979 to DM 3.3 at its peak in March 1985. During the same period it went up from ¥240 to ¥260, not nearly so large a jump. The loss of competitiveness caused the US current account to plunge into the red. From a surplus of $2 bn in 1980, it deteriorated to a deficit of $121 bn in 1985, when the dollar peaked. Helped by the 'J-curve' (the way in which a falling currency normally makes the trade balance worse before it gets better), the deterioration continued for a further two years to produce a massive $167 bn deficit in 1987. Germany, meanwhile, had a $14 bn deficit in 1980, which was converted into a surplus of $16 bn in 1985. Moreover the German surplus continued to increase throughout the 1980s reaching $46 bn in 1987 and $58 bn in 1989. At its peak the US deficit equalled 3.7% of GDP, while the German surplus climbed to 4.9%.

As the US economy recovered from the 1980–2 recession it sucked in imports, helping Germany to enjoy export-led growth. US supply-siders originally believed that Reagan's tax cuts would do little if any damage to the US budget deficit. The growth they would stimulate was expected to make tax revenues more buoyant to offset the fall in tax rates. But as usual the Americans had neglected the external effects. When increased demand sucked in imports, the incomes the extra sales generated were earned by foreigners. The additional tax revenues went to the German and Japanese governments, which were only too delighted. Both had embarked on protracted periods of fiscal consolidation to reduce bloated budget deficits. American fiscal profligacy took much of the deflationary sting out of Japanese and German stringency.

Chart 12.1 German and US Surpluses and Deficits

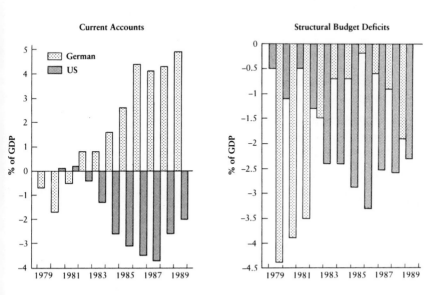

Even so, Germany's recovery from the 1980–2 recession was pitifully weak. It managed just 1% a year growth between 1979 and 1984, just slightly better than Britain's 0.8%, but well below rates achieved in the US and in Japan. Moreover, in 1985 the world economy seemed to be sliding back into recession. The term 'Eurosclerosis' was coined to describe the inferior performance of European economies, not merely in growth but also in creating jobs and limiting unemployment. The European response was to agree in 1985 to the Single Europe Act which, by the end of 1992, was to remove all remaining barriers to trade within the area (*see also* Chapter 14). Whatever the long-term effects of the Single Market, it came too late to help Germany improve its record in the second half of the 1980s. During the decade as a whole, German growth fell well behind British.

Table 12.1 International Growth Comparisons in the 1980s (GDP, % pa)

	US	Japan	Germany	France	Britain
1979–84	1.8	3.5	1.0	1.5	0.8
1984–9	3.1	4.5	2.6	3.1	4.0
1979–89	2.5	4.0	1.8	2.3	2.4

The 1980s ended with Germany and Europe facing a jobs crisis. The German, French and British labour forces had each increased by around 3 million during the 1970s and 1980s, 1% to 1.5% a year growth. Japan's labour force rose by 2% a year and the US by 4%. Germany and France found jobs for fewer than half of this increase, and most of that in public sector employment. Britain created more jobs, approaching 2 million, and almost all in the private sector. Part of this was due to privatisation, but when the effects of this are excluded, about half the rise in private sector employment was real. By contrast with continental Europe, the US and Japan found jobs for over 90% of the increase in their labour forces.

Low employment growth was reflected in rising unemployment. The jobless rate in Japan, while creeping higher, has remained exceptionally low. The US rate rose to the early 1980s, but has subsequently been on a downward trend. Unemployment in Europe, which was below American in the 1960s, is now considerably higher at an average of around 12%. The west of Germany has performed better than Britain

Table 12.2 International Employment Performances, 1969–89

	Germany	France	Britain	US	Japan
Labour force growth, 000s	3236	3189	3051	41,318	11,720
Labour force growth, % pa	1.16	1.42	1.14	4.07	2.09
Employment growth, 000s	1338	1414	1898	39,440	10,880
Employment growth, % pa	0.51	0.68	0.75	4.18	1.97
Employment/ Labour	41	44	62	95	93

and France but now has higher unemployment than the US. We shall return to the European jobs crisis in a later chapter.

CHAPTER 13

Unification

The two Germanies were reunited on 3 October 1990 – a political triumph for Helmut Kohl and an economic disaster for many ordinary east Germans. The triumph, however, would probably not have been possible without the disaster. (Time may show that the one-for-one-exchange of Ostmarks for D-Marks was best in the long run.) Unification came with breath-taking speed. A few weeks before the Berlin Wall fell, the author predicted (in a Radio New Zealand interview) that it would come – sometime towards the end of the century.

The train of events leading to unification began four years before the Wall fell, when Mikhail Gorbachev was elected General Secretary of the Soviet Communist Party in November 1985. With Gorbachev's election came recognition that the Communist economic system had failed. While people east of the Iron Curtain remained ignorant of growing affluence in the West, they endured the Communist system's short-comings. Everyone was cheaply clothed, housed, fed, kept warm – and there was plenty of vodka. If life was drab, so it was for everyone. But as Russians and Eastern Europeans became more exposed to the Western media, they learnt of our habits. Ordinary men and women in the West pushed piled-high trolleys through supermarket checkouts; so, not unnaturally, they wanted the same, hardly realising what this might entail for their 'job security'.

1848 WITHOUT BLOODSHED

Communism in Europe collapsed with hardly a shot being fired – in contrast to, say, Budapest in 1956 or Prague in 1968. Widespread popular uprising swept Eastern Europe, deposing dictators. East Germany's collapse began when its borders became porous. Before the Berlin Wall was built in August 1961, East Germans crossed to West Germany at a rate of over 200,000 a year. Between 1949 and 1961, migration totalled 2.7 million. After the Wall went up the numbers fell to a trickle. Then, in May 1989, Hungary relaxed its border controls with Austria and East German tourists found they could escape to the West. By August, a great exodus was under way. The Hungarians tried to stem the flood by tightening their controls again. Those who had got out of East Germany, posing as tourists, had no intention of going back. They invaded West German embassies, not only in Budapest but also in Warsaw and Prague. The invaders became so numerous that the authorities could do nothing but let them go.

Erich Honecker's East German Government tried to crack down on tourist visas. Spontaneous demonstrations began, notably at St Nicholas Church in Leipzig on 4 September. When it became clear that the Soviet military commander would not use force to break them up, the demonstrations grew and spread. Honecker favoured force, but other leading Communists preferred to avoid bloodshed, hoping that the mob could be bought off by concessions. With Moscow's approval, Honecker was ousted. But the demonstrations became massive, with millions on the streets chanting, 'We are *the* people.' Finally, on 9 November 1990, the borders between East and West were reopened. The Wall came tumbling down.

Once East Germans could vote with their feet, they did so in vast numbers. Despite the few weeks of the year during which the borders were opened, 344,000 East Germans went west in 1989, and they were not alone. A further 377,000 ethnic Germans poured into West Germany from other Eastern European countries. The loss of labour stalled the East German economic system. There was no turning back, although few people imagined that unification could come so quickly. Helmut Kohl was one who did. He saw the political opportunity and grabbed it. On 28 November 1989 he announced a ten-point plan, which pushed unification to the top of the political agenda. East German demonstrators started to shout, 'We are *one* people.' On 7 February Kohl offered full economic and monetary union to East Germany with the D-Mark replacing the Ostmark (O-Mark or OM). Free East German elections followed on 18 March and on 12 April Lothar de Maizière, the East German CDU leader, formed a coalition government and immediately accepted Kohl's offer. Economic and monetary union came into force on 1 July and the conversion of O-Marks to D-Marks began the next day.

Meanwhile Kohl had persuaded the four Occupying Powers – Britain, France, the United States and the Soviet Union – to attend talks on Germany's future. As these talks included both German governments they were called the '2 + 4' negotiations. On 31 September the Unification Treaty was concluded and on 3 October 1990 it came into effect. Five Länder were re-established in east Germany – Saxony, Saxony-Anhalt, Mecklenburg-West Pomerania, Brandenburg and Thuringia – which simply accepted west German law and became part of an enlarged Federal Republic of Germany. This procedure for unification had always been provided by the West German constitution, which meant that there was no need for a protracted debate on how to proceed.

Although the Americans were whole-heartedly in favour of German unification, both the British Prime Minister, Margaret Thatcher, and the French President, François Mitterrand, had serious reservations. Mitterrand pursued an active anti-unification campaign, visiting the East German and Soviet leaders in an attempt to talk them out of it. He could only be persuaded to join the 2 + 4 negotiations in return for German support for the Maastricht Treaty on European unity. Kohl was forced to make other concessions. Germany had to renounce all claims on lands to the east of the Oder and Neisse rivers and to provide financial assistance to the Soviet Union, particularly to rehouse Soviet troops on their return home. There was to be no restitution of property confiscated by the Soviet Union between 1945 and 1949. These concessions were a small price to pay for unification. The Federal Republic even remained a member of NATO.

'IT WON'T HURT AND IT WON'T COST'

Two months after unification, on 2 December 1990, there were elections in the old and new Länder to a new Bundestag. Helmut Kohl sold unification to the German people by telling east Germans that it would not hurt and west Germans that it would not cost. His Social Democrat opponents challenged him on both counts, presenting a more realistic picture of the pain and problems which lay ahead. But the 'Unity Chancellor' prevailed. Kohl and his coalition partners won a comfortable Bundestag majority.

Prior to unification, both East and West Germans harboured illusions about the efficiency of the East German industry and the productivity of East German labour. Comparisons are difficult because, in a Communist command economy, prices rarely reflect costs. They do not determine the allocation of resources or send signals to producers and consumers. But without realistic pricing, it is almost impossible to measure the value of output. Nonetheless, East Germany had been held up as the jewel of the Communist system and was thought to have performed rather well. Productivity was put at about 40% of the West German level, although it was probably nearer 30%. Table 13.1 provides a comparison between the two Germanies on the eve of unification.

The reality was that East Germany was a place of despair and decay, with an economic system in the final stages of collapse. The roads were full of pot-holes. Houses and flats were ancient and decaying. Over 70% of the housing stock was pre-war. Factories were full of rusting pipes and aged machines. Temporary sheds on the point of collapse contained stores. Even new factories were full of technologically old plant and equipment. The shops, such as there were of them, had mainly empty shelves. Banks were nearly non-existent and restaurants and theatres rare.

THE RUSH INTO MONETARY UNION

East and West rushed into monetary union. With 40,000 east Germans a week crossing to the west, they could not have done otherwise. The only way to prevent west Germany being flooded with immigrants was to promise that east German living standards would rapidly rise to west German levels. D-Marks had to move east to stop people moving west. There was talk of a slow integration process, as envisaged by the Maastricht Treaty for European monetary union, but the idea was rejected. Urgent action was needed to resolve the east German economic

Table 13.1 East and West Germany on the eve of Unification

	East	West	East/West %
Area, sq km	108.3	248.6	44
Population, 1988 m	16.4	61.5	27
GNP, DM bn current prices, 1989	285.7	2206.4	13
Working-age population (15–64), 000s, 1989	11,077	43,393	26
Labour force, 000s, 1989	8,886	29,779	30
Participation rate, 1989	80.2	68.6	117
Employment, 000s, 1989	8,886	27,208	33
Productivity, whole economy, DM per head, 1989	32,152	81,094	40
Value-added by sector, DM bn, 1989			
Agriculture	11.0	35.7	31
Mining & manufacturing	152.6	777.3	20
Construction	21.3	119	18
Wholesale & retail trade	17.9	194.3	9
Transport	23.0	126.4	18
Services	15.6	627.3	2
Government services	36.3	238.6	15
Private non-profit institutions	8.0	46.5	17
Total	285.7	2165.1	13
Employment, 000s, 1989			
Agriculture	960	1066	90
Mining & manufacturing	3655	9140	40
Construction	598	1810	33
Wholesale & retail trade	784	3600	22
Transport	624	1559	40
Services	899	4978	18
Government services	1746	4267	41
Private non-profit institutions	374	1203	31
Total	9640	27623	35

Table 13.1 East and West Germany on the eve of Unification (*cont.*)

	East	West	East/West %
Productivity, DM per head			
Agriculture	11,458	33,490	34
Mining & Manufacturing	41,751	85,044	49
Construction	35,619	65,746	54
Wholesale & retail trade	22,832	53,972	42
Transport	36,859	81,078	45
Services	17,353	126,014	14
Government services	20,790	55,918	37
Private non-profit institutions	21,390	38,653	55
Total	29,637	78,380	38

Source: OECD, *Economic Survey Germany 1990–1*

crisis. In fact, monetary union is never a matter of convergence, but of political will – the will to foot the bill which union imposes.

There was great uncertainty about how much German economic and monetary union would cost. Official estimates were pitched deliberately low. The speed with which east German living standards would catch up with west was grossly exaggerated. As late as 1992 Kohl still predicted this would take only 'three, four or five years'. Putting a narrow construction on his words, he could have been right. In 1991 employers and unions in the metal-working industries agreed that east German wages would be raised in four stages to west German levels between April 1991 to the spring of 1994. The employers, however, backed down from this commitment in 1993 and the date for parity was postponed until 1 July 1996.

COUNTING THE COST OF UNIFICATION

From the start it was clear that unification was going to be more expensive than the Government's official estimates. Appendix B, reprinted from *The Sunday Times*, gives an analysis done at the time. The problem could be simply stated in terms of three gaps. There was first the gap between east and west German productivity, the former about 30% of the latter. This was a gap which could only be closed slowly. Moreover to close it required substantial capital investment. Indeed to reach half the west German capital stock per head over the course of a decade would require investment in east Germany equal to 6% per annum of west Germany's GDP. Some of this could be financed out of east German savings, but much would have to be financed by west Germany.

The second gap was between east and west German incomes. The one-for-one rate at which, for many purposes, Ostmarks were converted to D-Marks meant that east German incomes were about 50% of west German. Unless this income gap were closed relatively quickly, millions more east Germans would migrate to west Germany in search of higher wages. But closing the incomes gap quickly, while the productivity gap closed only slowly, meant that a third gap would be increased – that between the value of east German output (when converted at the one-for-one exchange rate) and the level of east German incomes. This gap was equal to two-fifths German incomes (i.e. income per head was 50% of the west German levels and output per head, or productivity, was only 30%). It would have to be filled by transfer payments from west Germany to east. Since east German income was put at 10% of west German at the time Germany was reunited, transfers equal to 40% of east Germany's income had to cost 4% of west Germany's GDP. This 4% gave a sum of DM 100 bn for transfers to east Germany, which was far greater than any of the German Government's estimates. Moreover the bill was certain to rise as east German incomes increased faster than east German productivity. The cost of unification was clearly too large to be financed without higher taxation.

GOOD MONEY DRIVES OUT BAD

The precise arrangements for exchanging Ostmark for D-Mark were somewhat complicated. The conversion rate for money as a medium of exchange was one-for-one, meaning that all wages, salaries, rents, leases, pension and other public and private transfer payments remained unchanged in amount except that after 1 July 1990 they were paid in D-Mark. Money as a unit of account or store of value was converted at varying rates. Financial assets and liabilities were mostly converted at a rate of OM 2=DM 1, notably the debts which state companies owed state banks. East German residents were allowed to convert their savings at one-for-one up to stipulated limits: OM 2000 for a child up to fourteen years old, OM 4000 for each adult and OM 6000 for people fifty-nine years old or older. Foreigners who had speculated by buying O-marks on the black market were allowed to change them at OM 3= DM 1. Since the black market rates had been anything from DM 7 to DM 11, this still left a fat profit. The average exchange rate worked out at OM 1.6=DM 1. Various calculations based on purchasing power parities (i.e., the cost of a fixed basket of goods in each country) produced widely different answers for what the rate should have been. The Federal Statistical Office calculated that for a basket of goods matching East German purchases before unification OM 100 would buy as much as DM 132. All this meant was that East Germans spent very little on high (east) priced goods such as consumer durables, while their cheap food, housing, heating, clothes and travel cost much more in West Germany. But when a basket of goods matching West German consumption was priced in the two countries, OM 100 would only buy as much as DM 88. But so distorted was the pattern of East German prices, so poor the quality of their products, that such comparisons had little meaning. Basically the near-worthless money of a collapsing economy was changed into one of the most respected and valuable currencies in the world.

The one-for-one exchange sustained incomes but undermined the competitiveness of east German industry. On unification east German productivity – GDP per person employed – was around 30% of the west German level and at the end of 1990 wages were 50%. In consequence east German wage costs were about two-thirds higher than west German. But, as mentioned above, east German wages were raised rapidly towards west German levels. By end-1993 agreed rates had climbed over 70% and risen to four-fifths of the west German level. The actual gap was wider because many east Germans received less than the agreed rates – unions and the authorities turned a blind eye to this irregularity. East German wages were probably 60% and 65% of west German levels. Wage costs depend on productivity as well as wage rates. East German real GDP fell by about a quarter between 1990 and 1993, but employment also fell by about a quarter, so productivity was little changed. West

German productivity grew by 6% so that east German relative productivity fell below 30% of west German. Thus east German wage costs relative to west rose from about two-thirds higher to around double.

WORSE THAN THE 1930S DEPRESSION

Whether the collapse in east German output caused the rise in wage costs or vice versa is a moot point. But the result was that output in east Germany slumped by more than American or German output during the 1930s depression; industrial production dropped almost 80%, real GDP fell 40% (see Chart 13.1). But transfers from west Germany supported east German incomes in almost exactly the manner projected. In 1991 real GDP fell 31.4% while domestic demand rose by 9.6%. Fortunately real GDP started to recover in 1992 and is now growing at a rate of up to 10% a year (albeit from a very low base). Most of the growth continues to be financed by hand-outs from west Germany.

Chart 13.1 East and West German GDP

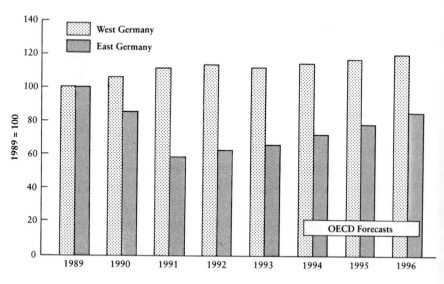

At current prices GDP was DM 186 bn but the total amount the east Germans were able to spend was almost twice this figure, DM 259 bn. The difference between the two was east Germany's current account

Chart 13.2 East German Output and Expenditure

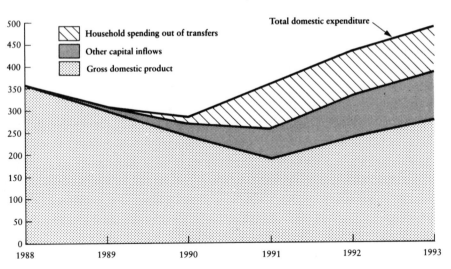

Legend:
- Household spending out of transfers
- Other capital inflows
- Gross domestic product
- Total domestic expenditure

deficit with the 'world' (i.e. including west Germany). This was financed by private capital inflows of DM 100 bn as well as west German transfers to east German households of DM 72 bn. By 1993 nominal GDP (i.e. at current prices) had risen to DM 276 bn due mainly to the rise in east German prices, while total domestic demand climbed to DM 488 bn. Capital inflows and transfers had fallen from 92% of GDP to 77%, but had climbed to DM 212 bn.

Unification still hurt. Employment collapsed. In total it fell by over a third between 1989 and 1991. But agricultural employment fell by three-quarters and manufacturing employment fell by two-thirds. The rise in unemployment was constrained by short-time working, early retirement, training schemes and, of course, emigration to west Germany. Daily and weekly commuters over the old border to work, called 'Pendler' numbered 75,000 in 1990 and increased sharply to over a million in 1991. Nonetheless the upheaval has been extremely painful to many east Germans. Ownership and control of some 12,559 state-owned enterprises, employing 4.8 million workers, was passed in 1990 to a special body, the Treuhandanstalt (often just called Treuhand). Its job was to rescue and sell all it could, while closing down those which could never become profitable. It had to carry losses and the burden of past debts. It has been remarkably successful in disposing of all but about 6% of the companies it inherited, albeit often for a pittance. Indeed some would say that the speed with which it has shed companies can have been achieved only by allowing their existing managers to grab ownership. Unfortunately, the companies which remain in public ownership include some very large ones. The Treuhand was wound up in 1995.

Unification has hurt east Germans in other ways as well. The decision was made to give back, rather than compensate, owners whose property had been confiscated by the Nazis or the Communist Government of the GDR after 1949. (Those dispossessed by the Soviets between 1945 and 1949 got nothing.) This has been rather a quid pro quo. Most of the claimants have been west Germans who fled from the east. They have got back their properties, as well as improvements. East Germans who suffered such hardship for so long under Communist rule have received their compensation by west German transfers.

Unification has proved costly. The total bill rose from DM 45 bn in 1990 to over DM 100 bn in 1991, climbing to DM 136 bn by 1994. Put simply, transfers accounted for about half east Germany's GDP in the early 1990s, which was about a tenth of west German GDP so that the cost to the west Germans was about 5% of their GDP. These are the back-of-envelope estimates the author made in 1991 and, as Table 13.2 shows, they were close to the mark. The cost to west Germany of bailing out east German incomes is currently some 4.7% of their GDP.

This is a bigger-than-expected bill. At the 1990 general election Chancellor Kohl promised the west Germans that there would be no need to raise taxation to finance unification. This was disingenuous. Like President George Bush and Britain's Prime Minister, John Major – who won elections after making similar promises not to raise taxation – Kohl did raise taxes. But he had an excuse. Germany, like Japan, contributed money instead of men to the Gulf War and, to help meet the bill, a surcharge of 7.5% was placed upon income taxes over the year from July 1991. There were further tax increases, including a hike in VAT from 14% to 15% on 1 January 1994. Social security charges were raised 2.5% points on 1 April 1991 and further increases followed to pension insurance.

Table 13.2 Public Transfers to former East Germany, 1991–4 (DM bn)

	1991	1992	1993	(1994 estimate)
1 Gross transfers	140	152	169	178
From Federal Government	75	89	116	127
Western Länder	5	5	10	14
German Unity Fund	31	24	15	5
European Community	4	5	5	6
Other	25	29	23	26
2 Receipts	33	37	39	42
Federal taxes etc. collected in east	31	35	37	40
Other	2	2	2	2
3 Net Transfers	107	115	130	136
% All-German GDP	3.8	3.8	4.2	4.2
% Western GDP	4.1	4.1	4.6	4.7
% Eastern GDP	58	49	47	44

Source: OECD Economic Survey, Germany 1994.

THE UNIFICATION BILL MET WITH BORROWED MONEY

Most of the money to pay for unification, however, has been borrowed. The German Government spent the 1980s pursuing a policy of fiscal consolidation. By 1989 it had succeeded in moving the public sector back into a small surplus. This was no mean achievement, particularly since taxes were reformed and reduced at the same time. Following unification, all the ground that had been gained was again lost.

The German budgetary system is complex because of the federal nature of the state. Länder and local authorities are responsible for more than half of all public spending. They do not collect taxes but are constitutionally entitled to a share of the taxes collected by the Federal Government. There is a revenue-sharing system which takes money from the richer Länder to give to the poorer. The new Länder were excluded from this when they first joined the old. Their needs were

Table 13.3 Public Sector Deficit, 1989–95 (DM bn)

	1989	1990	1991	1992	1993	1994†	1995†
Federal government	−20	−48	−53	−39	−67	−70	−70
Länder & local government	−7	−46	−70	−77	−71	−77	−61
Bundesbank profits, etc*	16	24	7	33	24	34	18
Social security system	15	20	25	4	12	18	16
General government	4	−50	−91	−79	−102	−96	−97
Off-budget items**	−12	−14	−36	−55	−59	−52	−10
Public sector total	−8	−64	−126	−134	−160	−148	−107
% of GDP	−0.2	−2.6	−4.9	−4.5	−5.2	−4.6	−3.2

Source: OECD Country Surveys, Germany 1991–2 & 1994.
* Includes adjustment to a national accounting basis.
** Includes Treuhand, Federal telecom, postal and rail losses.
† OECD projections.

looked after by special off-budget funds. The German Unity Fund was the most important, together with the Treuhand. East Germans also benefited by being brought within the west German social security system with entitlement to similar benefits. This did not mean they received the same pensions or unemployment pay as west Germans, but what they received was related in the same way to their lower (but rapidly rising) east German pay. This knocked the security systems surplus for six, plunging the Federal Labour Office into deep deficit, hence the rise in social security contributions.

Although the public sector's broadly defined budget deficit rose by an amount which corresponds closely to the transfers to east Germany, this gives a slightly misleading impression of Germany's finances. The rise in the public sector deficit also reflected the effects of the 1992–4 recession. The general government structural budget deficit – i.e. what the deficit would have been if the German economy had been working at its full potential rate – rose to a peak of 5.2% of GDP in 1991 and was steadily reduced to an estimated 2.3% in 1994. As the German economy recovers from the recession, the budget deficit will melt away; indeed it is already doing so.

The Germans are taking no chances on this. In 1993 a 'Solidarity Pact' was negotiated between the Federal Government, old and new Länder Governments (meaning the opposition parties), employers and trades unions, to place the on-going costs of supporting east Germany from 1995 within the normal system of Federal and Länder Government financial arrangements. Under this, the new Länder have been integrated into a restructured revenue-sharing system, with the help of an increase in the Länder's share of VAT revenues from 37% to 43%. The Federal Government has taken over Treuhand's debts and other special funds which were wound up. To help pay for this, the 7.5% tax surcharge was reimposed on 1 January 1995.

AN EXPLANATION OF OUTPUT GAPS

Unification caught the west German economy as it was on the point in the business cycle of overheating and needed to be slowed down. The best way to describe and illustrate the business cycle is to use the concept of output gaps. There is a certain level of activity, or GDP, that an economy can sustain without either overheating (causing inflation to accelerate), or stagnating (causing inflation to slow down). This level is called the economy's 'potential GDP'. Potential GDP is not, however, a constant. It grows over time as a result of labour force growth and investment in new capital equipment which increases productivity. This is called the economy's 'potential growth rate'. By definition, if an economy is working at its potential level and growing at its potential rate, it can sustain that growth indefinitely since inflation neither accelerates nor slows down.[1] Economies seldom if ever attain the ideal of hitting both potential level or rate. Normally GDP moves in a cyclical path about its potential level, at times being below it (i.e. having a negative output gap) and at times being above (i.e. having a positive output gap). When the gap is positive and the economy is overheating, action must be taken to slow it down. Either monetary or fiscal policy must be tightened, or indeed both. Growth must be reduced below its potential rate for a time to eliminate the overshoot on the up side.

[1] Economists cannot observe potential GDP levels and growth; they estimate them, but with considerable uncertainty.

Chart 13.3 West German Output Gap

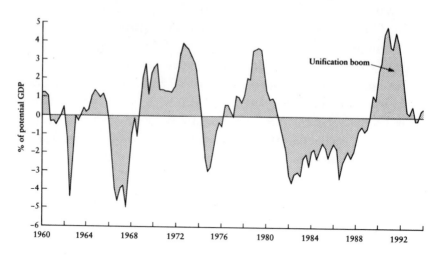

Equally, when an economy has a negative output gap, governments will normally want to stimulate demand so that the growth rate rises above its potential until the negative gap has been eliminated. They may not rush to do this if inflation is unacceptably high to begin with. A negative gap brings it down and may be tolerated until inflation has fallen to an acceptably low rate. German experience is illustrated in Chart 13.3.

THE UNIFICATION BOOM

German growth, far from slowing down in 1990, accelerated sharply after economic and monetary union, producing west Germany's largest boom in three decades. This was mostly the result of changing unspendable O-Marks into spendable D-Marks. People in Communist countries were paid more than they needed to spend on cheap everyday necessities, and thus tended to save a lot. Cars and consumer durables being dear and hard to obtain, rationing was by waiting and queuing more than by pricing. The result was a 'monetary overhang', meaning that east Germans had relatively more cash in the bank or in savings than west Germans, but little of value in the home or the drive. The normal capitalist methods of eliminating excess financial liquidity, lower interest rates or higher prices, were not employed in Communist countries. Gerlinde Sinn and Hans-Werner Sinn, in their excellent book, *Jumpstart: The Economic Unification of Germany* (1994), set out most of the following arguments. In 1990 East German money balances (M3) totalled OM 237 bn or 142% of east German income. West German M3 money balances totalled only 87% of disposable income. So for east German money balances to be reduced to west German levels, the exchange between the O-Mark and D-Mark had to average 142/89 = 1.6. East Germans would then acquire DM 150 bn. The actual conversion terms would have pulled this off, but for a miscalculation. Certain trading companies, which had been treated as banks before unification, were reclassified as non-banks thereafter. This meant their DM 30 bn of balances with real banks were redefined as part of M3, which consequently rose by DM 180 bn, or 13%. The east Germans brought more money into the union than they should have, given their GDP was less than 10% of west Germany's. Nonetheless it would have been unreasonable to expect them to have much the same cash balances, when they had nowhere near the same amount of consumer durables.

Immediately after unification, east Germans set out to change part of their valuable D-Marks into goodies. They went on a shopping spree in the west, particularly for second-hand cars. West Germans eagerly sold their old bangers and bought new cars, so much so that in the first year after unification, Germans bought one out of two of all new cars sold in Europe. East Germans also switched their regular spending from east German to west German goods. As trade with former Comecon countries was also crashing, the result of unification was a sharp slump in east Germany combined with a big boom in west Germany. West German real GDP reached a peak quarterly growth rate of over 8%. It grew by 6% at an annual rate in both the second half of 1990 and the first half of 1991. By the middle of 1991 a positive output gap of 5% of GDP had emerged. The result was an acceleration in west German inflation, which reached 5% at an annual rate a year later.

The unification boom in west Germany was caused by both the conversion of O-Marks into D-Marks and by the fiscal cost of bailing out east German incomes. The emergence of a public sector financial deficit at the height of the boom (when cyclically there should have been a surplus) meant that the structural deficit widened exceptionally rapidly. West German unions took advantage of falling unemployment and strong demand to push wages sharply higher. Wage increases in 1990–1 ranged from 6% to 7.5% and, helped by higher social security contributions, pushed up unit wage costs by a like amount. The union's response was natural. They had shown considerable restraint in the 1980s, during which the share of wages in GDP fell to its lowest level in 30 years. A large number of three-year contracts in 1987 had been agreed at a time when German prospects did not appear too promising. They turned out to be highly favourable to employers and the unions wanted to get their own (share) back.

With fiscal profligacy causing the economy to overheat, and inflation accelerating, the Bundesbank imposed tight credit conditions. Interest rates had started to rise before unification, discount rate was pushed up from 2.5% in mid-1988 to 5.5% by end-1989 and the Lombard rate from 4.5% to 8%. After unification, the Bundesbank hesitated for some time to see what would happen and then, at the end of the year, it started pushing rates higher again, to peaks in July to September 1992 of 8.75% and 9.75% respectively. Since then rates have been slowly but steadily reduced, notwithstanding M3 growth which significantly exceeded the Bundesbank target ceiling through most of 1994.

FOREIGNERS MEET THE BILL

The combination of fiscal profligacy with monetary stringency, meant that non-Germans met the bill for bailing out east Germans. Prior to unification, the west German economy was running a current account surplus approaching 5% of GDP. This measures the extent to which the nation was producing more than it consumed. The public sector was running a small financial surplus (0.2% of GDP), so that the current account surplus more or less matched private sector net savings of 4.7% of GDP. After unification, transfers to east Germany rose to 4.6% of west German GDP by 1993, while the public sector moved into a financial deficit of 5.7% (5.2% of all-German GDP). The current account moved to a deficit of 1.2% of west German GDP, a deterioration of 6.1% of GDP. The west German continued to save as much as before, but instead of lending to foreigners he lent to his own government, which gave his savings to east Germans. Instead of acquiring claims on foreigners, the west Germans (as savers) merely piled up claims on themselves (as taxpayers). This is seen in the rise in German public sector debts, which are projected by the OECD to climb from 43% of west German GDP in 1989 to 64% of all-German GDP by 1995. But it has to be added that part of the increase results from the Federal Government taking over the debts of former East German public institutions. The switch in west German lending from foreigners to their own government produced the deterioration in the German current account balance. The money they gave to east Germans was spent buying goods from west Germany which would otherwise have been exported to other countries. West Germans did not consume less. They merely transferred their surplus savings and output to east Germany.

HOW RESOURCES WERE SHIFTED

It is important to understand how this transfer was achieved. There are only two ways in which a balance of payments current account can be changed: through a change in relative prices or through a change in relative activity rates. Relative price changes can take place through differential inflation rates in advanced economies. This tends to be a rather slow process. Inflation rates do not usually differ by more than a few percentage points in any year. Exchange rate changes produce much larger and more rapid changes in relative prices (although they may subsequently be reversed where a devaluation leads to faster inflation). When relative price changes cause the balance of payments to adjust, the result is produced by a switch in expenditure. A stronger D-Mark makes German goods less competitive. Both foreigners and Germans buy fewer of them and more foreign goods. So German exports decline and imports rise. The current account deterioration reduces demand in Germany and increases it outside, leaving total demand unaffected. As the reduction in foreign and west German demand for west German goods was necessary to free resources to flow to east Germany, west German total demand was unchanged by the D-Mark rise, while demand in other countries was enhanced. Tight money and high interest rates following unification caused the D–Mark to rise against non-European currencies, setting in motion the adjustment process outlined above.

Exchange rate changes were banned for European countries whose currencies were pegged against the D–Mark in the ERM. They had to adjust by relative changes in activity rates. These do not shift expenditure between countries, they change expenditure levels within countries. To stop their currencies being pushed through the floor, ERM member countries had to match the Bundesbank's monetary stringency. But since their fiscal policies were less profligate than Germany's, their policy overall became more deflationary. Other European economies were also mostly overheating in 1990, so most did not initially mind the deflationary repercussions from German unification (Britain and France had large positive output gaps at the end of 1989 (see Chart 13.4) and needed monetary toughness. So while Germany boomed, growth elsewhere moderated. Frenchmen, for instance, spent less on everything – French and imported German products. Germans, because their economy was booming, spent more on everything, German and imported French products. This again resulted in a deterioration in the German current account balance.

Chart 13.4 Out-of-Step Cycles

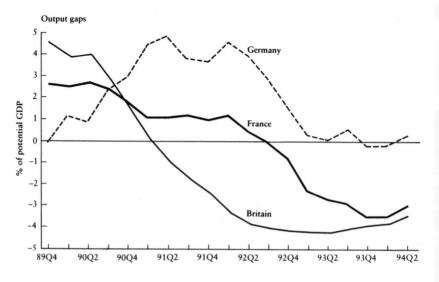

OTHER EUROPEAN COUNTRIES PUSHED BY GERMANY
DEEPER INTO RECESSION

Imitating Bundesbank monetary stringency was fine while the German economy boomed. But it did not go on booming. The conversion of excess D-Mark cash balances into consumer goods by east Germans gave a once-off boost to spending. Rising unemployment then led east Germans to become more cautious with their savings. The Bundesbank steadily raised interest rates while, after 1991, the Government tightened fiscal policy strenuously. This was not apparent in the actual public sector financial deficit, but the structural budget deficit fell from 5.2% of GDP in 1991 to 3.1% in 1993, a contraction of 1% of GDP each year. Growth slowed sharply and the positive output gap was eliminated. West German unemployment rose and wage increases ran below the rate of inflation. Real wages fell. In 1993, the unions reluctantly agreed to slow down the rate of wage convergence between east and west Germany. Price inflation abated to 3% in 1994 and would have been lower but for the increase in VAT at the start of the year.

When the German economy slowed down, the cyclical component of the budget deficit rose, offsetting the reduction in the structural deficit. German government borrowing and transfers to east Germany were little reduced, so the current account remained in deficit. But as activity in other ERM member countries had to remain below Germany's, the slow-down there caused slumps elsewhere. The need to match Bundesbank monetary stringency to protect ERM parities increasingly conflicted with domestic requirements to ease monetary policy to counter growing recessions.

BRITAIN'S STUPID ERM ADVENTURE

Pressure upon Britain was intense. The economically illiterate John Major, as Chancellor of the Exchequer, had persuaded the Prime Minister, Margaret Thatcher, to let sterling join the ERM in September 1990. It did so at demonstrably the wrong time, the wrong (i.e. grossly overvalued) rate and for the wrong reasons. But these were the dying moments of Margaret Thatcher's premiership, when she was beset by opposition on all sides. Her reluctant consent showed her end was near. In support of ERM membership were such eminent Tories as Sir Geoffrey Howe (who had resigned over Thatcher's anti-European attitude), Douglas Hurd, Nigel Lawson, Michael Heseltine and Sir Edward Heath. With such political heavyweights plus a majority of the economic establishment calling for ERM membership it is hardly surprising that Thatcher capitulated.

Since the terms of German unification were already known, it required little wit or wisdom to foresee the result (see Appendix C). Possibly the British Treasury were as blind to European developments as most of the press. More likely it underestimated the strains and overestimated Britain's ability to survive them. At any event, when John Major succeeded Margaret Thatcher as Prime Minister in October 1990, he wasted no time in compounding his folly. Forced to follow Bundesbank monetary stringency, he matched German fiscal profligacy. The British public sector financial balance went from a surplus of 0.9% of GDP in 1989, the year John Major became Chancellor, to a deficit of 7.7% of GDP in 1973 – a record peacetime deterioration of no less than 8.6% of GDP. Part was due to recession; nonetheless the structural deficit deteriorated from 2.1% to 5.3% of GDP in 1993 – a larger deficit than Germany's, when it faced the full cost of unification.

By 1992 the British economy had slid deep into recession. The positive output gap of 4.5% at end-1989 had, by June 1992, become a negative gap of nearly 4%. Nigel Lawson's bubble boom of the late 1980s had been burst. Ordinary people were up to their ears in debt and house prices had collapsed. In this environment the last thing the economy needed was high and rising interest rates. It became increasingly clear that Britain could not follow the Bundesbank rate rises. Consequently massive speculation ejected Britain from the ERM fixed rate system on 17 September 1992. The result was that the economy could recover. The Government belatedly embarked upon a policy of fiscal consolidation, reversing the damage John Major and ERM membership had done.

The French story is different and exemplifies why there can be little room in Europe for rival British and French economic systems. The French have long been committed to the *franc fort* or strong franc policy. The establishment saw this as necessary for the creation of a single European currency which would tie Germany into the west. The establishment has been willing for the past decade, whatever the sacrifices, to keep the franc strong. The French people objected to slow growth and higher unemployment, but no politician offered any alternative. Sectional interests were bought off from time to time, but that was all. The franc survived the speculation in September 1992, which pushed sterling out of the ERM, and faced another massive attack in August 1993 when the Bundesbank refused to reduce rates as fast as the domestic French economy required. After France's foreign currency reserves had been exhausted through intervention the franc was forced through its ERM floor. It seemed that the ERM system was at its end. Instead member countries agreed to widen fluctuation margins to 15% either side of their Ecu parities. The French, unlike the British, did not then cut interest rates and the franc gradually climbed back into its old narrow margins against the D-Mark. But to win the 1995 presidential election Jacques Chirac promised to lower unemployment. He will not be able to do so unless he abandons the *franc fort* or is pushed off it.

German unification should have been followed by change in ERM parities, but the system had become politically too rigid. The French would not devalue, nor the Germans revalue, while the credulous British had just chosen to go in. Bundesbank policy, quite rightly, was determined by the requirements of the German economy and the stability of the D-Mark; German law says it must be. The French have no say in Bundesbank policy. This is one reason they want a single currency. They would have a say in the European Central Bank which will run it, as will other member countries. The Bundesbank is deeply concerned by the prospect.

THE RUSH TO GERMAN MONETARY UNION WAS RIGHT

Was the rush to monetary union a ghastly mistake? Karl Otto Pöhl, after he had resigned as President of the Bundesbank, said it had been a 'disaster'. Detlev Karsten Rohwedder, Chairman of Treuhand, claimed it had caused a 'catastrophic change in output potential' in east Germany. If the exchange had been at a lower rate and if east German wages had not risen so rapidly, more of east Germany's enterprises would have survived. The bill for supporting east German incomes, which has taken four-fifths of all transfers, would have been less, and both public and private investment could have been larger.

Pöhl and Rohwedder spoke for their own special interests. The jobs of managing Germany's money supply and of selling off east German state enterprises would undoubtedly have been easier. But the arguments are not nearly one-sided. Private investment through Treuhand sales were hindered more by Government policies, particularly the right of former owners to restitution, rather than compensation. Obligations to help clear pollution, with the Treuhand's contribution capped, as well as commitments to future investment and employment levels, also reduced the saleability of east German enterprises. The shock therapy of a move to high west German wages should, in the long run, result in high-tech industries moving to east Germany, in which labour productivity is commensurately high. The east Germans are not badly educated, they are wrongly educated. Certainly, with low wages they could have got work in low productivity jobs. But now they are being forced to make an effort to earn those high wages. Singapore employed the same strategy in the 1970s, deliberately raising wages by 20% for three years in a row, while holding down prices. The policy did wonders to raise the value-added by industry establishing there. It will be shown later that the last thing Europe wants is employment of low-wage cheap labour in competition with developing countries. To have converted the O-Mark for the D-Mark at a lower rate would have condemned Germany to just that.

East Germany had a Communist-style bloated industrial sector, far too large relative to other kinds of economic activity. High wages forced it to shrink rapidly to levels more appropriate to an advanced modern economy. While the spotlight was on industrial collapse, it missed the great strides being made to build decent modern service sectors. Now that the industrial collapse is virtually complete, 10% a year growth in east Germany has become a source of dynamism for the country as a whole. In the middle of 1994 it helped propel West German GDP growth forward at an unexpected 4% annual rate. The net cost of supporting east German incomes will disappear as growth brings in buoyant tax revenues. More resources will flow into investment, increasingly financed by east German savings.

EAST GERMANY IS NO PROBLEM

From a ten-year perspective, the rush to unification is more likely to be regarded as producing a miracle than a disaster. Had the Germans wanted a *mezzogiorno* in east Germany, they would have made it a low-wage, dependency economy. Meanwhile, for a time the unification boom dispelled concern about the deteriorating performance of the west German economy. The recession which followed has reawakened it. The next chapter looks at the German social market system and its rivals, and considers which is likely to perform best in the current world environment.

CHAPTER 14

The German Social Market

In the debate on Europe's future, a distinction is often drawn between Anglo-American laissez-faire and French dirigisme. The former traces its descent from Adam Smith and his *Wealth of Nations*, published in 1776. French dirigisme goes back even further, to Louis XIV's finance minister, Jean-Baptiste Colbert (1619–83). Laissez-faire is probably superior in economic terms. Dirigisme does not perform as well as the free market, but it is more socially just. The Germans have a third model, somewhat neglected as it is not connected to a famous name. It is the social market. It tries to balance social justice against economic efficiency. Arguably that is what we should all aim to do.

The systems can be compared to games of football. The Anglo-American version has few rules, no referee and no teams. Everyone tries to kick the ball to score goals for themselves. The French game has many rules. The referee makes them up as the game goes along. He also joins in and cheats. Rival teams are less interested in winning the ball than in bullying the referee to give them penalty kicks. When likely to lose, particularly to an away side, they stop playing until the rules are changed. The German game also has many rules, but the referee keeps out of it. The rival team captains invent many of the rules themselves and enforce them. Sometimes they come to blows deciding what the rules should be. But thereafter they make sure nobody cheats. Germans play as teams; if they lose they practise harder for the next game, buy new boots or change their tactics. Their long-term aim is to head the championship table at the end of the season.

Britain's attachment to laissez-faire and the free-market model is not only recent, but tenuous. Despite its charismatic new leader, Tony Blair, and his pro-market rhetoric, the Labour party remains wedded to the social market model. Labour's support for a minimum wage and willingness to accept the Maastricht Social Chapter signals a retreat from laissez-faire.

PITY THE FRENCH

French dirigisme is understandable in its historic context. In sharp contrast to the Federal Republic of Germany, France is a highly centralised state, run from Paris by an élite establishment of bureaucrats. They are known as the *Enarques*, after the prestigious Ecole Nationale d'Administration, at which all high-flyers receive their education – the French equivalent of Oxbridge, but much more exclusive. The majority of Enarques are from Paris and the offspring of Enarques. As a class they dominate business, finance and politics. They are the French establishment and it is exceedingly monolithic and more venal than its British equivalent.

The French establishment looks back to the seventeenth and eighteenth centuries, when France and French culture led the world, the days of the 'Sun King' and of Colbert's masterly administrative reforms – centralisation and internal liberalisation combined with external mercantilism. It thinks long term, seeking to restore, at least in part, French greatness. The French take their history, glory, honour and culture very seriously – hence their obsession with the purity of the French language and their zealous laws to prohibit the use of 'Franglaise' and other foreign words. The Paris élite thinks it knows best how a nation should be run. It regards free markets as jungles. A prime object of policy is to maintain domestic tranquillity, meaning that pressure groups and special interests must be appeased to maintain peace, rather than opposed to promote efficiency. The European Union is a vehicle, which the French are determined to drive where they want it to go.

THE GERMANS SEEK CONSENSUS

The German social market involves keen competition, but within a prescribed framework decided by consensus and co-operation. German corporate structure has evolved differently from the Anglo-American joint-stock corporation, German companies relying less on shareholders' capital. Only 600 German companies have stock-market quotations, accounting for 10% of GDP and over 40% of their shares are owned by other companies. By comparison, there are 3000 British quoted companies covering 30% of GDP and very little cross-shareholding. Most medium and small German companies are privately owned, as are some large ones. German companies rely little upon equity issues for finance. Two-thirds of the money they need for investment comes from retained profits, compared with less than half for Britain – but a high corporate tax rate, plus generous allowances encourage companies to plough back profits rather than distribute them. For tax reasons, shareholders prefer capital gains to dividends. German companies are heavily reliant upon long-term bank loans for capital, whereas bank lending to British companies is overwhelmingly short term.

Table 14.1 Corporate Financial Structures
Average 1989–92; % of financial resources

	Germany	France	Britain
Self-financing	60.5	52.9	45.0
Equity issues	6.0	11.7	11.9
Debt	33.5	35.4	43.1
Direct bank borrowing	12.8	5.7	14.4
Short-term	7.3	0.0	14.4
Long-term	5.5	5.7	0.0

British and American companies are run for the benefit of their shareholder-owners and their main aim is to maximise profit. As shareholding is defused and there are strict laws against insider trading, shareholder control is limited. If a shareholder does not like the way a company is run, he or she can do little about it. Only very large (institutional) investors can force management changes, and even they have a struggle. Most shareholders sell their shares if the company is doing badly. This exercises discipline on management. If a falling share price exposes a badly run company to a hostile take-over bid, then the management gets sacked. Meanwhile most managers vote themselves large salaries and long contracts so that, when fired, they receive golden hand-shakes. The Anglo-American system produces substantial income inequality between workers and management. Because of the importance of today's share price, management takes a short-term approach to profit maximisation. Projects must pay off almost immediately or they are not worth undertaking.

THE STAKEHOLDER CULTURE

German companies operate for the benefit of its 'stakeholders', all of whom have an interest in the company's survival and success. In addition to shareholders, stakeholders include employees, unions, bankers, customers and suppliers. The determination of what is in their collective best interests is formalised through the system of supervisory boards, which all large companies must have. One-third of the seats on these boards (one-half in the iron and steel industry) go to workers' representatives. Thanks to cross-shareholdings, customers and suppliers are usually represented, as are the company's bankers. The supervisory boards oversee the strategic decisions of the executive boards covering such matters as investment in new plant, closure of old and redundancies. The supervisory boards, together with long-term shareholders, determine how German companies develop. Bad management in theory can be changed more readily – in practice, it isn't.[1] Payment to management is not so outrageous, thanks to worker representation on supervisory boards. Hostile take-overs are virtually unknown. Managers are not constantly looking over their shoulder at share prices. They concentrate on the long-term prosperity of the company.

[1] The *Financial Times* in a leader on 21 December 1993 observed: 'For all its well-deserved reputation for taking industry seriously, Germany offers a surprisingly large number of case studies where various failures of management supervision have led to highly publicised corporate losses or even, in extreme cases, financial collapse. The list of well-known companies which during the last 10 or 15 years have been dealt severe blows through spectacular incapacity to exert proper control over aspects of their business include AEG, Nixdorf, Grundig, Krupp, Kloeckner & Co. and Volkswagen.'

Workers have a hand in the day-to-day running of their companies. Where more than five people work together in an establishment they can set up a works council if they wish. Such councils have legal status and a statutory right to be consulted about many things, such as working hours, as well as having a near veto over redundancies. Disputes go to special labour courts for adjudication, separate from the normal civil and criminal courts. Labour courts have a record of siding with workers over redundancies. It is extremely difficult for German companies to fire workers, and job security is controlled within a complex legal framework which protects workers against dismissal. Short-term work contracts are limited to a fixed period of eighteen months (increased from six months by the 1985 Employment Promotion Act). If a company wants to dismiss above a certain number of permanent employees, it must present a 'social plan' involving support and retraining. If challenged, the Labour courts can ignore economic criteria in favour of social justice.

Many German employers actively dislike the Anglo-American practice of hire-and-fire, so that, in consequence, workers enjoy something approaching the Japanese lifetime employment system. This arrangement encourages long-term relationships between companies and their workers, their customers, suppliers and banks. When times get difficult, the German company looks to improve its product or raise productivity, not to reduce employment. Banks usually see companies through difficult periods as their loans are long term.

One-third of German workers belong to trade unions, not a very different proportion from their British counterparts. But in Germany an employee does not have to belong to a union to benefit from its activities. Workers, not unions, are represented on works councils, although in larger companies the worker representatives tend to be unionists. Unions are represented on supervisory boards, and German workers are organised into a federal system of sixteen nation-wide industry-based unions under a single umbrella organisation. Designed by the British after 1945, it is a much better system than Britain's mixture of craft- and industry-based unions. Demarcation disputes are unknown in Germany. The unions are confronted by powerful employers' organisations, which play a more important role in Germany than in Britain. They organise training and are dominant in wage-bargaining.

Wage deals are negotiated between the sixteen unions and employers' organisations at regional level. Negotiations concern working hours, holidays and other fringe benefits as well as pay. Once a settlement is reached in a leading region, all other regions follow suit along similar lines. Some 40% of settlements involve agreements to implement decisions reached by other groups of workers. Wage deals set pay rates for workers under a system of job grades, which are classified regionally. Once a deal has been reached, it becomes a legally enforceable contract between unions and employers. All employers belonging to the employers' organisation must pay at least the going rate. Most pay more than the minimum, but not much more. Strikes and lock-outs are illegal until the contract expires, and occur only while a new contract is being negotiated. Germany loses fewer working days resulting from industrial action than almost any other country. Where a deal covers more than half the employees in an industry and region, the union or the employers can ask for it to be legally extended to cover all employers in that region. This is done where employment tends to be in relatively small units, such as retail distribution.

The employers' role in training is managed by local Chambers of Commerce, to which most employers belong. There are some 400 nationally standardised occupational training programmes which employers operate. The Chambers of Commerce ensure that all companies contribute to training programmes, thereby preventing non-trainers poaching trained workers. They help to provide training for companies too small to do their own. The Chambers of Commerce apply both moral and legal sanctions against companies which do not pull their weight. The ratio of skilled (i.e. with qualifications of some sort) to unskilled workers in Germany is nine-to-one. In Britain it is one-to-one. The British National Institute for Economic & Social Research reckons that half Germany's productivity lead over Britain is due to better training. David Goodhart, in his Institute for Public Policy Research pamphlet *The Reshaping of the German Social Market* (1994) – on which this chapter draws heavily – put training into its broader social market context:

If all companies pursue their own short-term interests *against* each other it prevents the creation of public economic goods. The classic case is training. Pressures for short-term profit maximisation and an opportunistic business culture are particularly damaging for training needs of a modern economy, argue the institutionalists. Unless companies are legally or institutionally compelled to train there will be an overwhelming temptation to free-ride by poaching skilled workers.

A NON-INTERVENTIONIST GOVERNMENT

The German Government is not interventionist after the French style. Partly this is because it is a federal Government with many powers in the hands of the Länder. Due to fears of strong central government in Germany, following experience under Bismarck and Hitler, the Basic Law set out deliberately to create weak government at the centre. The power of the Federal Government has been increased, particularly under the Kiesinger Grand Coalition in the 1960s, but is still limited in comparison with other countries. Many other functions are devolved. The Government sets the rules, but does not intervene, in the wage-bargaining process. Companies and unions, as already indicated, collectively determine pay and working conditions. The independent Council of Economic Advisers, the 'Six Wise Men', defines a norm for allowable wage increases each year, calculated as the sum of expected productivity growth per hour and 'unavoidable' inflation. At times of high unemployment it calls for moderation and, as a rule, unions have followed the Council's guidelines.

Bismarck's welfare state involved accident, unemployment and old age insurance, financed by employers and employees, not by the state. Health, unemployment insurance and the pensions system remain more in the private than in the public sector. The independent Federal Labour Office looks after unemployment insurance, training grants and other labour-related expenditures, such as subsidies for re-hiring unemployed workers aged over fifty. It also has had a near monopoly of labour placement services. Until 1994 the only private employment agencies allowed were for artists and senior management. The main health insurance and pension funds are officially self-financing from employees' and employers' contributions, independent of the state and run by representatives of employers and unions. But the benefits and services they provide are regulated by the state, and the state guarantees them.

The pension fund is a privately run 'pay-as-you-go' system. Given the ageing of the population and the increasing cost of modern medicine, the state makes a significant contribution out of general taxation, which is set to rise substantially.

From the start, the banking system has been independent of the Federal Government. Neither the Bank deutscher Länder nor its successor, the Bundesbank, have been controlled by the Government. Monetary policy is determined independently and with sole regard for preserving the external and internal value of the D-Mark. Germany economic policy-making differed sharply from British and French, where the Bank of England and the Banque de France were under government control. This has now changed. In 1994 the French Government, in accordance with the requirement of the Maastricht Treaty (Stage 2), granted the Banque de France full independence. The British Government has not gone so far; but, de facto, the Bank of England currently controls credit and interest rate policy. The Chancellor of the Exchequer consults with the Bank's Governor every month and between them they decide what to do. Six weeks after the event the minutes of their discussions are published. The Chancellor retains the last word, but he dare not overrule the Governor for fear of the financial markets' reaction when he is found out.

Public ownership of industry (Treuhand apart) is limited in Germany. Until Thatcher's privatisations, it was lower than in Britain. The Federal post, telecommunications and railway systems are publicly owned, as was Lufthansa until 1994. The Federal Government has privatised in recent years, in whole or in part, nine public enterprises, the two largest being Industrieverwaltungsgesellschaft AG (assets, DM 663 m), an industrial holding company and C&L Treuarbeit Deutsche Revision AG (assets, DM 558 m), an audit company. Total receipts from privatisation, at DM 1.7bn, were minuscule compared with over £50bn raised by British privatisations over the past decade.

INTERVENTION BY LÄNDER GOVERNMENTS

Below the Federal Government there is considerable Länder ownership and intervention in industry. The states own or part-own Landesbanks, which account for about 40% of banking business. They operate in a semi-commercial, semi-public manner. Westdeutsche Landesbank, for example, is building up its portfolio of company shares, while commercial banks are under pressure to reduce theirs. It recently bailed out Gildemeister, a bust tool-maker. Landesbanks seek to support local companies and jobs. The Land compete to attract businesses to locate within their boundaries, with various financial incentives, infrastructure spending and the like. Land themselves have shareholdings, usually small, in many companies and provide subsidises. The level of public subsidisation of industry in Germany is high, but not excessive compared with many countries. At the Federal level it runs at around 1.2% of GDP, while on a broadly defined basis to include Treuhand, coal subsidies and tax breaks (but not Länder subsidies) the total is around 4.5% of GDP.

But if direct ownership, intervention and subsidisation are limited, regulation is excessive and all-pervasive. The difference between Germany and the Japanese system of 'administrative guidance' under which bureaucrats decide everything, is that the Germans have written rules covering everything. Terrestrial telecommunications is a public monopoly. The provision of energy is generally a local monopoly. Local government grants a monopoly in its area to gas or electricity suppliers who provide the supply network of pipes or wires. The energy companies pay the local authority for the privilege and everyone in the area is forced to buy from them. Competition is completely ruled out. There are national restrictions on shop hours and Sunday opening. Road transport operators, taxi drivers and the like require public licences to operate. Individuals cannot set up companies unless they possess the appropriate qualifications. Regulations are stifling developments in such high-tech sectors as biotechnology, where it can take two years to obtain a licence to enter a business while the necessary environmental impact studies are conducted – against six weeks for similar studies in the United States. Laws regulate working hours and Sunday working, redundancies (as already explained) and all manner of things in the work place. Yet in fairness to Germany, most other countries are bound up with red tape. England, for instance, has only recently caught up with Scotland by reforming its drink licensing laws to enable pubs to remain open during the afternoons and scrapping restrictions on shops opening on Sundays.

SOME PRAISE FOR THE SOCIAL MARKET

The Germans defend their social market system, claiming it performs better than the Anglo-American free market system and that it is fairer. David Goodhart can again be quoted in this context:

> Also relatively unknown in Britain is the school of economists – loosely described as 'institutionalists' – who by examining real markets in their institutional settings have come up with some compelling explanations for why social market economies like Germany or the Netherlands have performed so strongly. Their explanation of the 'institutional comparative advantage' of such economies is that they have succeeded because of – not despite – their tendency to offend against neoclassical assumptions about opportunistic, profit-maximising behaviour of companies and individuals. Competitive success in markets for goods and services, argue the institutionalists, depends upon restraining or guiding other kinds of markets, for labour and capital in particular.

The German stakeholder system leads to secure long-term relationships which pay off in industrial harmony. There is still a degree of cartelisation of the German market. Companies in the same industry, probably with knowledge of each other's investment plans through overlapping supervisory board directorships, specialised on different product ranges. German industry has concentrated on capital goods which are more quality-sensitive than price-sensitive, so this approach seems to have paid off. Moreover determination of wages between co-operative unions and management has produced modest inflation at the macro-level.

There is a lot to say for the German social security system. It is certainly generous and should be as long as Germans feel it is worth the price. But the result of the shortest working hours in Europe, the best holidays and amongst the best welfare systems, has been to feather-bed the west German worker. There is virtually nothing to be said for the regulatory system. As in Japan, it represents a triumph of producers' over consumers' interests. It limits competition and leads to inefficiency. It is not, however, essential to the functioning of the social market and is, in any case, being ameliorated through Single Market legislation.

ANGLO-AMERICAN MODEL MORE FLEXIBLE

It is hard to say which system – German, French or British – is best. It probably depends on the circumstances. The German social market has been successful, but that does not make it the only successful system or always the most successful. Free markets also work. The contention here is that, in the 1950s and 1960s, when the going was good, Germany's social market system performed remarkably well. But as Germany was catching up and repairing wartime destruction, that was not too surprising. In the 1970s, when the going got tough, it withstood the shocks better than most. Union moderation in pay demands, when confronted by rising prices, led to less serious recessions in Germany than elsewhere and fewer lost jobs. But through the 1980s and into the 1990s, with the world environment changing more rapidly, the German system has been slow to respond. In consequence, the decline in West Germany economic performance had become a matter for concern during the 1980s.

Growth in Germany, as in almost all European and OECD economies, has slowed down in every decade since 1950. But with countries marching out of step through the cycle, comparisons between growth rates can vary substantially according to the starting and ending dates chosen. Long period comparisons are best, but they are slow to reveal changes in relative performance. Comparisons over 1984 to 1994 are not too bad. In 1984 most countries had climbed out of the early 1980s recession, while in 1994 they were similarly recovering from recession. A slightly earlier starting date would be unflattering to Germany. In the four years 1980–3, German growth averaged less than 1% and never climbed above 2%. Other countries dug deeper into recession and then climbed more rapidly out again. So if the starting date is the trough of the recession, they perform much better relative to Germany. If, however, the date is pushed back to the beginning of the recession, Germany does well once again. Within the period, however, German growth trailed other countries through the second half of the 1980s and only surged ahead again in the 1990–2 unification boom. Without that boom, Germany would have continued to lose ground.

BRITAIN'S BETTER PRODUCTIVITY PERFORMANCE

Over the last ten years as a whole, there is hardly anything to choose between German, French and British growth. But the US, which used to be a slow-growth country, outperformed Europe. Looking ahead, the OECD forecasts west German GDP will grow by only 1.7% a year between 1992 and 2000 (*Country Survey: Germany 1994*), compared with 2.2% in Britain and 2.3% in France. Both US and Japanese growth are put at 2.6% a year.

Growth comes from higher employment and increasing productivity (output per employee). In West Germany employment grew moderately strong during the second half of the 1980s, but was well behind British growth. The unification boom changed the picture in the 1990s, as German employment surged ahead of British and French. More recently Germany has lost ground again. But Europe has been well behind the US and Japan in creating new jobs.

Chart 14.1 Manufacturing Productivity Growth 1979–93

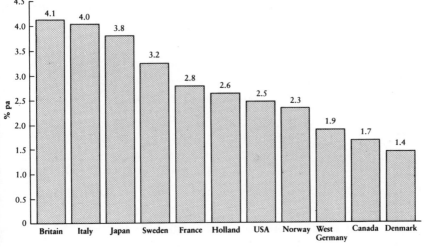

Productivity growth is compared in Chart 14.1. Taken from a US Bureau of Statistics study published in October 1994, it shows how Germany is slipping down and Britain accelerating up the international productivity growth league. Britain was one of the few countries in which manufacturing productivity rose as rapidly in 1985–93 as it did over 1979–85. This put Britain at the top of the league over the decade as a whole. US GDP growth created lots of new jobs and in consequence productivity growth was disappointing. Germany has lagged well behind, third from bottom. In the 1980s, the Anglo-American laissez-faire system had a slight edge on growth and employment over the German social market system, which the unification boom temporarily reversed.

EUROPE'S JOB CRISIS

The real weakness in Europe's performance is to be seen, however, in long-term labour market developments, which have caused many commentators to claim that Europe faces a jobs crisis. Unemployment has shot up in Europe with each economic cycle. West Germany has performed better than most and has lower unemployment today than both the EU and American average. But whereas US and Japanese unemployment figures have oscillated around a flatter trend, unemployment in all EU countries, west Germany included, has been on a long-term rising trend.

Demography helps to explain the more rapid growth of employment in the US and Japan than in Europe. Population growth has been more rapid in both countries than in Europe, nearer 1% a year over the three decades to 1991, compared with 0.5% in the EU. Germany and Britain had amongst the slowest growing populations, whereas France enjoyed rather faster growth. The population of working age, 15–64 years old, grew faster everywhere than the total population.

Britain's weak population growth was partly offset by a sharp rise in participation rates. The labour force increased by more than the population age 15–64, as more married women went out to work. Participation rates also rose sharply in the US and were stable in Japan. But in continental Europe they fell. While this was partly the effect of youngsters spending more time in education, it also reflected a lower level of female participation and a tendency towards earlier retirement.

BRITAIN'S MIXED RECORD

The US working-age population rose by 57 m between 1961 and 1991, the labour force rose 55 m and employment by 51 m. The increase in

Chart 14.2 Unemployment, 1974–94

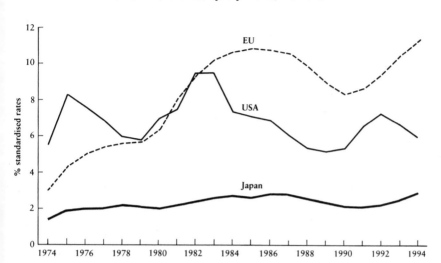

employment thus equalled 90% of the increase in the population of working are. At the other extreme, the German working age population rose by 6.6 m, the labour force by 3.8 m and employment by only 2.3 m, barely more than a third. The French performance was little better than the German, while Britain did markedly better with employment rising by half the rise in numbers of working age. But Britain also created more jobless in that the growth in the labour force exceeded the growth in the population of working age and the result was more unemployed as well as more employed than elsewhere in Europe. In more detail, Britain created private sector jobs, whereas almost all the growth in employment on the Continent has been in public sector jobs. This remains true even when account is taken of the shift in employment in Britain from public to private sector through privatisation. After adjusting for this factor, British public sector employment has remained flat while private sector employment has risen.

FREE MARKETS ARE BEST AT CREATING JOBS

Labour market experience lends support to the view that the free market system, with its easy hire-and-fire rules and no minimum wages, is superior in creating employment than the continental European systems. Rising unemployment may be seen as predominantly a European failure. Yet this misses a crucial point. The dispersion between the highest and lowest paid workers in the United States and Britain has increased significantly since the 1970s, whereas wage differentials in Europe have remained little changed or have declined. Wages amongst the lowest paid in the US and Britain have fallen in real terms. Thus Europe's problem is the unemployed poor, living on public support, whereas in Britain and the United States it is the working poor. Many of the jobs that have been created are female, low paid, part-time and service sector jobs. Adult male unemployment is higher everywhere. In Britain and the United States there is no longer any pretence that the income of a lower paid worker will be sufficient to support a wife and family. Two incomes are needed for that, which is another reason why participation rates are higher than in continental Europe.

How will the rival systems adapt and perform in the future? The appearance of German weakness in relative economic performance was far more pronounced in the mid-1980s than it is now. That was largely because fiscal consolidation led to such slow growth in the first half of the decade. The German response was to try and improve its social market model to enhance its performance. Between 1986 and 1990 a three-stage income tax reform package was introduced, cutting marginal tax rates, but also ending some reliefs. Company taxes have been lowered in the 1990s, not withstanding the need for extra revenues to cover unification costs. Steps have also been taken to cut costs in the welfare system by reducing unemployment benefits by 3% and raising the retirement age. At the same time long-term care for the ill has been improved. Laws have been introduced to increase labour market flexibility by allowing more work on Sundays and public holidays. The quotas and licensing system for long-distance transport has been retained, but its operation somewhat eased.

All in all, however, the structural changes that have been made in Germany have been marginal and incremental, not massive and brutal, as were those introduced by Margaret Thatcher in Britain during the 1980s. But then the West German political system was specifically designed to prevent powerful and autocratic leaders, in the mould of Margaret Thatcher, from taking control. Consensus politics leave little room for conviction politicians. Foreign affairs is the only area in which Chancellor Kohl has had the same power as Margaret Thatcher, and that mainly because most Germans pay little attention to it.

DOUBTS ABOUT EUROPE'S COMPETITIVE FUTURE

Economists' doubts today about Germany's (and Europe's) performance rest upon structural weaknesses. The first stems from the burdens placed on business by high levels of public spending and generous welfare systems. These reflect both the size of the burdens and the ways in which revenue is raised. Public spending in all-Germany was 50% of GDP in 1994. In France, Italy and the Netherlands it was around 55%. In Britain it was 7% to 10% points lower at 43%, while in the US and Japan it was a full 15% to 20% points lower at 35%.

It can be seen from Chart 14.3 (on page 160) that German public spending is now on a rising trend while Britain's is again falling. The composition of public spending matters. Differences in detail between German and Britain are revealing. Germany spent less on defence and public goods (such as the police, civil service, courts, etc); less on education and housing; less on public sector investment and on debt interest. If spending on everything else had been the same, German public spending would have been 3.9% points of GDP lower than Britain's. It was higher because Germany spent over 1% more on subsidies, nearly 1% more on health and over 5% more on transfers, mostly pensions. State pension entitlements are more generous in Germany and France than in Britain, as Table 14.2 (on page 160) shows. The British state pension is only 20% of assessed earnings (32% for a married couple) against 50% to 60% in France and Germany. It is indexed to prices not wages and it takes fifty years to obtain a full pension.

GERMANY IS AGEING MORE RAPIDLY THAN BRITAIN

Although Van den Noord and Herd in their study (on which Table 14.2 is based) concluded that unfunded pension liabilities in Germany and Britain were much the same and lower than in France (all have pay-as-you-go systems), contribution rates in Britain are lower. Moreover, the German and French populations are ageing more rapidly than Britain's.

Chart 14.3 Public Spending, 1978–95

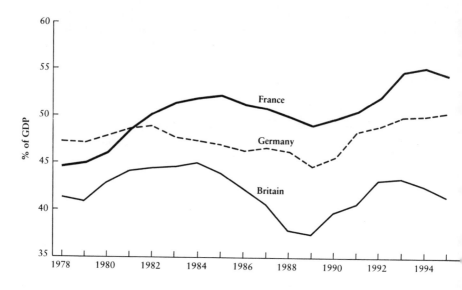

Table 14.2 Pension Entitlements, 1994*

	Germany**	France	Britain
Retirement age m/f	65/65	60/60	65/60
Flat rate	No	No	Mostly
Other help	Social assistance	Guaranteed minimum	Social assistance
Assessed income	Career	Best 10 years	Career
% of Assessed income	60%	50%	20%
Spouse supplement	No	No	12%
Indexation to	Wages	Wages	Prices
Minimum contributions	5 years	10 years	25% of working life
For full pension after	40 years	37.5 years	50 years
Accrual factor	1.5%	1.75%	0.4%

* From Table 1.1 in *Pension Liabilities in the Seven Major Economies*, OECD Economic Department Working Paper by Paul Van den Noord & Richard Herd.
** West Germany

The ratio of pensioners to the population of working age is currently 0.24 in Britain compared with 0.22 in Germany. But while the British ratio does not start seriously to rise until after 2010 and only reaches 0.31 by 2020, the German ratio climbs to 0.33 by 2010 and 0.39 by 2020. More rapid German ageing will also push up health care costs faster. Germany and France are both faced with the choice between reforming their pensions and health care systems to make them less generous (which to some degree they are doing), increasing employee and employer contributions or bailing their systems out from higher general taxation.

THE DOLE IS MEANER AND CHEAPER IN BRITAIN

The average unemployment benefit in Britain is 18% of the average wage, against 47% in Germany and 48% in France. These figures are based on expenditure on unemployment relief related to the numbers unemployed. They understate the level of relief actually received as the unemployed (except in Britain) include some who may not be entitled to receive benefits. In 1991, the year to which these figures relate, west German unemployment was 4.4% and Britain's almost double at 8.7%. Yet Germany spent 1.4% of GDP on paying the dole against Britain's 0.6%. If German unemployment had equalled Britain's, Germany's bill would have been 4.6 times larger.

TAX WEDGE FAR WIDER ON THE CONTINENT

Higher public spending has to be paid for out of higher taxes or larger borrowing. Germany and France are doing both. For every £100 that a British worker takes home in his pay package, his employer pays out £143. The equivalent figures for Germany and France are DM 162 and Ffr 176. The tax burden in Italy is even higher. These extra tax payments come on top of higher wages in the first place. The hourly cost of employing a German worker was DM 43 in 1993. This was DM 20 more than it cost to employ a British worker for one hour. But the German's hourly take-home pay was DM 27, only DM 9 more than the Briton's. Moreover Germans work fewer hours, which narrows the take-home pay gap, but widens the cost gap. German machines are worked for fewer hours in the week.

Table 14.3 Taxes & Social Security Contributions*

% average earnings, 1991	Germany	France	Britain
Social security contributions			
Employers'	18.2	43.8	10.4
Employees'	18.2	17.1	7.6
	36.4	60.9	18.0
Average income-tax rate	8.7	1.0	15.5
	45.1	61.9	33.5
% of average earnings plus employers' contributions			
Average total tax rate	38.1	43.1	30.3
Marginal total tax rate	45.6	47.0	38.9
Effective tax rates in 1993** as % of GDP			
Income tax	23.6	17.4	20.7
Employers' tax	19.1	28.1	12.5
Indirect taxes *less* subsidies	11.7	12.2	13.3
	43.6	44.5	32.2

* Taken from OECD *Economic Outlook*, June 1993, Table 9.
** From Table 32, OECD *Economic Survey* of Germany, 1994.

WAGE COSTS ARE HIGHER IN GERMANY

The German belief is that their higher wages are affordable because of their superior productivity. A recent study (reported by Andrew Lorenz in *The Times*, 31 Oct. 1994) by the German motor manu-facturers' & traders' organisation, the VDA, maintained that although German hourly wage costs in the motor vehicle industry were DM 52.06, more than double Britain's DM 25.9, German productivity was so superior that British wage costs were 18% above the equivalent

German level. German hourly productivity is undoubtedly higher, but this is ridiculous. German workers have taken a large part of the benefit by working fewer hours. Moreover, as already shown, the growth of output per employee in Germany has slid to the bottom of the international league table during the past decade (see Chart 14.1 above). Absolute levels of productivity are rarely compared. Normally people look only at percentage changes. But a chart in the 1994 OECD *Country Survey, Germany* suggests that British manufacturing productivity may now almost equal Germany's. This fits in better with evidence from the Ford Motor Company, which reports lower costs in Britain than in Germany although still higher than in Spain and Belgium. It also fits with the choice of Britain as a manufacturing base by so many foreign investors. Britain takes the lion's share of foreign direct investment into Europe.

Chart 14.4 Labour Costs

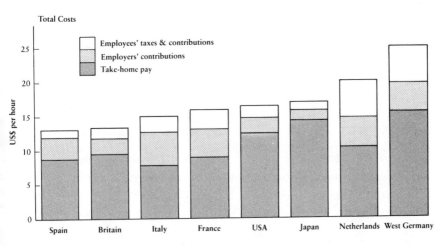

There can be little if any difference between German, French and British productivity amongst computer programmers and systems analysts. If anything the British will be amongst the best. Table 14.4 shows where pay differences can really hurt the continental economies. It also reveals the greater cost differentials in Britain between qualified, skilled and unskilled or semi-skilled workers.

Table 14.4 Selected Pay Differences, 1994 (US $s)

	Germany	France	Britain
Computer programmer			
Salary per year	40,124	26,311	25,529
Non-salary costs*	13,951	19,210	5718
Total costs	54,075	45,521	31,247
Britain = 100	173	146	100
Systems analyst			
Salary per year	49,286	44,050	41,808
Non-salary costs*	15,821	27,113	9680
Total costs	65,107	71,163	51,488
Britain = 100	126	138	100
Textile worker (hourly)			
Salary per year	13.12	9.73	8.23
Non-salary costs*	7.38	6.76	2.04
Total costs	20.50	16.49	10.27
Britain = 100	200	161	100

Source: *The Economist,* 30 July 1994.

SERVICE SECTORS ARE MORE RESTRICTED AND LESS EFFICIENT

The macro-economic results of German national wage bargaining are enviable wage moderation. But the cost is considerable micro-economic distortions. The result has been little regional variation in pay combined with rather large variations in unemployment rates. The differential between the pay of skilled and unskilled workers is also narrow. Real wages amongst lower paid workers have risen rapidly in Germany despite high unemployment amongst the unskilled. One must also recognise a weakness of the British performance relative to Germany's. Britain's superior productivity growth in recent years was caused largely by falling employment rather than by rising manufacturing output. In industry, which includes construction, mining and quarrying as well as manufacturing production, British employment fell by a third between 1979 and 1993 against a German fall of less than a tenth. There is no question that Britain was becoming leaner and meaner, but was British industry in danger of dying of anorexia? Probably not. Germany (with Japan) is more the exception with a higher proportion of employment in industry than is normal for a high-income advanced economy. The danger is more that German industry is suffering from obesity.

GERMAN TECHNOLOGICAL WEAKNESS

Germany's labour market failings are compounded by technological failings. Germany and the rest of Europe are lagging far behind the US and Japan in areas of high-tech production. High-tech products, for instance, account for a remarkably small proportion of European exports. Walter Eltis, in a report published by the *Bank Credit Analyst* in August 1994, cites the German share in 1990 as 20% with France on 22%. By comparison high-tech products account for 33% of Japanese exports and 38% of American. Britain comes in at 28%. The British level is boosted by pharmaceutical companies such as Glaxo, which is world class. This is largely because the British National Health Service buys drugs wherever it can get them cheapest. The contrast is with semi-conductors, in which Europe's share in world production and trade is pitifully small. This can be blamed directly on state protection. In France, Group Bull is a prime example of the baleful effect of protection and subsidisation. In a much criticised decision in October 1994, the European Commission sanctioned a Ffr 11.1 bn ($2.1 bn) government bail-out for the ailing computer-maker, which will simply encourage it to avoid hard decisions.

Studies of revealed comparative advantage show where German industrial strengths and weaknesses lie. These look at the share of different products in German and other countries' exports, as a ratio to their shares in OECD total exports. Where the German share, say, in car exports, exceeds the average share, German manufacturers can be assumed to have an edge over their competitors. Germany's performance is weak in high-tech products such as telecommunications equipment, aircraft and aerospace, cathodes, sound recorders, optical goods (surprisingly), photographic equipment, computers and office machinery. In all these categories the ratio of exports to imports is lower than the ratio of exports to manufacturing production as a whole. Germany is strong in machine tools, vehicles, mechanical handling equipment, printing machinery, tools and technical apparatus and so forth. This reflects the German emphasis on improving quality, reliability, design and service when the going gets tough. The trouble is that the Germans are not especially gifted at design, while modern manufacturing methods are increasingly designing out skills and designing in quality and reliability.

A simple but dated example shows how this can be done. Britain was amongst the world's leaders in precision engineering. Then Nissan of Japan started to produce better engines cheaper. They did this without greater skill in cutting metal to finer tolerances. Realising that it is easier to measure accurately than to cut accurately, they simply measured and matched over-sized cylinders with over-sized pistons, achieving thereby a more perfect fit (although repairs became harder).

Using reliable, skilful and well-paid workers to make medium-tech goods well is a wasting asset. Medium- and low-tech products are increasingly being made by high-tech machines and methods. This is undermining another of Germany's advantages, its education and training system. Because training is so closely connected to the company, it reflects the same balance as existing work and skills. This is enshrined in the rigid categorisation of apprenticeship qualifications and courses. In a world in which the structure and size of industry is rapidly changing, the German system produces too many workers with the unwanted skills of the past and too few with the desired skills of the future.

The ability to create new and dynamic companies is another part of the problem of adapting a successful model to a rapidly changing environment. German manufacturing companies tend to be large, with a median size of 318 employees in 1987 against 263 in the US and 166 in Japan. The average size was much smaller: thirty employees in German against forty-nine in the US and sixteen in Japan. But Germany is not a good breeding ground for new technology advanced companies. German banks, as the main source of capital, are highly cautious. They have a good record of backing winners, but only because so few ventures meet their demanding standards. Those that do tend to be in well-tried areas rather than innovative. The total capital of the twenty-five venture capitalist enterprises in Germany (somewhat datedly), was $500 m at end-1986. The comparable British figure was 110 venture capital enterprises with $4.5 bn, nine times as much.

The corporate stakeholder system performs best in periods of relative stability and in large manufacturing companies where relationships between the stakeholders must necessarily be formalised. In an environment of rapid change, where small service companies are replacing large manufacturers, the formalisation of relationships and rigidity of wage structures are positive obstructions. Small companies cannot afford a hire-and-fire mentality. Their existence depends upon the loyalty of their employees, customers, suppliers and bankers. Relationships are close, often ones of personal friendship. These combine flexibility with long-term stability. Germany has yesterday's model industry, not tomorrow's. But it can change.

CHAPTER 15

The Single Europe Act and the Maastricht Treaty

Germany's response to its relative poor 1980s performance has been considered. It is time now to discuss Europe's response. When Euro-sclerosis set in, pressure for further progress towards integration increased and, in 1986, the Single Europe Act was signed. It aimed to complete, by end-1992, the common market originally envisaged in the Rome Treaty, in which goods, capital and labour could move freely throughout the European Community. This mainly involved removing non-tariff barriers to trade, notably regulatory restrictions. (For those who have the time to wade through it, the way in which the European Union works is set out in Appendix D.)

The Brussels Commission was set the task of preparing directives – in all 282 – harmonising regulations throughout the community covering trade in goods, but also in services such as insurance, pensions, tele-communication and transport. For Germany harmonisation means opening up its insurance market, in which life insurance and general insurance have been legally separated. Transport regulations had also to be liberalised, notably the prohibition on trucks from foreign countries picking up loads from Germany for delivery in third countries on their way home. The Single Market ought to mean, ultimately, open skies in Europe. But Germany and France are dragging their heels, while trying to bail out their loss-making national carriers. France was ordered by Brussels, under Single Market legislation, to allow British airlines landing slots at Orly, which is nearer to Paris than Charles de Gaulle airport. The French said Orly could only take small aircraft, which was untrue.

It only gave way when British Airways threatened to land without permission. France was also ordered to open up domestic routes, notably the profitable Orly-Lyons one, but resisted, appealing to the European Court of Justice as a delaying tactic. It lost its appeal, but continued to use delaying tactics.

The directives devised by the Commission had to be passed by the relevant Councils of Ministers. To expedite the creation of the Single Market, the Single Europe Act had to change the way the Union operates. Back in June 1965 France found itself alone opposing Commission proposals on CAP and budgetary matters. De Gaulle ordered the government to boycott the community by leaving its chair empty at all council meetings. Business was brought to a halt until, in January 1966, the 'Luxemburg compromise' was reached by which members could veto majority-vote legislation when they claimed that 'very important interests' were at stake. There was no hope of completing the Single Market by its end-1992 deadline if countries retained the Luxemburg right of veto. Single Market directives were therefore made subject to qualified majority voting, meaning it needed two large nations and one small to block a decision. The deadline was still missed. Some 222 of the 282 Single Market directives had to be transposed into national legislation. By late-1994 only half had been passed by all the then twelve member countries. Britain had the best record for implementation; Greece, France, Spain and Ireland the worst. Even under the Single Market agreement, the deadlines for opening some areas were deferred until after end-1992. Insurance was not opened to European competition till mid-1994. Investment service will not be opened until 1996, nor basic telephone services until 1998. The motor trade still employs competition-denying restraint over dealerships, with Brussels' blessing. State aid to ailing industries continues to distort competition, with the commission apparently willing to give way at all turns.

A SINGLE PRODUCTION LINE

The Single Market was a misnomer. The Single Europe Act, by allowing the free movement of factors of production – labour and capital – as well as their products and services, also established a single production line. Whereas the original common market meant that anything made anywhere could be sold everywhere on the same terms, the single production line meant that anyone could make anything anywhere on the same terms. The 'same terms' must be defined. It does not mean the same for everyone everywhere in Europe. The Single Market did not impose uniformity on tax and social security systems, or on broader regulatory systems which differ from country to country over such things as shop opening hours, regulations limiting working time, redundancies, pollution and the environment, speed limits on roads, wage levels, pension entitlements and age of retirement, etc. The 'same terms' do mean that a British, French or Spanish company would be allowed to operate in Germany under the same rules and conditions as a local German company. The qualifications for entering a particular business or profession had to be the same across Europe. The Single Market approach has been to lay down minimum standards and, while not obliging any country to apply them to its own nationals, obliges them to accept foreign nationals who qualify under them.

COMPETITION BETWEEN TAX SYSTEMS

Because the Single Europe Act did not impose uniformity, it created free competition between national tax, social security or regulatory systems. Output and employment was allowed and encouraged to move to where tax and social security costs were least, labour cheapest and where the regulatory environment was the most benign. The Single Market benefits low wage, low tax economies at the expense of high tax, high wage economies. Germany (as we have seen), France, the Benelux countries (and, to a degree, Italy) are the most closely regulated and penally taxed production centres. British taxes are low by comparison. One clear example of the effect of such competition was the decision by the South Korean industrial giant, Samsung, to invest £450bn in a new high-tech plant (providing 3000 jobs) to make microwave ovens and computer monitor screens at Wynyard in north-east England. Samsung also plans to move its European company headquarters from Frankfurt to London. Meanwhile, nearby Swan Hunter Shipyard on Tyneside is being broken up and sold by receivers. In low-cost Britain, old jobs are going but new taking their place. In high-cost Germany and France, government subsidies and regulations on redundancies keep old jobs going and prevent new ones coming.

Europe as a whole stood to gain from competition between systems and the high-cost countries, which stood to lose, did not like it. For example, when Hoover proposed to close its plant in Lyons and transfer production to Cambuslang in Scotland, where labour costs were £234 per man week against £407 in France, French ministers went so far as to threaten Hoover's management with criminal prosecution. The term 'social dumping' was coined to describe what the French regarded as unfair competition. In this way the Single Europe Act automatically spawned the Maastricht Treaty, designed, *inter alia*, to level Europe's playing fields.

UNIFICATION AND MAASTRICHT

German unification added political momentum to the move towards economic and monetary union amongst the then twelve EU members. Circumstances in 1990 were very similar to those in 1955, when Germany gained full sovereignty in return for raising a national army. The Treaty of Rome was proposed to tie a sovereign and rearming West Germany into a deep relationship with France and Western Europe. As already mentioned, President Mitterrand made German support for Maastricht a condition for French agreement to take part in the 2 + 4 talks, which paved the way for German unification. This was as brilliant opportunism as Kohl had shown in seizing his chance to get Soviet agreement to unification. Mitterrand said France would agree to unification only if Germany were tied more tightly to the West through political, economic and monetary union. It was the only hope the French had of influencing Europe's development. A united Germany, as Europe's largest and most powerful economy, would be able to dictate Europe's future on its own. French fears of German political hegemony and British economic competition spawned Maastricht.

A BOTCHED JOB

The Maastricht Treaty was a hurried and botched job. Even Jacques Delors, President of the European Commission from 1984 to 1994, admits that now. It was raw power politics, in which all Europe's leaders bar one, ignored public opinion while committing their countries to a timetable leading irrevocably to economic and monetary union (EMU) by 1999 at the latest. In addition, they created a mechanism (the Social Chapter) by which the EU could come to replicate the French dirigiste model. Its signatories agreed to accept EU legislation – covering working conditions, such as minimum earnings, consultation rights, works councils, supervisory boards, equal pay and so forth – on the basis of qualified majority voting. Under this, national Parliaments could be forced to accept laws designed by Brussels bureaucrats. It was a very considerable surrender of sovereignty and to a secretive and undemocratic system. In addition, the eleven agreed that social security entitlements should be determined and hence harmonised at the European level, but subject to unanimity. The French hope, through the Social Chapter, to reduce, if not eliminate, competition between rival welfare systems. But what the French mean by a level playing field is that if Britain had good harbours and France a rocky coastline Britain should fill in her harbours with rocks.

The British Prime Minister was the only European leader who refused to follow the Franco-German lead. John Major knew that he could not get Maastricht through Parliament at Westminster – if he had tried, the Conservative party would have been split and thrown out of office (as when Peel pushed through the 1846 Corn Laws). Major therefore prevaricated. He negotiated an opt-out of Stage 3, when countries meeting convergence criteria move to a single currency. The British Government has been left free to decide what to do, as and when the time comes. Britain also refused to sign the Social Chapter. Major did not veto other European countries going forward with monetary union or harmonising their labour market and social security systems, provided they did not go backward from Britain's right to stay in the Single Market while staying out of Maastricht. This was brilliant but unrealistic. If European economic and monetary union does go ahead and Britain stays out, it will inevitably be pushed out of the Single Market.

MONETARY UNION IS NOT THE PROBLEM

Maastricht combines German terms for monetary union with French terms for suppressing 'unfair' competition. The Germans set out to make the common European currency, the Ecu, as strong at the D-Mark rather than as debauched as the pound or lire. This was a simple task. All it required was two conditions. First, the European Central Bank (ECB) president and governors should be totally independent of their national governments. As the governors include national central bank governors, the Maastricht Treaty requires that national central banks become independent in Stage 2, prior to the move to EMU in Stage 3. Secondly, the ECB should be given the single objective of preserving the value of the Ecu. It would then be possible to rely on central bankers and the ECB executives to perform their unambiguous task with Bundesbank fervour.

The trouble was fiscal, not monetary, policy. As this would remain in the hands of national governments, it was necessary to ensure that the work of the ECB was not undermined by fiscal profligacy. To this end Maastricht contained rules to test and impose fiscal prudence on national governments. In the run-up to EMU these became 'convergence criteria', designed to determine when countries were ready for EMU. Maastricht allows a majority of members, if they qualify under its convergence criteria in 1996, to go ahead with EMU on or after 1 January 1997. The minority who do not qualify would join as and when they could. If a majority do not qualify, EMU is postponed, but only until 1 January 1999. At that date all the countries which qualify under the convergence criteria go ahead with EMU, even if they still comprise a minority of EU members. After EMU, obedience to criteria for prudent fiscal behaviour will be enforced by sanctions against miscreants, including fines imposed by Brussels.

TUNNEL-VISION CRITERIA

The criteria were designed by central bankers for central bankers. They reflect the view that all that matters in economic policy is to avoid inflation. Countries must keep their inflation rates within 1.5% of the average of the three best EU performers. Prior to EMU, they must not devalue their currencies in the ERM. Their Government bond yields must not be more than 2% above the average for the three best inflation performers. Their public sector deficits must not exceed 3% of GDP or their public sector debts exceed 60% of GDP. But these limits can be exceeded if it is the result of temporary and exceptional circumstances (e.g. German unification) or if sufficient progress is being made towards meeting them. In 1994 Ireland was judged to be one of only two countries to meet the convergence criteria (Luxemburg was the other), despite public sector debts of 90% of GDP. It qualified because this ratio had been steadily reduced from a peak of 117% in 1987.

Chart 15.1 Franco-German Convergence

There is nothing in the Maastricht criteria to address today's and tomorrow's problems: growth and employment. No country need have any difficulty in the short run in meeting them, provided it is prepared to accept whatever degree of deflation is necessary to do so. The French Government is determined to see Maastricht succeed. Ever since 1983 it has pursued its *franc fort* policy, giving overriding priority to reducing inflation below German levels and maintaining the franc's D-Mark parity. It has largely succeeded. But convergence in the product market has been bought at the price of divergence between German and French unemployment in the labour market. Criteria which do not include growth, employment and unemployment are worthless. No country can persevere with deflationary policies to achieve price stability if the cost is massive unemployment. Europeans seem to have forgotten that it was deflation, *not* inflation, which brought Hitler to power in 1933.

The convergence criteria were made to be bent. The Commission and Council are given ample room to apply them flexibly. As things stand in late-1994 it is easy to envisage a situation in 1996 in which they could declare that a majority had qualified for EMU (see Appendix E for details). Italy, however, would not be amongst them. Monetary union, as German unification has shown, is not a matter of criteria and convergence but one of political will and willingness to foot the bill.

SOCIAL CHAPTER NONSENSES

The Social Chapter would impose German and French generous welfare provisions and job-destroying labour market laws on other countries. It is a fundamental mistake for governments to legislate benefits for existing employees and impose the cost upon employers. This merely places a tax on jobs, meaning fewer will be bought. An employer should have no statutory financial obligation to his workers, other than to pay for the work he buys. (Statutory obligations to ensure strict safety standards and the like should, however, be enforced.) He does the employee enough of a favour by supplying a job. This is not a hard-hearted plea for bosses to be able to exploit workers, it is a common-sense call for a system which ensures a maximum of work. Maternity leave, sick pay, unemployment relief, health insurance, redundancy pay are all things which no advanced democracy should be without. But the entire burden should fall on the generality of taxpayers, companies and employees, not upon individual employers. This would not increase costs or taxes, but shift the burden away from job-destroying levies. By the same token, there is no need for Europe to impose works councils, supervisory boards, regulations governing working hours, minimum wages and redundancy notices. National governments and employers can judge whether such things are necessary. Countries will adopt the system which turns out to work best. It could be closer to the German Social Market than the Anglo-American free-for-all. But there is no need to pre-judge the issue. That is the beauty of competition between regulatory systems.

Harmonising social security and welfare benefit rates and conditions must mean moving up to the most generous, rather than down to the least. Brussels would hardly advocate cutting German and French pensions. This would raise the share of public spending in poorer EU countries and the tax burden on employers and employees. With the exceptions of Greece and Portugal (the EU's poorest member countries), the share of public spending tends to rise with incomes. The tax costs would not depend upon the ability to meet them out of income and tax revenues, but on the numbers of unemployed, sick, pregnant, elderly and so forth. Unemployment tends to be higher in countries with low incomes – Greece and Portugal are again exceptions. But the number of pensioners tends to be higher in richer countries. On the whole there would be little correlation between income levels and welfare bills.

While harmonising welfare systems would impose public spending costs which were not correlated with incomes, harmonising tax systems and tax rates would produce revenues which were so correlated. If tax rates were harmonised at the level required to balance the poorest country's budget, they would generate massive surpluses in the richest countries. If, however, tax rates were set to balance the budgets of the richest countries, the poorest would run massive budget deficits. If, finally, rates were set to produce enough tax revenue for the EU as a whole, to cover public spending in the EU as a whole, poor countries would run deficits and rich countries would run surpluses. This would work perfectly well, provided the rich did not mind giving their surpluses to the poor. This is what is happening following unification between east and west Germany, where the same tax and welfare systems apply in both. If the political will exists to make large, quantifiably and identifiable transfers, taxes and welfare systems in Europe can be harmonised. If not, countries must charge different tax rates or pay different benefits in order to balance their budgets. They cannot both balance their budgets and pay the same taxes and benefits. It is an impossibility.

Such transfers could take place smoothly and efficiently if Brussels were made responsible for collecting the greater part of European taxes and financing most of European spending. Where taxes are pooled and spending comes out of the same pot, transfers are less readily identifiable or quantifiable. A federal Europe with a large federal budget is the only way out of the dilemma posed above – even if the 'F'-word still means different things to different people.

Partial harmonisation is almost as bad as none at all. Problems are posed by differing VAT rates and excise duties in different European countries. The British, for example, take vans and trucks over (and now under) the Channel to Calais to load up with cheap French beer. There is a proposal broadly to harmonise VAT with a two-rate system. But if VAT rates were harmonised, countries where they were raised would have to reduce other taxes, and, in countries where VAT rates were cut, other tax rates would have to go up. As long as the proportion of GDP taken in taxation varies between countries, harmonising one part of the tax system simply results in even greater disharmony between other parts. Pushing down British excise duties, for example, might stop the British crossing to Calais to shop. But if it meant higher income taxes, more British might prefer to retire to the South of France.

PART III

THE WORLD SCENE

CHAPTER 16

Lessons from the Great Depression of 1873–96

This section sets the contemporary world economic scene in its historical context. The late nineteenth century was a period of explosive technological advance and massive structural change without precedent (although it now provides one for the late twentieth century). Change is always a mixed blessing. New industries kill off old. New producers in old industries drive out old producers. Millions of new jobs are created, but at the expense of millions of old jobs that are lost. The changes which occurred around a century ago were extremely painful to many people. So much so that the world was believed to have suffered the 'Great Depression of 1873 to 1896'.

The Great Depression was thought to be the trough of a long, fifty- to sixty-year, Kondratiev business-cycle, named after the Russian economist who first identified them. Kondratiev cycles reflect structural and technological innovation. World investment demand is boosted by invention. The steam engine, for example, led to great railway building booms. The jumbo-jet led to massive investment in planes and airports in place of docks and liners. The trough of such a cycle is associated in theory with a dearth of technological progress and low investment. But the reverse was far from the case in the late nineteenth century.

What went wrong with the theory? Kondratiev mistakenly identified long cycles with reference to price movements. This was because output data was then scarce and patchy, while price data was more plentiful. Kondratiev simply supposed that prices always rose in booms and fell in slumps. Between 1873 and 1896 prices fell 40%, as Chart 16.1 shows.

Chart 16.1 Commodity Prices 1860–1994

The Economist Index, log scale, 1860=100

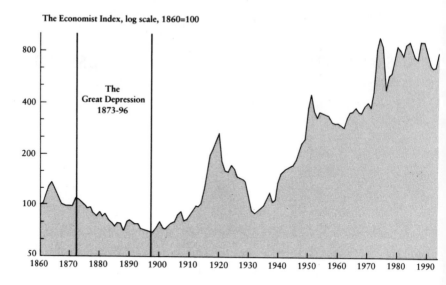

That was one reason why this period was called the Great Depression. Another was that, in this period of rapid change, the declining old industries in Britain and agricultural depression on the continent of Europe were better documented than the rise of newer industries and of agriculture elsewhere in the world. Output estimates have been compiled in recent years going back to the nineteenth century. These show that, for the world as a whole, growth was faster in the last quarter of the century than at any other time until the 1950s. The world did not suffer a depression though some countries and industries did. It enjoyed a remarkable 'falling-price boom'. Sir Walter Layton, in his book *The Study of Prices* (1912), observed:

> As regards actual production, it appears that during the 'seventies, 'eighties and early 'nineties the expansion in the world output of all kinds of commodities far outran that of any previous period of history. While the New World began to flood European markets with food products and raw materials, the art of production made enormous strides; manufactures were, moreover, stimulated in Germany and the United States by the opening up in both countries of new sources of iron and coal – a development which made these

countries industrially more independent of Great Britain than they had previously been.

A FALLING-PRICE BOOM

Rapid technological advance caused the late nineteenth-century falling-price boom, in which 1870 marked a watershed. The first phase of the industrial revolution began for well-known reasons in Britain in the late eighteenth century. It was based on textiles, iron (not steel), steam power and rail transport. It changed *how* goods were made and transported, rather than *what* was made. A rich man's home in 1870 differed little from that of a rich man's in 1770, except that it was bigger. There were also many more rich men. The industrial revolution changed the conditions by which ordinary people worked, by herding them together into rapidly growing cities and towns and employing them in factories instead of fields. It did not greatly change how they lived at home, other than substantially to reduce the quality of their (urban) lives. The second phase of the industrial revolution began in the last quarter of the nineteenth century. Based on steel, refrigerated steamships, electricity, chemicals, telephones, the internal combustion engine and automobiles, it revolutionised how people lived. Life by 1913 was vastly changed from life in 1870.

The contrast during the late nineteenth century between the appearance of recession and the reality of boom can be understood once the distinction is drawn between core or advanced countries at the centre of the industrialised world and developing countries at its periphery. Industrialisation spawned real income growth, a phenomenon virtually unknown amongst agricultural economies. (It also spawned unemployment and the business cycle, as distinct from agrarian fluctuations which were driven at random by the hazards of harvest failures and wars.) Industrialisation had three characteristics: it pushed forward; spread outwards as more and more countries industrialised; and it divided the world into industrial economies and primary producers.

From 1820 to 1870 Britain dominated the forward movement. The first phase of industrialisation depended on fairly simple inventions and their exploitation by entrepreneurs. But in the second phase Britain's lead was rapidly eroded. The inventions driving this phase required a deeper knowledge of science and hence a higher level of education. In this Britain was at a deep disadvantage. In 1776 the majority of American colonists were literate. Compulsory education began in some German states in the late eighteenth century and progressed to most following the Napoleonic Wars. By 1830 most Germans were literate. Publicly provided elementary education did not begin in Britain until 1880 and did not become compulsory and free until 1892. Secondary education remained rare well into this century. (My father left school in 1908 aged eleven.) An industrial economy needed then, as it needs today, an educated labour force of operatives and clerks. So Britain lagged in the second phase of industrialisation, while the United States and Germany took over the running.

THE ROLE OF GOLD

Falling prices and Britain's poor showing can also be blamed on the gold standard. In the latter part of the nineteenth century more countries converted to gold, Germany and Japan in particular, adding to demand. At the same time gold production dwindled until new discoveries were made in South Africa and Australia towards the end of the century. Inadequate money-supply growth kept world price increases in check. At the same time Britain, at the centre of the international financial system, suffered from its leading role as supplier of capital to the world. The Bank of England, with limited reserves, reacted rapidly to any undue gold outflows by raising interest rates. As such it continually caused British recoveries to abort at an unnecessarily early phase. The outflow of investment from Britain, which averaged 5% of GDP during the three decades before 1913 and peaked at 10%, starved British industry of capital. Britain financed its competitors' industrial and agricultural development and then suffered severely from their competition.

Until the second half of the nineteenth century, the outward thrust of industrialisation to other countries was slow. Britain alone was industrialised by 1800 (defined as where agricultural employment falls below 50%). By 1850 industrialisation had spread to the United States, France, Belgium and Germany, in that order. But these economies were far behind Britain in their development. Then the spread of the industrial revolution from the core to the periphery accelerated rapidly over the end of the last century. Another half-dozen countries joined the industrial world by 1870 and a further fifteen by 1913. There were thus twenty-six industrialised countries in 1913 against five in 1850.

THE GROWTH OF WORLD TRADE

Increased international specialisation was the third factor in late nine-teenth-century industrialisation; until mid-century there was remarkably little international trade. Most countries were agricultural economies and largely fed themselves. Until they industrialised, they had little need to export on a growing scale in order to obtain food and raw materials. But from the mid-nineteenth century onwards railways opened up the interiors of great continents, while steamships replaced sail, iron and steel replaced wood, connecting continents together by cheap and reliable ocean transport. Two massive migratory movements provided the labour to develop the new worlds which had been opened up. During the second half of the century roughly 50 million Europeans emigrated to the United States and other temperate zones such as Australia, New Zealand, South Africa and Argentina. Another 50 million Indians and Chinese were moved to work in tropical countries. Temperate zone grain and meat imports, together with tropical foodstuffs, flooded into Europe. The result was a deep agricultural depression in which farm prices tumbled. Landowners and farm workers suffered severely, but industrialists and their workers benefited from supplies of cheap food.

Advanced economies did badly in the late nineteenth century. Britain, way out ahead of all others, managed only 2% a year industrial growth over 1873–96. But those catching up did exceedingly well. US industrial production rose at a trend rate of 4.9% a year. Germany's trend growth was 4.2%. Older industries did badly – British textiles faced Indian competition for the first time. Iron-founding declined, though steel and chemicals increased. The agricultural depression in Europe created severe political stress between landowners, rural dwellers, industrialists and their employees. Much of twentieth-century history, particularly its turbulent first fifty years, can be explained by the social and political strains imposed by nineteenth-century industrialisation. This is why the study of this period is more relevant to today's world than experience in the interwar years or during the past three decades.

The last decade of the twentieth century is the first since the first decade in which the world has been one economy. The remaining eight decades were abnormal in one way or another. The First World War tore the world apart. Efforts to put it back together again in the 1920s failed so badly that the world relapsed into protection and depression (and in Germany, Italy and Spain into Fascism) in the 1930s. After the Second World War Communism spread until by the 1950s nearly one-third of the world's population lived in centrally planned command economies. They cut trade and economic relations with capitalist economies to a minimum.

Nearly one-third of the world population live in former colonies, many of whose first leaders were educated at left-leaning universities, such as the London School of Economics. Numerous intellectuals in the 1930s and 1940s believed, understandably, that market capitalism had failed. They preached Socialism and future African and Asian leaders listened. When their countries gained independence in the 1940s and 1950s they adopted Socialist development strategies, involving extensive state ownership and control. They endeavoured to build infant industries by import-substitution behind high protective barriers to trade. Exchange controls prevented domestic enterprises falling into foreign ownership and control. The infant industries were often ill-chosen – large capital-intensive integrated steelworks or chemical plants – the last thing poor cash-strapped overpopulated developing countries required. These Socialist strategies mostly failed but Third World leaders rarely cared. Public ownership and control gives ample opportunity for graft. Third World leaders often spent more on their armies than on education, which they used to repress their own citizens rather than to repel foreigners. Not all Socialist economies were badly run, not all leaders were venal. But the system itself retarded development, reduced trade and inhibited the free flow of international capital. It failed to produce growth, while with export-oriented development strategies, the Asian tigers bounded ahead. Market economies accounted for less than 40% of the world's population in 1990 and the OECD for only 15%. But that 15% produced 54% of the world's GDP.

During the 1980s the world started changing. Communism collapsed, as has already been related, because it was unable to satisfy its citizens' aspirations. Developing countries increasingly abandoned their failed socialist models, liberalised their economies, opened them to trade, freed capital from controls and opened stock markets. During the past decade, two-thirds of the world's population have rejoined the world market economy. They have done so just as technology and modern communications have made financial and physical capital more mobile than ever before. Conditions which last existed almost a century ago have been restored. The ramifications are immense.

CHAPTER 17

The World's Greatest Boom Ever

Mature advanced economies, such as most members of the OECD, normally suffer suppressed symptoms of chronic depression. Their rich and ageing populations tend to save rather than to spend. But investment opportunities offering high returns have mostly been exploited. Fast growth and large profits come from catching up with existing technology, rather than pushing ahead with new. Excess saving in mature economies was no problem a century ago. The old world surplus savings were lent to the new, opening its continents with railroads, linking them to the new with steamships, developing agriculture, industries and exploiting natural resources. The new world used the old's surplus savings to buy the old's surplus products.

That has not been the story most of this century. The rate of world development slowed down after 1914. In the 1930s excess savings caused the depression. After the Second World War many feared it would return. But first Europe and Japan had to be rebuilt, which absorbed all the money anyone wished to save. When that task was completed, there were three decades of neglected technological progress to repair. Profitable investment opportunities remained substantial well into the 1960s. But then the problem of excess savings in advanced countries re-emerged. It was worst amongst devastated wartime losers, Germany and Japan. Their economic systems had been reconstructed from the ground up after the war. They were designed to generate extremely high savings and to channel them into productive investment at home. Tax systems, for instance, favoured savings over spending. These biases were not eliminated when the need for a very high investment disappeared. High benign savings became malign excess savings.

EVEN BRITONS AND AMERICANS SAVE A LOT

The United States and Britain seem to be exceptions to this thesis. They are not. Americans and Britons save a lot, not a little. Savings create wealth. A fascinating table in each semi-annual OECD *Economic Outlook* shows household wealth as a ratio to household disposable income. British gross assets were worth seven times income in 1991, split almost equally between real and financial assets; American were six times; Japanese were nine times, but only because of higher land and house prices; financial assets were lower in the United States and Britain. No figures are available for the value of real assets in Germany. But gross financial assets were smaller relative to income than in Britain and the United States. Britain and the United States also had larger gross assets than Italy and France.

One cannot accumulate wealth without a high level of savings. Nor for that matter can one have large financial services sectors unless there are ample funds to be transferred from savers and lenders to borrowers and spenders. But look at the British and American figures for net household assets, after taking into account financial liabilities. These are lower as a proportion of income than in Japan or continental Europe. American and British households save and lend more, but also borrow and spend more, than other nationalities. Middle-aged Americans and Britons are big savers. But it is easy in both countries to borrow while one is young. Mortgage lending borrowing is much higher than elsewhere. The efficient Anglo-American financial systems transfer the high savings of older workers to younger workers, enabling them to buy and set up homes, furnish them and raise their children without too great an immediate sacrifice.

The transfer of savings from older to younger households cancels out within the personal sector, lowering the observed household savings ratio. It also leads to a reverse wealth transfer from young to old. As the young use borrowed money to buy assets, principally homes, they drive asset prices higher relative to product prices. Since real wealth is concentrated amongst the older generation, they benefit most from rising asset prices (until their fortunes are passed on at death to middle-aged sons and daughters).

The dynamics of this system depend on demography. It needs more young spenders (baby-boomers) than old savers. In the United States the ratio of people aged 45–64, relative to those aged 25–44, declined steadily from 1971 to 1991, falling from 0.87 to 0.55. In Britain there was also a decline, from 1.00 to 0.75. But the post-war baby-boomers are now becoming middle-aged. Their too few sons and daughters are not entering the 25–44 age range at the rate the boomers are leaving it. Immigration apart, the trend in the ratio of older to younger workers has been abruptly reversed. By the year 2011 the ratio will have climbed to over 1 in both countries. The result should be a gradual but significant rise in the American and British household saving ratio.

PALLIATIVE TO DEAL WITH EXCESS SAVINGS

Low observed savings rates do not, however, disprove the existence of excess savings. Efforts to save too much are confounded by falling incomes, until what is actually saved falls to match the required level of investment. This is what makes mature economies chronic depressives. Since the late 1960s a series of palliatives have rescued the OECD from plunging back into depression. Excess savings first became a problem in Japan and Germany. Both countries escaped through export-led growth which gave them big payment surpluses. The world as a whole cannot enjoy export-led growth. Germany and Japanese current account surpluses usually ended up as American and British deficits, helping to cause the Bretton Woods fixed exchange rate system to collapse. They reappeared in the 1970s and early 1980s, when President Reagan's supply side tax cuts led the United States to run a large deficit.

OPEC oil price rises helped mop up surplus savings for a time. They turned the terms of trade against advanced oil-importing economies, channelling income to Arab oil sheikhs. Unfortunately, the oil sheikhs saved rather than spent, depositing their money with Western banks. These banks recycled it to developing countries, largely as sovereign loans to governments, where it was used to sustain LDC consumption despite falling incomes. But while this sustained OECD exports and growth from the mid-1970s to early 1980s, after the 1982 LDC debt crisis, resource flows were reversed, inhibiting OECD growth.

Growth slowed down everywhere in the 1970s and 1980s. It would have slowed further but for government action. In the 1950s and 1960s most advanced countries ran balanced budgets over the course of the economic cycle. But in the 1970s structural deficits emerged almost everywhere. For a period public sector dissaving offset excess private saving, but like all such palliatives, rising budget deficits were a temporary expedient. Big deficits caused big debts which could not be increased indefinitely. By the 1990s all major countries, except for Japan, had embarked upon policies of fiscal consolidation designed to eliminate structural budget deficits. These then inhibited growth.

Inflation was another palliative, particularly asset price inflation in the bubble economies of the late-1980s. Continental Europe largely sat this one out. The Anglo-Saxon countries and Japan all participated. Asset price inflation discourages savings and encourages (often conspicuous) consumption. As house prices and share prices rise, people become identifiably and quantifiably richer without anybody becoming identifiably and quantifiably poor. But rising asset prices do nothing to make society as a whole richer. Nonetheless as many people become effortlessly wealthier, they are tempted to cash in on part of their new-found riches by 'equity withdrawals'. They borrow against assets to finance consumption. But bubbles always burst and, when they do, they leave a legacy of bankruptcies, loan losses and burdensome debts. These inhibit borrowing and boost savings, as was seen in the early 1990s recession.

THE RETURN OF THE JUGLAR CYCLE

With fiscal policy on auto-pilot and monetary excesses impossible in today's nervous international capital markets, the nature of the business cycle has changed. The dominant 1950s to 1960s cycle in developed countries lasted from four to five years from peak to peak (or trough to trough). These short cycles are called Kitchin cycles, driven by inventory swings, usually caused by mistaken expectations about income and sales growth, and by official stop-go policies. When economies boomed and overheated, fiscal and monetary brakes were applied, usually involving increased taxation. When they slowed down and inflation fell to tolerable levels, monetary and fiscal policy was eased (fiscal ease usually involved increased public spending, so its share in GDP ratcheted up). Governments did their best to ensure that Kitchin cycle peaks coincided with the electoral cycle.

The Kitchin cycle is still with us, but it is no longer the dominant cycle. As governments have lost their ability to reflate at will, markets now dictate the length of the business cycle. It is longer, eight-to-ten years, and known as a Juglar cycle. Juglar cycles are driven by longer-term construction booms, usually caused by mistaken expectations about asset prices. They involve excess credit creation during the upswing, followed by a debt shake-out and a prolonged period during which banks are hesitant to lend, other than on the best security, while companies and individuals are reluctant to borrow. Big booms have occurred at the end of the 1970s and 1980s, big recessions at the beginning of the following decade. Between, in the mid-1970s and mid-1980s, there were weak booms followed by mild recessions. (Juglar cycle peaks are defined as being higher than the previous peak and at least two years later.)

Chart 17.1 Return of the Juglar Cycle

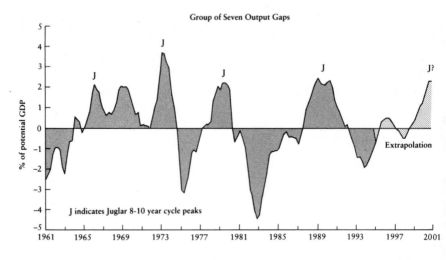

The source, strength and durability of recovery from the early 1990s recession has always been in doubt. Even in the United States, where the upswing began while Japan and much of Europe were still sliding deeper into recession, the recovery remained unusually weak until it was two years old. Forecasters in December 1993 made gloomy noises about prospects in 1994 and were confounded by the strength of OECD growth during the year. There were good reasons for this. They had forgotten to factor into their thinking the changed world environment and the growing importance of developing countries in world output and trade.

DEVELOPING ECONOMIES ARE BIGGER THAN WE THOUGHT . . .

For most of the postwar period, economists have tended to treat the OECD as if it was the world economy. It was thought that it accounted for some 85% of world GDP. But this share was calculated using exchange rates determined by international trade. These produced absurd results. The average Chinese annual income, for example, worked out at just $200 in 1990. But on this the nation was well fed and adequately housed and clothed. It would be impossible to survive on such a low income in the US, and it was the average, meaning a majority of Chinese lived on even less (i.e. the median income is below the average in a distribution including a lot of poor and a few very rich).

Exchange rates are not a bad guide to the relative prices of traded goods in different countries. The dollar price of a hair-dryer made in Thailand and sold in New York is probably not very different from its price (converted into US dollars at the going exchange rate) when sold at home in Thailand. But as wages in Thailand are far lower than in the United States, the cost of non-traded goods and services are far lower there relative to both traded goods in Thailand and non-traded goods and services in the United States. A haircut in Thailand may cost one-twentieth of a haircut in New York when valued at current exchange rates.

A more realistic way of comparing incomes and GDP size between different countries is to use 'purchasing power parities' (PPPs). These are calculated using a standard basket of goods and seeing what it costs in each country. The PPP exchange rate is derived from the relative cost of each basket. The baskets can have the same composition or can include what people normally buy in each country. The use of PPPs is not without difficulty. But the results are much less misleading that those obtained using exchange rates. The Thai haircut plus the hair-dryer cost far less in Thailand at current exchange rates that the New York haircut and Thai hair-dryer cost in New York. Hence the PPP of the Thai dollar (calculated from the ratio between the two) is much higher than its exchange rate, making Thailand's GDP using PPPs relatively much larger.

... AND THEY ARE GROWING VERY FAST

In 1993 the IMF came out with new PPP estimates of shares in world GDP (Annex IV, *World Economic Outlook*, May 1993). The OECD share was revised down to 54.4% and developing countries share rose to 34.4%, leaving former Communist countries with a bit over a tenth. Moreover these shares are fast changing as growth in developing countries outstrips OECD growth. In 1995 the developing countries share will rise, on 1993 IMF forecasts, to over 40%. The OECD won't, however, lose much ground owing to the collapse in GDP in the Soviet Union and East Europe. But thereafter, if all but the former Communist countries maintain their 1990–5 growth rates (and the former Communist countries grow at 5% pa) developing countries will account for over half world GDP in fifteen years' time and the OECD will account for less than a third in another ten years after that. A quarter of a century hence, the OECD will take a smaller share of world GDP than the developing countries do now. Moreover, assuming a continuation of today's growth rates in developing countries is extremely pessimistic (see below). The rest of the world can no longer be ignored on account of its size. It is big, growing fast and it matters.

There is another, possibly more important, reason for paying increased attention to developing countries. They are no longer marching in step with the OECD through the business cycle. They missed out on the mid-1970s oil shock recession (thanks to petro-dollar recycling) and have boomed in the early 1990s while the OECD slumped. The developing world's business cycle has decoupled from the developed world's. Because advanced industrial economies are chronic depressives, forecasting their growth is like guessing the speed of a cyclist going uphill; the question is, 'Who's pedalling?' The possibilities are consumers saving less, businesses investing more, governments running bigger budget deficits or foreigners buying exports. OECD forecasts are made by analysing demand. This is not the way to forecast developing countries. They are cyclists freewheeling downhill. There is no shortage of potential demand, because of the massive and profitable investment opportunities which exist while they are catching up with developed countries. The question is: 'what stops them?' Their growth is limited by supply-side bottle-necks — such as inadequate electrical power or limited port facilities. Bottlenecks can be removed moderately quickly when adequate foreign exchange is available, i.e. to buy generators and cranes. Problems arise when foreign currency is scarce.

THE IMPACT OF LIBERALISATION

When this distinction is drawn, much becomes clear about the changed workings of the international economy in the 1990s. While developing countries pursued illiberal policies, capital inflows were inhibited. (Government borrowing and the 1982 LDC debt crisis hardly helped matters.) Without capital inflows, export earnings determined the level of developing countries' imports and hence the rate of growth in their economies. As the OECD provided their main markets, export prices and volumes declined when industrial countries suffered a recession. Imports and growth in developing countries had therefore to be cut. Their business cycles were driven by the OECD's.

Liberalisation has changed this. First, it has led to a surge in capital flows from developed to developing countries. It is not yet on the pre-1914 scale, but these are early days. It will mount rapidly if the ageing of Americans leads to a sustained rise in the US household savings rate. The US current account balance has been in deficit for over a decade and to most young economists this has become the accepted and normal state of affairs. But from a much longer historical perspective, it is an absurd anomaly. One of the richest countries in the world should not be borrowing to support consumption in excess of income. From 1890 to 1980 there was no period of ten years in which, in total, the United States had a current account deficit. For a century after American real income caught up and passed British, it was a capital exporting country. It will be again in the late 1990s.

Liberalisation has also changed developing countries trade per-formance, relative to the OECD's. Between 1950 and 1975 OECD trade volumes (exports as well as imports) rose twice as fast as OECD real GDP, meaning the share of trade in GDP steadily increased. This was largely due to the benign effects of increasing trade freedom under successive GATT agreements. But from the mid-1970s, when OECD growth slowed down, trade volumes rose by only 1.5 times real GDP growth. Almost exactly the opposite has happened to developing countries' trade, but over a different time scale. From 1963 to 1985 trade volumes rose by 1.5 times GDP, but since 1985 trade growth has sprinted to 2.5 times GDP growth. Much of it is with each other, particularly in Asia where the old 'tigers' (Singapore, Hong Kong, South Korea and Taiwan) and the new (China, Malaysia, Thailand, and Indonesia) now do more trade with Asian partners than with the OECD. That area's business cycle has already largely de-coupled.

There is growing evidence that the developing world is now pulling the developed world out of recession. World current account balances, which ought to sum to zero, never do. The world generally records a deficit. With this in mind, the turnaround in the payments positions in the OECD and developing countries in the early 1990s is striking. The OECD almost earned a surplus in 1993, compared with a $120 bn deficit in 1990, while the developing countries' balance mirrored this in moving from near surplus to a $120 bn deficit. Capital flows to developing countries, which grew so rapidly in the early 1990s, allowed them to go on importing and growing when their export revenues suffered from the OECD recession. The deterioration in their current account balances, which capital inflows financed, gave OECD countries export-led growth in return.

THE COMING WORLD BOOM

The importance of trade and capital flows between developed and developing countries has increased massively since the world became one market. But this is as nothing compared with what is now in store. The world is on the brink of its biggest boom.

There is always a tendency for world growth to accelerate even when no individual country is growing any faster. This surprising proposition is true except on the completely unrealistic assumption that all countries grow at the same rate.

A simple illustration shows why. Take a two-country 'world' in which in 1995 Country A's and Country B's GDPs are the same size, so that each has a 50% share in 'world' GDP. But suppose Country A is growing at a rate of 6% a year, but Country B by only 3% a year. 'World' growth will be the average of A's and B's growth, each weighted by the size of its GDP. In 1995, since GDPs are equal 'world' growth will be 4.5%. But after ten years, A will have increased its share in 'world' GDP to 57% and 'world' growth in 2005 will average 4.7%. After thirty years A will account for over 70% of world GDP and the 'world' growth rate will have risen to over 5%. To estimate world growth and world GDP shares in some future year, it is necessary to break each area down into fine detail before calculating the effect of unchanged growth rates. But it is also likely that growth will accelerate in some countries, like India, which are now in the middle of liberalising.

Chart 17.2 World Growth 1800–2015

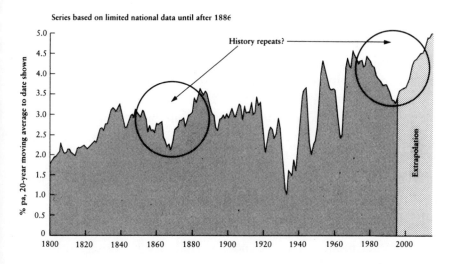

World growth should accelerate strongly as long as there are backward countries catching up with the leaders' growth. (It slowed down during the 1970s and 1980s because the leaders themselves had been catching up in the 1950s and 1960s to make up for the losses and damage suffered during the 1930s and 1940s.)

There are two utterly compelling reasons why the world now faces its biggest boom ever:

1. The later a country industrialises, the faster it does so.

2. More and bigger countries are industrialising today than ever before.

These reasons are shown in bold because they are amongst the most important statements in this book.

LATE STARTERS GROW FASTEST

Until Britain led the world into the industrial revolution in the late eighteenth century, real income growth was rare. Agrarian output expanded with the world population (or possibly the other way round), but from one century to the next output per head was largely static. It varied from place to place and from year to year as a result of the vagaries of harvest and climate. But until industrialisation, living standards in one age differed little from those a century earlier or a century later. Growth became the norm only after countries started to industrialise, which they did at different times. Real income growth was combined with rising populations to produce more rapid real GDP growth.

Britain's industrial revolution is reckoned to have begun around 1780. Between 1700 and 1780 real GDP is estimated to have risen by about 0.7% a year. But this was only marginally faster than the rise in the population. Although output growth accelerated in the closing years of the eighteenth century, so did population growth and real income growth actually slowed down. It was not until the first three decades of the nineteenth century that real incomes started to rise significantly, by around 0.75% a year. Thereafter it accelerated. Even so, the fastest growth in GDP per head over an extended period was 2% a year during the 1950s and 1960s. The average for the whole period 1780 to 1995 was 1.1% a year. Fast growth has always come from those at the back catching up. Britain never had the chance to do this. It may have lagged behind in the twentieth century, but it has always been amongst the leading pack of industrialised countries.

US GDP estimates go back to 1789. US real income growth was

more rapid than Britain's through most of the nineteenth century, except when interrupted by the War of 1812 with Britain and the American Civil War in 1861–5. Real GDP per head caught up with Britain's in 1890 and surged ahead to a 60% lead by 1950. (See Chart 17.3 on page 200). But thereafter British growth was slightly faster and America's lead was slowly whittled back to 40%. Over the entire period 1789 to 1995 US GDP per head grew by 1.75% a year, beating Britain's by 1% a year.

French statistics go back to 1815. France merely matched British growth through the nineteenth century and by its end French GDP per head was still only about half the British level. France did not seriously start to catch up until after the Second World War. Nonetheless, over the period from 1815 French GDP per head growth has averaged 2%. German statistics, covering the countries which comprised the Second Reich in 1913, go back to 1850. German real incomes were then about 60% of British and double the level the United States had enjoyed in 1789. Germany caught up with Britain less rapidly than the United States, but largely because its progress was interrupted by wars. After the Second World War, German growth was spectacularly fast. Consequently the average per capita rise in real GDP over 1850–1992 was 2%, just slightly faster than the US longer-term average.

The starting point for Japanese statistics is 1875, reasonably close to the beginning of Japanese industrialisation. The policy of *Sakoku*, under which the Tokugawa Shogunate bolted Japanese doors against the rest of the world, had ended in 1868 with the Meiji Restoration. But this was followed by civil war in 1873. From 1875 to 1995 Japanese real incomes grew by 2.75% a year, 1% a year faster than American and 2% faster than British.

South Korea is the next country to consider, largely because it has the longest back-run of GDP figures. Taiwanese statistics are hard to come by as it is no longer an IMF member, while Hong Kong is a British colony and cannot be a member in its own right. Singapore did not break away from Malaysia until 1965. South Korean real incomes have risen by 5.5% a year since 1953. China, the latest and most important country to begin industrialisation, has achieved 5.75% real GDP per head growth since 1961. But more recently, over the past fifteen years, Chinese per capita growth has accelerated to average 7.7% pa.

Chart 17.3 Real GDP per Head, 1790–2015

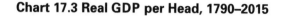

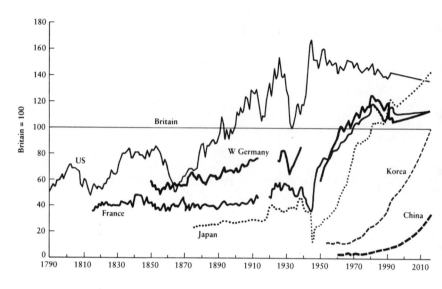

Chart 17.2 (on page 197) also shows extrapolations over the coming twenty years. It is assumed that real GDP per head growth in Britain and France are much the same, slightly faster than in the United States, but slower than in Germany, where real GDP per head fell following unification. Japan is assumed to continue to catch up with the United States. If South Korea keeps up its recent performance it will catch up

Table 17.1 Long-Term Growth in GDP per head

Country	Period from	Growth % pa
Britain	1780	0.75
US	1789	1.75
France	1815	2.00
Germany	1850	2.00
Japan	1875	2.75
S. Korea	1953	5.50
China	1961	5.75
China	1978	7.70

with Britain within twenty years, but China's real GDP per head will have climbed to only one-third of Britain's.

MORE AND BIGGER COUNTRIES ARE NOW INDUSTRIALISING

The proposition that more and larger economies are now industrialising and catching up hardly needs substantiation. China and India between them accounted for 40% of the world's 5 billion population in 1990. The extrapolation shown in Chart 17.2 of world GDP growth is based upon a breakdown of the world into its major regions and countries. Population growth forecasts are readily available for virtually all countries. These were combined with what seemed plausible real income growth assumptions. The analysis was carried out by the author in August 1993 and is therefore a little dated. But the results are so robust that updating it is unlikely to change the conclusion. This was that world GDP growth would accelerate to 5% pa over the coming twenty years, its fastest ever rate. Admittedly, much of this forecast turns on extrapolating Chinese GDP per head growth at 7% pa. But this only means assuming the economy will perform almost as well over the next twenty years as it did over the last fifteen when GDP per head grew by 7.7% pa. Given China's 1995 GDP per head of less than 10% the American level, such growth would still leave it a bit below a quarter of the American level by 2005. This is not implausible.

The implications for world trade are truly staggering – but not as dramatic as unchecked compound arithmetic would suggest. In 1990 Asia's GDP was 17.2% of the world's and the OECD's was 55.7%. Asian GDP was thus just under a third of OECD GDP. If Asia's GDP grows by a conservative 6% a year for twenty years to 2010, while the OECD grows by an optimistic 3% a year, Asia's GDP will double to two-thirds of OECD GDP. Now combine Asia's faster growth with the higher Asian exports-to-GDP ratio. If the Asian ratio remains at 2.5:1, Asian exports will rise by 15% a year, while the OECD ratio of 1.5:1 gives only 4.5% a year export growth. In 1990 Asian exports amounted to under 15% of OECD exports. But with these compound growth rates they would thunder to over 150% of OECD exports by 2010.

But notice that exports currently account for a much lower share in

Table 17.2 World Growth to 2013

	Share in world GDP 1992	Growth % pa to 2013:			Share in world GDP 2013
		GDP/head	Population	GDP	
OECD*	55	2.1	0.5	2.6	34
Latin America	9	4.6	1.5	6.2	11
Asia	20	6.7	1.4	8.2	37
Africa	4	0.8	3.4	4.2	3
Middle East/ Europe	5	3.1	2.3	5.5	5
Former Communist Countries	8	5.0	0.9	5.9	10
World	100	3.4	1.5	5.0	100

Asian GDP than they do of the OECD's. This can be seen from the difference between GDP weighted in 1990 and export weights. It again comes back to purchasing power parities, which increase the size of the non-traded goods and services sectors in developing economies, thereby reducing the relative size of the trade sector. This is quite realistic, as the example of the Thai haircut and hair-dryer shows. Unindustrialised countries have small traded goods sectors. Fast growth results from industrialisation, which expands trade even faster until an economy matures. There is no doubt that the ratio of trade growth to GDP growth will fall in developing Asian economies over the coming two decades. But it is still likely to remain above the OECD's ratio.

Developing countries export and import growth will be considerable during the coming world boom. Much of the expansion will be in trade between developing countries. But none the less, the developing world is going to make extremely deep inroads upon OECD countries' trade with developing countries and into OECD countries' home markets. World trade in those goods whose production requires only moderately skilled workers will be increasingly captured by developing world producers, particularly Asian. These will include products such as cars where quality and reliability can now be designed into the manufacturing process. The only areas in which high-cost European producers will be able to compete will be at the very top of the range, such as high-tech products and in services such as banking, stockbroking, insurance, air transport, computer programming, biotechnology and telecommunications.

But perhaps the most important conclusion of this chapter is that the boom has hardly yet begun. The job losses and rising unemployment in Europe over the past decade were largely home-grown, as a consequence of technological change. They were not, to any great extent, the result of inroads made by developing countries exporting into European markets. Imports into Europe from non-oil-developing countries were 3.2% of nominal GDP in 1992, *down* from 3.8% in 1982. Exports to non-oil-developing countries were *down* from 3.8% to 3.1%. (By comparison, imports from other OECD countries rose from 18.2% of GDP to 18.3% during the decade, while exports to the rest of the OECD rose from 17.3% to 17.6%.) A deterioration of 0.1% of GDP in Europe's trade balance with non-oil-developing countries could not have caused unemployment to rise by 2% points or five million in the decade. Obviously there were industries in which foreign competition led to a loss of European jobs. Trade with dynamic Asian economies – China, Hong Kong, Singapore, South Korea, Taiwan, Thailand and Malaysia – did expand. Imports from these countries rose from 0.63% of GDP in 1982 to 1.1%; exports to them grew from 0.28% to 0.81%. None the less, to date as much as been gained in terms of trade and employment from supplying developing economies with the capital equipment they need to set up their infant industries, as has been lost as a result of rising exports from those infant industries. The tidal wave of competition from cheap imports has yet to come – but it will.

PART IV

INTO THE TWENTY-FIRST CENTURY

CHAPTER 18

German Domestic Prospects

After the Second World War many Europeans feared that when the Germans regained their independence, they would rise again to dominate and bully Europe. West Germany did, but peacefully and economically, and in a way which would nurture the growth of a healthy democracy. Unlike the Weimar Republic, the great mass of Germans respect the Federal Republic of Germany and its Basic Law. Only a tiny minority of extremists remain opposed to the present system. Democracy, now secured, is unlikely to be relinquished. Moreover democracies do not normally make war on one another. Britain's Prime Minister, John Major, summed up the situation concisely in his William and Mary Lecture in Leiden on 6 September 1994:

> The European Community was born to end divisions in Western Europe. It has succeeded. With NATO, it has given us peace and prosperity in our part of the continent, and made war unthinkable. The determination of the founding fathers has succeeded far beyond the estimations of most people in their time. Their vision was proved right for its age. But it is outdated. It will not do now.

True to form, John Major offered no new vision to replace the old. This will be the task for Europe's statesmen as they cross the threshold into a new millennium.

GERMANY IS POLITICALLY STABLE

Helmut Kohl is far and away Europe's foremost statesman. He heads the EU's largest and most powerful economy, and has been German Chancellor longer than any other European leader has been head of government. If he serves out his fourth term in full which ends in 1998, he will have held the job for sixteen years, the longest-serving post-war German Chancellor. Konrad Adenauer was Chancellor for fourteen years. Admittedly Kohl's victory in the 1994 General Election was narrow. His CDU–CSU/FDP coalition saw its Bundestag majority cut from 134 to ten. But under the German system this is a workable majority. It won't be dented by by-election defeats; there can be none. When a member of the Bundestag dies or resigns, his place is taken by the next candidate on his party's proportional representation list.

The SPD opposition controls the upper house, the Bundesrat. They can block legislation, particularly 'concurrent' measures such as changes in taxation, over which both houses have a veto. But there is nothing new in SPD control of the Bundesrat – this was the situation long before the 1994 election. Kohl has had to govern with the consent of the Opposition and has done so with considerable success. The solidarity pact, to regularise support for east Germany within the normal federal budgetary system, was negotiated between the Federal Government, the Länder (many controlled by the Opposition), employers and unions. The pact may not have gone far enough, but it showed a willingness to compromise on all sides. The SPD has a real share in German Government in a way that British Opposition parties can never enjoy.

During the October 1994 Bundestag election campaign, Kohl unfairly raised the red menace, arguing that a vote for the SPD would bring former East German Communists, the Party of Democratic Socialism, into government. In the event, the Red Socks, as he called the PDS, performed well enough to obtain thirty Bundestag seats. Their 4.4% share of the vote fell below the 5% level, but they gained a share of the seats allotted by the proportional representation by winning at least two constituency seats. In fact, they won three, all in east Germany. The PDS has a strong following in the east amongst the many whose expectations of unification have been disappointed. Its leaders were charismatic and closer to their local communities than most other candidates. Their support was a protest vote, but more one concerned with the way unification had been handled. The PDS is no threat to the stability of the enlarged FRG. On the contrary, its representation democratically in the Bundestag allows its supporters to seek redress for their grievances within the system.

The far-right Republicans failed miserably in the Bundestag election. Despite fears fuelled by isolated strong performances in the odd Länder election, nationwide support for them proved minimal, less than 2% of the vote. Right-wing extremists are, however, a threat to internal security. Further outrages, such as the murder of two Turkish women and their three daughters by skinheads in December 1992, are likely. The fall in support for main-line parties following unification and the increase in support for extremists or single-issue parties, is neither surprising nor seriously worrying. The same phenomenon was observed in the first Bundestag election in 1949. By the 1960s, however, all minor parties had been wiped out and only the four major parties obtained Bundestag seats. It is hoped that support for extremists and protest parties – the Greens apart – will diminish as the east German recovery moves forward. Germany today has decent, democratic government, run by highly responsible (if often rather dull) politicians, which should be capable of handling most problems it is likely to confront. The FRG enjoys a high degree of political stability – more so than Italy, for example; and far more so than Russia, where a military dictatorship could well re-emerge.

EAST GERMANY IS RECOVERING STRONGLY

Domestically, some problems facing Germany are easing. Five years after unification, east Germany is at last recovering strongly. The OECD estimates that GDP grew by 9% in 1994 and forecasts that it will continue to grow at this rate during 1995 and 1996. East Germany will continue to absorb real resources from west Germany, but their nature will change. As east German output and incomes rise, unemployment will fall and east German tax revenues will prove buoyant. Transfer payments from west Germany will diminish, helping to cut the Federal budget deficit, which the OECD forecasts will fall to under 2% of GDP by 1996. At the same time, private capital investment flows from west to east will increase. Private transfers, unlike public, have statistically disappeared.

Monetary union in July 1990 eliminated the exchange frontier between the two Germanies, since when payments from one to the other have not been recorded. Separate east and west German balance of payments statistics are no longer available, thus making it impossible to know the aggregate size of private capital flows between the two. Separate GDP figures continue to be published; the east German figures appear months after the west. Both include guesstimates for trade flows between the two. But these are little more than guesses and soon all-Germany GDP estimates will be the only ones worth publishing.

The net flow of private capital from west to east need not be substantial. East Germans may not save enough as a share of income to match the share taken by investment in east German expenditure. None the less they have emerged as high savers, like their west German neighbours. Doubtless there will be a high level of direct investment by west German companies into east Germany. But this will be largely offset by short-term capital flows in the opposite direction.

MISTAKEN POLICIES ARE THE MAIN DANGER

The German economy none the less faces short-term cyclical and longer-term structural problems. It should be able to handle these, but there are dangers which need to be recognised it they are to be avoided. One is that the independent Bundesbank will impose an excessively tough monetary policy in pursuit of an unrealistically low inflation rate for what is potentially an extremely dynamic economy. It will do so if it sees its task narrowly, as the guardian of the domestic and external value of the D-Mark, and adheres uncritically to current economic orthodoxy. This maintains that governments cannot, by stimulating demand, permanently raise the level of employment. This supposition rests on the proposition that when unemployment is reduced below a certain level, inflation accelerates. This level is known as the non-accelerating inflation rate of unemployment (NAIRU). Fiscal profligacy, which causes accelerating inflation, cannot be sustained. It must either be reversed or negated by monetary stringency.

This argument has led most governments to abandon full employment targets and to concentrate upon achieving stable or near-stable prices. Stable prices, they say, are a necessary condition for sustained growth and reduced unemployment in the longer term. Macro-economic demand management policies have been abandoned as a means of promoting employment and replaced by micro-economic supply-side measures. Nobody would question the importance of supply-side measures to improve competition, increase capacity and enable an economy to grow more rapidly without overheating (i.e., lower NAIRU and raise the economy's potential growth rate). They doubtless produce results, but these are extremely modest except over a decade or two. In any case, supply-side reforms can be pursued regardless of the macro-economic demand management policy a government adopts.

Orthodox analysis neglects the supply-side damage which can be done by protracted demand deflation. Assume GDP in an economy is at its potential level (with unemployment at its NAIRU rate). Inflation is therefore stable, meaning that it is neither accelerating nor slowing down. But suppose it is stable at an unacceptably fast rate, say 5% or more. Conventional wisdom dictates monetary or fiscal tightening to slow growth below its potential rate and thereby produce a negative output gap. This gap will cause inflation to slow down. Once price increases have fallen to an acceptably low rate, deflationary policies can be abandoned and the economy allowed to recover until the negative output gap has been eliminated once more. When real GDP again equals its potential level, inflation will stabilise at its new lower rate. The size and duration of the required negative output gap will depend upon how far the initial inflation rate exceeds the level regarded as acceptable and how responsive wages and prices are to recession.

Conventional analysis assumes that the supply side of an economy (its potential growth and NAIRU) are unaffected by recession, however deep or long it may be. Recessions rarely produce beneficial supply-side effects. Where they are short and sharp, the damage they do may be limited. Large and long-lasting negative output gaps, however, are a different matter. They imply that above-average levels of unused plant and unemployment labour can persist for years rather than months. But when there is no prospect of surplus plant being used profitably again for years – if ever – it is scrapped. Even if demand does pick up three or four years later, plant will have been scrapped because it costs too much to maintain while lying idle. Moreover, by the time demand picks up once more, old plant will be obsolete. Workers, forced to spend a year on the dole, rapidly become unemployable. Their availability for work, as outsiders, has little effect on the wage settlements which those in employment, as insiders, can obtain. Scrapped capacity and reduced capital investment in a recession reduces the productive potential of the economy. Persistently high levels of unemployment raise NAIRU. Unless a negative output gap is rapidly closed by a rise in demand, it will be closed by a fall in potential supply. The potential for sustained inflation-free growth is thereby reduced. Repeated severe doses of demand inflation increase inflationary pressure in the medium term leading to both higher inflation and higher unemployment from one business cycle to the next. The growth in industrial capacity in developing countries, and the greater availability of cheap imports when demand recovers, means long or repeated recessions are now likely to do even greater damage to supply potential than before.

The obverse of the argument that macro-economic demand-management measures cannot permanently raise the level of unemployment is that nor can they permanently lower the rate of inflation. They can be used as a short, sharp, shock-therapy treatment to bring down an excessively fast inflation rate. But they cannot be employed, over a protracted period, to reduce inflation to an unrealistically low level without the most baleful consequences. This is a lesson the Bundesbank must heed in dealing with Germany's current situation.

GERMANY'S OUT-OF-STEP ECONOMY

When measured by the fall in output, the west German recession during 1992–3 was unusually severe, the worst since the war. (The east German recession was worse than the inter-war depression.) But measured by the output gap, the west German recession was unusually mild. The post-unification boom caused extreme overheating leading to the emergence of a record 5% positive output gap in 1991, which the fall in output eliminated rather than reversed. It was not until late 1993 that a negative gap emerged and then it never exceeded −1% of GDP.

The west German recovery in 1994 was unexpectedly strong. By the middle two quarters of the year the economy was growing at an annual rate of 4–5%, twice its potential GDP growth rate. As a result, the small negative output gap was eliminated. Exports and investment largely explain the economy's unexpected strength. West German GDP figures count sales to east Germany as exports, and these were thought to be particularly buoyant. Consumer spending remained subdued. Real wage incomes were squeezed as nominal increases negotiated in 1993–4 fell short of the rise in consumer prices. OECD estimates reveal that real wages fell 0.5% between 1993 and 1994. Strong growth coupled with wage moderation increased productivity and raised corporate profits by up to a half.

With the economy recovering and profits rising sharply, German unions obtained wage increases of 4% in 1995, well ahead of inflation. They managed to protect their real living standards from the effect of the 7.5% 'solidarity' income tax surcharge (re-imposed on 1 January 1995). As incomes rise, growth will be boosted by a recovery in consumer spending. Unfortunately there may not be enough domestic capacity available to meet this.

Since unification, inflation in west Germany has been faster than in most other major EU countries. If a recovery in consumer demand keeps growth above its potential rate during 1995, a positive output gap will emerge and domestic inflation will begin to accelerate. This does not mean that German prices will soar. The strong D-Mark helps keep prices down. The Bundesbank's target is to limit inflation to around 2% a year (i.e., somewhat below the actual rate of inflation experienced in early 1995). It may move speedily to raise interest rates at the first hint of resurgent inflation.

Unification has added an extremely dynamic element to German demand. Spending on and in east Germany will continue to boost west German investment and 'exports'. At present the west German economy has not the capacity both to meet these demands and those from a substantial recovery in west German consumer spending. The post-unification boom was not a unique phenomenon, but reflected the greater autonomous demand pressures in unified Germany than in the former West Germany. East Germany has absorbed west Germany's surplus savings, with the result that all-Germany can no longer be likened to a chronic depressive. Conditions exist for a sharp acceleration in west and all-German potential GDP growth. But this will require that the economy runs 'hotter' than hitherto, with an inflation rate of around 4%, double the Bundesbank's current target.

A LESSON FOR THE BUNDESBANK

If the Bundesbank sticks rigidly to its 2% inflation target, growth in the economy will have to be checked sharply during 1995–6. (The strong D-Mark helps to do this. If it weakens, interest rates must rise.) The shallow 1992–3 recession will then be followed by a weak 1994–5 boom, before the economy relapses into recession once more. It is unlikely that high interest rates will have a large and immediate effect of consumer spending. They are more likely to affect investment and exports. The D-Mark became overvalued after unification, the means by which the excess west German savings were transferred from west Germany's balance of payments surplus with the rest of the world to supporting east Germans. Tough monetary policy, in pursuit of an unrealistically low inflation rate, will keep the D-Mark overvalued, damaging all-Germany's exports and increasing imports. The all-German current account will remain in deficit. The weak boom will fail to raise employment and renewed monetary stringency will damage the east German recovery. The adverse supply-side effects of excessive monetary stringency in an economy experiencing a major structural adjustment will be severe.

Killing Germany's recovery shortly after its birth will exacerbate the country's long-term structural policies. The social market is being liberalised, slowly and partly thanks to the move to the European Single Market. Much more needs to be done, always in the teeth of opposition from the special interest groups adversely affected. At the same time, the post-unification budgetary situation has so far only been stabilised. Further measures will be needed to lower the level of public spending from its 50–55% range (as a per cent of GDP) to a more reasonable 45–50% range. Reductions of this magnitude were achieved during the 1980s and could be repeated during the late 1990s. But it will require a considerable willingness to compromise by all the German political parties at Federal, Länder and local level. The task will be far easier if the economy is allowed faster growth, even at the expense of somewhat faster inflation. Moreover, inflation will probably be lower in the medium term as a result.

Fortunately the Bundesbank is pragmatic. Despite its reputation for anti-inflationary rigour, it has always taken into consideration the wider economic consequences of its actions. It is already proceeding much more cautiously than the Bank of England, which began raising interest rates in 1994 on the mere fear that, in 1996, inflation could move higher. Germany already suffers faster inflation than Britain. Moreover Britain, with a large negative output gap, could afford one or two years of above potential GDP growth before inflation need move higher. So while Germany may face some of the problems outlined above, it should be spared the worst.

CHAPTER 19

The European Dimension

Europe's future is under constant review. Heads of government meet twice yearly. But once every five years major inter-governmental conferences (IGCs) are held to review progress towards deepening and widening the Union. The Single Europe Act was the product of the 1986 IGC, the Maastricht Treaty (signed in 1992) was the product of the 1991 one. The next IGC is scheduled to begin in 1996, but could be stretched into 1997 on the prospect of a British general election (which could produce a Labour Government more favourable to Europe). The 1996 IGC will re-examine the Maastricht Treaty, under which the Council is required to decide whether a majority of countries are ready for stage three in the treaty's timetable for progress to economic and monetary union. The IGC will also attempt to strengthen common defence and foreign policy links (matters not further discussed here) and issues related to the further enlargement of the community. Enlargement from fifteen to twenty or more members in the next century must involve the further development of European institutions, dealing in particular with what is known as Europe's 'democratic deficit' (of which more anon).

If there is the political will, the convergence criteria that are set out in the Maastricht Treaty could be bent to allow a majority to qualify for a move to stage three as early as 1 January 1997. This seems unlikely, but its chances would be increased if Labour were returned to Government in Britain. More likely, the Maastricht plan for economic and monetary union will have to be postponed or even abandoned.

The Maastricht Treaty's most serious flaw is its widespread unpopularity. Europe's political establishment formulated it with arrogant disregard of public opinion and then, for the most part, cynically imposed their will on their countrymen. Only the Irish, the Danes (twice) and the French held referendums on Maastricht. The Irish, who gain greatly from EU membership, voted solidly in favour (69% yes); the Danes rejected it on the first count (51% no) and only accepted (57% yes) after modifications giving them, like Britain, an escape route from stage three. The French, whose leaders are amongst the most pro-Europe in the union, voted in favour by a whisker (51%). Opinion polls show that, in most countries where electorates were given no say, Maastricht would have been heavily defeated. Moreover opinion against the Treaty has been hardening. A poll in late 1994 showed that only 23% of Germans favoured the move to a single European currency, lower even than the 25% of Britons in favour. The strength of public opposition makes it unlikely that Europe's leaders can push ahead with the move to stage three at the pace the Treaty makes possible.

Maastricht's second most serious flaw was its obsession with inflation. Convergence criteria pay no heed to rates of growth or levels of employment. Prices can always be stabilised in the short term by driving an economy deep into recession, but it is politically impossible to sustain price stability by extending the recession until it becomes a depression. By the time the 1996 IGC meets, the obsession with inflation will have evaporated. Europeans will be more concerned about jobs.

THE TRILEMMA THE BUNDESBANK POSES FOR EUROPE

There is no knowing how severely the Bundesbank will need to tighten monetary policy in 1995–6 to prevent the German economy from overheating. But however late and little that tightening may be, it will be too much and too soon for other European economies. When German GDP reached its potential level in late 1994, all other EU member countries were still suffering from large negative output gaps (France and Spain −3.2% in the third quarter of 1994, Britain and Italy −2.5%). ERM members will be obliged to follow the Bundesbank's lead and tighten, regardless of domestic economic considerations. The conflict between internal and external policy requirements, which drove Britain and Italy out of the ERM in September 1992 and, in August 1993, caused margins to be widened to 15%, will return in late 1995 or 1996.

As long as German monetary policy is set solely according to domestic considerations and the German business cycle is out of step, other countries will be forced to choose between unpalatable options. They can match Bundesbank monetary stringency (which central banks will want to do) and kill their recoveries prematurely; they can refuse to follow German monetary policy and leave the ERM; or they can offset monetary stringency with fiscal laxity in an effort to keep their recoveries going. The first option is the only one compatible with a move to stage three under Maastricht criteria. But it would exact an intolerable price in increased unemployment. The lesson of Britain's departure from the ERM and subsequent non-inflationary recovery is there for all to see.

The one remaining possibility is that persistently above-average German inflation, together with an increased all-German current account deficit, could undermine the credibility of the Bundesbank and the D-Mark. In which case, the D-Mark would lose its anchor role in the ERM (probably to the French franc) and German interest rates would have to rise to a premium over those of other ERM member countries. If the Bundesbank pursues its 2% inflation target to the bitter end, this will become a probability. It is unlikely to happen in time to rescue other ERM countries from their trilemma.

THE COMING WEAK MID-DECADE RECESSION

European prospects cannot be considered in isolation. By 1996 the OECD as a whole is likely to be moving in to a mild Kitchin-type recession, following its moderate, mid-decade boom. (Big Juglar-type booms now occur at the end of each decade, big recessions at the beginning of the next.) Despite fears of resurgent inflation, there will be little acceleration in prices during the weak mid-decade boom. (The OECD forecasts that EU consumer price deflators will fall from 3% on average in 1994 to 2.6% in both 1995 and 1996.) The governments of all major industrial countries, except Japan, are pursuing policies of fiscal consolidation to reduce bloated budget deficits and to halt the rise of government debts. Monetary policy is also now largely outside their control, determined by central banks and at the mercy of markets, which punish monetary authorities perceived to take risks with inflation.

Long-term interest rates rose everywhere in 1994. The change from bull to bear bond markets began in the US in October 1993 and ended five months later in Europe in February 1994. Synchronisation of bond market movements, at a time when business cycles were de-synchronised, meant that long rates started rising in cycle-laggards (e.g., Japan, France and Germany) much earlier than normal in the business cycle. The rise in long rates at a time of declining inflation has pushed real rates to historically high levels. This market behaviour is one reason for expecting the 1994–5 boom to be weak and short-lived.

But what explains it? Markets now march in step because they are globally integrated. When the US Treasury had to pay more to borrow, so had everyone else. The rise in long-term interest rates in 1994 was substantial, because hedge funds and banks had speculated heavily on bonds in 1993, pushing their prices to unsustainably high levels. Rising US short rates forced them to unwind their heavily leveraged positions, causing bond prices to crash. A third reason for rising interest rates was a world shortage of capital. Developing countries returned to the world's capital markets as borrowers to compete for limited funds. Industrial countries' government budget deficits could not be turned off as rapidly as the demand for funds by developing countries was turned on.

A further and frequently cited explanation was that markets saw the danger of resurgent inflation sooner than economists. A sharp rise in commodity prices (probably driven by demand from developing countries as their economies boomed) supported such fears. They seem ill-founded. Rapid real money supply growth normally heralds inflationary excesses to come, but everywhere – with the exception of Germany – real money growth remains negligible. None the less, the fact so many people fear future inflation is, in itself, of significance. It means that when recoveries falter in 1996, without there having been any serious increases in inflation, the lurch back towards recession will be blamed on today's unfounded fears.

This sentiment is likely to be reinforced by world trade developments. The tidal wave of cheap imports from developing countries, forecast at the end of Chapter 17, will be evident in industrial countries by 1996. Its impact will limit the ability of domestic producers to pass on cost increases in higher prices. Cheap imports will reduce output and employment in countries whose exports to developing countries remain feeble. Continental Europe is particularly exposed. Compared with the US, most Europeans are high-cost producers. Economies whose currencies are locked to the D-Mark in the ERM will suffer from its excessive overvaluation. The United States and Britain are the countries likely to suffer least, both having competitive currencies and flexible labour markets. American productivity remains the highest in the world – while in Britain most of the industries which could be wiped out by competition from developing countries have already been wiped out by competition from developed ones (such as Japan).

THE 1996 IGC WILL BE DOMINATED BY EUROPE'S JOBS CRISIS

The dominant theme at the 1996 IGS will be the return of Eurosclerosis and Europe's jobs crisis. Governments and markets will no longer be obsessed by inflation but will be fearful of growing competition from developing countries. The battle between British laissez-faire and French dirigisme will be on with a vengeance. Europe's relationship with the rest of the world will be one of four questions facing Europe's leaders. The issue is whether we should build a 'fortress Europe' to defend old jobs, or remain open to foreign imports and concentrate upon creating new ones? The other issues are whether and at what speed we move towards a single currency. (If we move at different speeds, the issue of free trade versus protection will also arise within Europe.) Should we seek to build a federal Europe or remain essentially a Europe of sovereign nations? The final issue concerns the speed with which the EU expands by admitting new members. All these issues are interrelated.

The single market has created competition between rival regulatory, tax and welfare systems. Unfettered competition within it means production and employment will migrate to those countries whose taxes are lowest, social security system the least generous and regulatory system (particularly labour market regulations) the least onerous. In so far as this is regarded as unfair competition or 'social dumping', countries losing out will either retreat from the single market or demand that the winners accept increased harmonisation of taxation, welfare and regulatory systems.

Harmonisation of social security systems will impose public spending costs that bear little relationship to per capita income. This is illustrated in Chart 19.1 by the horizontal line showing shares of public spending in GDP for countries with varying levels of per capital GDP. (This is an extreme case in which shares of public spending in GDP are the same everywhere, whatever the level of income.) Harmonisation of tax systems and rates will generate government revenues which are correlated with per capita GDP. Thanks to the progressive element in direct taxation, tax revenue as a share of GDP will rise with per capita GDP. This is shown by the lines rising from left to right in Chart 19.1, which represent high, medium and low rates of taxation.

Chart 19.1 Budgetary Consequences of EU Harmonisation

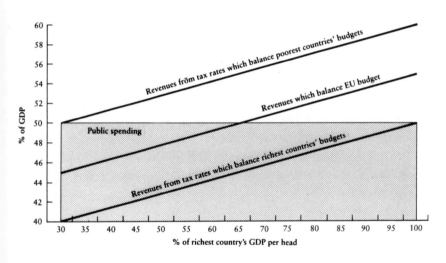

Tax rates which in aggregate balance the combined national budgets of EU member countries (the middle line in Chart 19.1) will produce budget deficits in poor countries with low incomes and surpluses in rich countries with high incomes. The tax rates which would balance budgets in poor countries (top line) would produce large surpluses in rich and an aggregate surplus for all taken together. Similarly, tax rates which balanced the budgets of rich countries (bottom line) would produce large deficits in poor countries and a deficit in aggregate. It is impossible both to harmonise tax rates and social security systems and achieve balanced budgets in all countries. The bigger the income differentials, the greater the budgetary problems from harmonisation.

A single currency and tax harmonisation are incompatible unless large and identifiable transfers are made between rich and poor countries, taking the surpluses from the former and *giving* them to the latter. Such transfers could be made only within a federal system in which substantially the greater part of taxation was levied at the European federal level and substantially the greater part of social security payments fell on the European federal government. Under such a system, tax and social security frontiers, like currency frontiers, would disappear. Transfer payments would become opaque. Indeed if tax and social security systems and rates are to be harmonised, decisions on what systems and rates to adopt would have to be taken at the European level and hence national governments would become mere collecting and paying agents. It is possible to meet the Maastricht fiscal criteria for moving to a single currency or to harmonise tax and social security systems (but not perhaps rates). It is not possible to do both.

The federal solution makes monetary union a practical proposition, although it is not a complete solution. In the absence of currency adjustments, certain regions within Europe would become and remain depressed areas. Linguistic and cultural differences are bound to limit labour mobility in a federal Europe as compared with the linguistically and culturally more uniform United States. Budgetary transfers would have to be boosted by special regional grants and tax incentives. These should be easier under a federal system.

If a 'Europe of nations' moved to a single currency without harmonisation, unfair competition or 'social dumping' would be greatly facilitated. The results would be different growth rates and employment levels in different countries. The common exchange rate with the outside world at which high-tax, high-wage EU countries (the inner core, i.e. Germany, France and the Benelux) could compete would provide a substantially undervalued rate for the low-tax low-cost members (such as Britain, Ireland, Portugal and Spain), and vice versa for an exchange rate reflecting low-tax low-wage countries' costs. If the inner core countries wanted to go ahead with a single currency and harmonisation, their taxpayers would have explicitly to foot the bill for the higher social security benefits paid by the poorer countries.

Movement by an inner core minority of countries to economic and monetary union ahead of the rest, or indeed by a majority of countries on Maastricht criteria after 1 January 1997, does little to resolve these problems. Within an inner core with much the same per capita income levels, budgetary transfers would be substantially less. But while tax and social security harmonisation within the core would be easier, its members would remain at a competitive disadvantage compared with those outside. As with a motorway, the outer lane would be the fast lane, the inner lane would be for the crawlers. The problem of 'unfair competition' would *not* be resolved within a two-speed, or multi-speed, Europe.

Economically, a single currency and harmonisation are only feasible within a federal Europe. The EU can remain a Europe of nations only if further progress towards economic and political integration grinds virtually to a halt. Europe could continue as a single market without progressing further towards economic and monetary union, provided its members were all willing to accept competition between rival tax, social security and regulatory systems. Widening Europe to include five or more Eastern European member countries, poses similar questions. For Europe then to evolve from a single market will require further development of its federal institutions to facilitate decision making.

FEDERAL GOVERNMENT NEED NOT BE UNPOPULAR

A federal Europe is widely suspect as undemocratic. We are, it seems, ruled by idiotic edicts from Brussels in which we have no say at all. Absurd examples abound, such as the maximum curvature of the Euro-banana. In fact, it is the Europe of nations which is undemocratic, because national politicians prefer it so. The Brussels Commission is Europe's government (or its executive branch of government). It proposes all European legislation and, within areas of its own delegated competence, issues executive directives which have the force of law throughout the EU. The Commission's President is Europe's Prime Minister. The Commissioners are European ministers. But they are neither elected by, nor answerable to, the European Parliament. They are, with few exceptions, lackies appointed by national governments. New European laws are not passed by Europe's elected representatives to the European (federal) Parliament. Europe's Parliament has a right to be consulted as well as now exerting modest powers of veto. The first use of this power was in March 1995.

European laws are enacted by 'councils of ministers' drawn from member countries' national governments, meeting and voting in secret conclave. According to subject, laws are passed by qualified majority voting or unanimously. Diktats from these councils of ministers become the law in all EU countries without further reference to national parliaments. In those areas of government (such as agricultural and competition policy) which national governments have collectively abrogated responsibility to the European level, power has not been transferred from the national to federal level. It has been transferred from national ministers acting individually and answerable to their parliaments, to national ministers acting collectively and in secret and answerable to nobody. This is not federalism. It is not democracy, but usurpation of power by the establishment.

The manner in which citizens are governed at the European level is profoundly undemocratic, which is why Brussels is so unpopular. US federal laws are not hated in the same way. The process by which they are passed is both public and difficult. Major laws are passed by Congress and President only when a large majority of people support them; thereafter there is a considerable willingness to abide by them. Germany's federal system is not unpopular for similar reasons. Laws emerge as a result of compromise and conciliation. They are not thrust down people's throats.

Europe's system is also highly inefficient. It is impossible to envisage further enlargement without changes and reforms to many of its basic institutions. The Common Agricultural Policy (CAP), for example, was a political device by which Europe's farmers were bribed to produce a greater quantity of highly priced food than Europe's consumers wanted to eat. (It has recently been reformed so that farmers are now bribed not to produce so much.) Without further CAP reform, or preferably its abolition, the European budget could not stand the strain of including Eastern European countries with their large farming sectors. Only 8% of the EU's labour force are farmers. The share is 12% in former

Czechoslovakia, 19% in Hungary, 20% in Bulgaria, 27% in Poland and 28% in Romania. Equally, East European countries would be hard put to meet the Maastricht criteria for membership of the single currency area. But if they did, the problems of transfer payments from rich to poor would be exacerbated.

ENLARGEMENT REQUIRES A FEDERAL SOLUTION

Enlarging the community will involve changing it. Changing it is difficult, if not impossible, without reform of its institutions and decision-making processes. Extending qualified majority voting to cover more areas of policy and weakening the blocking power of the existing larger member countries is a solution. But it would require unanimous support at the IGC, which it won't receive. The better solution would be truly democratic federalism. There is no need here to spell out precise constitutional details. The general principles are simple enough. For every area of government there is a level of government at which it is best performed; and at every level of government there must be a democratic system for taking decisions. Brussels should not be responsible for emptying Broadstairs residents' dustbins; nor should Broadstairs Town Council be responsible for air traffic control over the Isle of Thanet. The principal of subsidiarity fully applies. Democracy demands that decisions be taken at the lowest possible level. In a world of diversity there is no intrinsic merit of imposed uniformity. There must always be overwhelming justification for the imposition of standardised rules. Secondly, at every level of government there has to be democratic responsibility for all decision-taking. There is not merely a need for responsibility over certain areas of government to evolve upwards to the federal level, there is an increasing need in countries such as the United Kingdom for greater powers to devolve downwards. But so far as most national politicians are concerned, 'subsidiary' only starts *above* them.

The EU, as currently constituted, falls down on both federal counts. Areas of European responsibility are defined by subject – agriculture, transport or competition policy – in a way that hands Brussels the task of making silly regulations covering some subjects while being prevented from making sensible regulations concerning others. European law-making and the exercise of executive powers are, as already explained, undemocratic. Brussels is thereby hated and federalism given a bad name. If Europe is both to broaden and to deepen, this must change.

POLICY STANCES

The analysis of the interconnections between the issues facing Europe's leaders becomes fascinating when compared with the matrix of the different countries' policy stances on these issues. Table 19.1 is limited to the positions held by Germany, France and Britain, the major members (with Italy) in the EU.

FREE-TRADE GERMANY

West Germany (despite, or possibly because of, its Second Reich past) emerged after 1945 as one of the most dedicated supporters of international free trade. This was understandable. Under the Bretton Woods fixed exchange rate system, the Germans enjoyed two decades of artificial currency undervaluation, which gave them a competitive edge. Their stance was not based on principle; free trade was to the Germans' pragmatic advantage. The proof lies in the continued tradition of restraint over competition within the German domestic economy. Thus one of the major issues over the coming few years is the degree of German commitment to the external free trade model.

Being a country, broadly, of rule-obeyers rather than problem-solvers, Germany probably favours harmonisation. But the belief that the social market out-performs both laissez-faire liberalism and mercantilist protectionism means that Germany is less determined than France to impose uniform standards on other countries. It is also undecided on moves to a single currency. This is seen, quite rightly, as a dilution of the D-Mark. German public opinion, constantly egged on by the Bundesbank, is against the single currency. It is inevitable that Germany favours a wider and more open Europe. The Soviet Union, after 1945, captured Eastern Europe as a cordon sanitaire against capitalism. Today, Germany must recapture Eastern Europe as a cordon sanitaire against the chaos which has accompanied the collapse of Soviet Communism. Helmut Kohl would have the greatest difficulty in pushing legislation through the Bundestag and Bundesrat taking Germany into a single European cur-

Table 19.1 Positions on Europe's Future

Issue	Do you favour?	Germany	France	Britain
Fortress Europe	European markets should be closed to unfair competition from cheap foreign imports	No	Yes	No
Harmonisation	Europe's tax, social security and regulatory systems should be harmonised?	Undecided	Yes	No
Single Currency	An early move to a single currency, even by a minority of member countries?	Undecided	Yes	No
Federal Europe	The reform of European institutions to give more power to the European Parliament and Commission?	Yes	No	No
Wider Europe	Admitting new member countries as soon and as many as possible?	Yes	No	Yes

rency, unless he could obtain the quid pro quo of agreement to a truly democratic federal Europe. Since this could not be part of any deal by which an inner core moved in advance of others to a single currency, such proposals must be suspect. (The CDU report on Europe's future, published by the party's Parliamentary leader, Wolfgang Schauble, a month before the German 1994 Bundestag elections, came down heavily in favour of a federal Europe but was spoilt by the proposal that a hard core of five members should go ahead on their own to monetary union.)

AT ODDS WITH DIRIGISTE FRANCE

Europe's development, from the 1957 Treaty of Rome to the 1992 Treaty of Maastricht has been founded on Franco-German co-operation. Yet a glance at Table 19.1 shows how little the two countries now have in common. On most issues they are on opposite sides. Even where they agree, German support is far from whole-hearted. The issue of free trade versus protection clearly divides the two countries. Edouard Balladur, as prime minister, expressed the French view with startling frankness in an interview with *The Financial Times* (31 December 1993):

> Can we [west Europeans] take it for granted that we will remain sufficient leaders in a sufficient number of sectors to survive – in face of countries with populations infinitely larger than ours and with levels of social protection infinitely lower? I say we should leave this to the market, but only up to a certain point. What is the market? It is the law of the jungle, the law of nature. And what is civilisation? It is the struggle against nature.

adding, according to that newspaper's interviewer:

> The European Union should use its new-found unity over trade to push for protection against unfair foreign competition which is based on lower wages, currency rates and environmental standards.

The same view was expressed more stridently in another *Financial Times* article (1 June 1993) by Claude Imbert, editor of the French magazine *Le Point*:

> I suggest we abandon the absolutism of free trade. This was the doctrine established in our most glorious period of economic growth, when the coolies of Asia were restricted to pulling rick-shaws. These times have passed: the coolies now sit at computer screens.

It is wrong to quote individual views and ascribe them to nations. But when the views are expressed by a leading and highly popular French politician, one must believe that they both reflect the stance of the establishment (Enarques) and strike a chord with public opinion at large.

The French position on harmonisation is equally explicit. France wants everyone to be forced to apply the same system as the French do. During Mitterrand's period as President of the European Council, for example, a determined effort was made to impose restrictions on European television to ensure at least half the programmes were made in Europe and a quarter of revenues were spent producing programmes in Europe. In a leader in *The Financial Times* (10 January 1995) the French attitude was summed up admirably:

> No French minister has seriously contended that EU broadcasting quotas are intended to increase the amount of British, German or Italian programmes shown on French television – or that that is what French viewers want. France's real interest is to shore up the elaborate regulatory edifice of programming quotas, subsidies and restrictions which it has created to protect its national film-making and television production industries. French broadcasters have long complained that they are placed at a competitive handicap by measures such as the requirement that they pay out as much as 25 per cent of their turnover to finance local production. The French Government's objective appears to be to 'level the playing field' by getting Brussels to impose similar burdens on the rest of the EU broadcasting industry.

Germany, together with Britain, opposed these French efforts.

The French Government and most French politicians are strongly in favour of the move to a single European currency and as soon as possible, even if only amongst an inner core of EU members. The majority of French people are probably opposed. The referendum on Maastricht was virtually a draw. While Phillippe de Villiers' anti-Maastricht movement won 12.4% of the French vote in the June 1994 European election, it was almost as big a share as the socialists. (In the first round of the French presidential election on 23 April 1995, however, de Villiers polled only 5%, while the Socialist, Lionel Jospin, won with 23%.) But despite their support for both a single currency and harmonisation, the French Government is strongly opposed to a federal Europe. It, least of all, wants democratic decision-making in Brussels. Finally, the French want to see relations between existing EU member countries deepened before the doors are flung wide to new members.

BRITAIN'S ATTITUDE IS AMBIVALENT

Britain is the most ardent supporter of free trade, a position largely shared by Germany. It also supports the expansion of the EU to include former Communist East European countries. On other matters a distinction must be drawn between the views of senior figures on both the Government and Opposition front benches, back-bench Members of Parliament and the general public. The overwhelming majority of front-bench MPs supported the pound's entry into the ERM in 1990 and many would like to see Britain part of any move towards a single European currency. Only a few right-wing Conservative ministers are opposed. (The Labour Party and Liberal Democrats also support the Maastricht Social Chapter.) In the present Parliament, a majority of MPs support Maastricht and following the next election – which Labour looks like winning – that majority could be increased. The establishment is equally opposed to a federal Europe. Given that this is the only significant issue on which the British and Germans differ, it is hard to see why Europe's development should continue to be founded on Franco-German co-operation.

The British public is firmly opposed to Maastricht and to Brussels. This is of no consequence as long as the electors are never given a say on Britain's future in Europe. Unless the Conservative Party becomes unambiguously anti-European before the next election, the British voter will again be denied a choice. In desperation, John Major, in an attempt to unite his party, has allowed the Cabinet's policy stance to drift towards the Eurosceptics' position. He has promised to veto any extension of majority voting at the 1996 IGC, and has stated that Britain could hold a referendum on the issue of a single currency. These moves, resisted by pro-European ministers, have made divisions in the Tory party more obvious. But the fact remains that leading British politicians are traditionally unswayed by public opinion. They are an interest group which seeks to retain power in its own hands, whether it be at the expense of the nation's elected representatives in Parliament, local government or the European institutions. The public opposes a federal Europe largely because it sees this as an extension of the powers of the hated European Commission in Brussels. Were it seen as it really should be — as an extension of democratic control over Brussels and a reduction in 'elective dictatorship' at home, perhaps views would change.

CHAPTER 20

The Task of the Fourth Reich

The European Union stands at a crossroads. It could disintegrate. If a small group moves ahead of the rest to monetary and economic union, it won't be long before the retreat begins from the single market. Thereafter, there will be little point in expanding the EU's membership and, in consequence, existing members, such as Britain, might question whether the costs of EU membership exceed the gains. It is implausible to suppose the EU can continue in a state of suspended animation. Too many members, such as France, will not settle for a Europe confined to a single market. The Union could move towards greater economic and monetary union à la Maastricht, while becoming the 'fortress Europe' which France wants. There will be considerable pressure from the jobs crisis to seek a solution along these lines. 'Fortress Europe' will not be created by a big decision taken at the next or some future IGC. Protectionism will come creeping in like the tide, restrictions spreading from one area of competition to another piecemeal. Finally the EU could develop into an open and democratic federation. (The author makes no secret of his belief that eliminating the 'democratic deficit' at the heart of the EU is a necessary prior condition for further progress towards political and economic union.)

Germany will decide Europe's fate. But first the Franco-German axis must fracture. For the past forty years, Franco-German co-operation has been based on personal relations between the leaders of each country, first between Konrad Adenauer and Charles de Gaulle, then between Helmut Schmidt and Valéry Giscard d'Estaing and finally between

Helmut Kohl and François Mitterrand. But with Mitterrand's departure this personal relationship is at an end. The passage from John Major's William and Mary Lecture in Leiden quoted in Chapter 18 is worth recalling. 'Franco-German co-operation' could well be substituted for 'the European Community'. It too was 'born to end divisions in Western Europe'. It has 'given us peace and prosperity in our part of the continent, and made war unthinkable'. But it is 'outdated. It will not do now.' It depended too much on German concessions to French demands. The time has come for Germany to grow up as a nation and stand against the disastrous course which the French want Europe to pursue.

THE COSTS OF 'FORTRESS EUROPE'

'Fortress Europe' would be an unmitigated disaster. It would impose on Europe the policies which the French prefer, but know will stifle their own economy within the single market if they continue to apply to them alone. Were French policies applied across Europe and cheap imports shut out, the costs would be concealed but remain none the less. The opening up of the world economy – the ease with which technology and capital can now be transferred from one country to another – has created irresistible forces for economic change. The world is now experiencing a process which economists call 'factor cost equalisation'. This means simply that, if workers are paid less in developing countries to do the same jobs as workers in developed countries and if what they produce can be freely exported to the developed countries, workers there will either have to accept lower real wages or be priced out of their jobs.

Europe has chosen higher unemployment (the US, lower real wages). Those out of work are unable to bid for it by offering to work for less than those in work. Protecting existing and identifiable old jobs, however, obstructs the creation of new jobs. Europe could close its frontiers to 'unfair foreign competition which is based on lower wages, currency rates and environmental standards' as Balladur suggests. It would thereby save old jobs at European real wage levels – but only at the expense of destroying new, higher value-added jobs and impoverishing Europe as a whole. When the real wages of European workers, doing jobs that 'coolies with computers' can do better and cheaper, are prevented from falling to lower levels, they are also sustained at unjustifiably high levels at home relative to the real wages of Europeans doing jobs that coolies cannot yet do (e.g. programming those computers). This levelling of real wages impedes the shift in employment to more productive jobs. It cannot prevent European real wages from falling. It merely shares the loss amongst everybody, unproductive and productive.

Unemployment, caused by cheap foreign competition, is either painful to those who become unemployed or, where welfare benefits are particularly generous, financially burdensome on the nation at large. Equally, a reduction in real wages to maintain old jobs, as in the US, causes hardship and the phenomenon of the working poor. It is natural that there is a hysterical reaction in Europe to the threat to jobs from foreign competition and growing support for protection. The hysteria will worsen. The temptation will be irresistible to some of Europe's politicians to channel this outcry in a move to strengthen the political and economic unity of the Union. Protectionism enhances the power of the state and spawns nationalism. People, threatened by change, feel the need for an enemy to blame for their predicament. Protectionists supply one: the coolies 'sitting at their computer screens'.

Deliberately to abandon Europe's generous welfare system would be wrong, in that the pain of change would be concentrated on those least able to afford it. Yet unless free traders come up with an alternative to the grim choice posed by factor cost equalisation, an increasingly impoverished society will be forced to abandon its generous welfare. The alternative is to create new jobs. A catalogue of micro-economic reforms is unnecessary at this point. The single market as it stands provides the biggest spur to such reforms in that governments will be forced into adopting the tax, social security and regulatory regimes which prove the most successful. Indeed the single market should be carried further into areas such as telecommunications, car distribution and aviation, where it has been delayed. Reform of the CAP represents an area in which distortions to prices and production impose an unnecessarily high cost on European consumers and taxpayers. Were savings on the CAP shifted to boost expenditure on education, the benefits would be even greater.

The goal of a single currency need not be abandoned. It would be the most important individual measure integrating the markets of Europe into a single mass market. It is no accident that productivity is higher in the US than elsewhere in the world; the US has the world's largest single market. The lesson to be learnt from Maastricht is not that the single currency *per se* was a bad idea, but that the method by which Europe was to progress to it was absurd.

Germany stands for much that is best for Europe's future. Its commitment to a social market is genuine, but so is its willingness to adapt, albeit slowly. It is the country which can thwart French plans for 'fortress Europe'. It cannot, however, lead Europe forward in the old way. It is not only the old visions of Europe that are outdated, but also the old methods of achieving them. Politicians in secret conclave, pursuing their own interests, cannot create a community which enjoys the mass support of its people. They can capture no imaginations; impart no visions. They can only display bickering self-interest as each endeavours to maximise national advantage from any new agreement. The 1996 IGC has all the makings of a disaster.

Without popular support for greater unity, no further progress will be made on Europe. While if the EU does not move forward, it is bound to sink back and fragment. A new initiative, transcending national politics is needed, appealing over the heads of politicians to the people of Europe.

TIME FOR A EUROPEAN CONSTITUTIONAL CONVENTION

The Germans in general, and Helmut Kohl in particular, must recognise that Europe's future and methods of operation need to be re-examined – but not by governments and ministers. There is a precedent for the creation of a successful, vibrant, democratic federal republic – the United States of America. It began life as a confederation of the thirteen original rebel colonies. In eighteenth-century parlance a 'state' was a sovereign country and as such the original colonies were bound together by Articles of Confederation agreed between them in 1781. Independence was won in 1783, but the confederation failed. By the winter of 1786–7 the Confederate States of America were in deep crisis. In desperation the Confederal Congress and the governments of all the states (with the exception of Rhode Island) agreed to establish a Constitutional Convention in Philadelphia. It comprised fifty-five delegates representing the states, most with a knowledge of political theory or public affairs, but also including men with business and other experience. The Constitution, when agreed by the Convention, was put for approval, not to the governments of the individual states, but to elected conventions. These conventions voted whether to ratify the Constitution and the federal United States of America came into existence when nine had done so.

The importance was less the result than the means by which it was achieved. The Constitution was not perfect and the American Civil War was one of the consequences of its defects; but it was produced by some of the best brains of the time through a process of discussion, debate and compromise. It had then to pass the test of public acceptability which, in its turn, produced intense public debate. The American Constitution emphatically was not the product of self-interested national politicians bargaining in secret enclaves. It was not foisted upon the people. Europe's founding fathers could not have followed this precedent in 1957. European national statehood was too deeply rooted. Governments had vastly more control over their nation's destinies than they do today. Memories of the war were too recent and vivid, the hatred it left behind too bitter. But over the coming years, with the possibility of Europe sliding deeper into economic crisis, the necessity becomes all the more urgent to learn afresh how nations can work together instead of against each other.

Helmut Kohl unified Germany. He could leave behind a still greater memory if he were to launch the drive which unified Europe. He will not achieve this by bargaining at the 1996 IGC. He will not achieve it by bowing to France or by turning to bully the French. The 'Europe of Nations' is in a cul-de-sac. It needs to back out. Kohl should call for a European Constitutional Convention. Its task would be to plan a democratic Europe and to determine (that is, limit) the powers of the European federal government within it. The European Convention, like its American forebear, would be one of delegates representing the people, not ministers representing governments. Its debates would be public and probably protracted. Its results, should it produce any, would be put to the people of Europe directly. It might fail to agree on the way forward. In which case further progress towards a deeper European Union is doomed. However unrealistic such a proposition may appear to politicians, it is no more unrealistic than to suppose they can make further progress. The 'Europe of Nations' will never, for example, agree to abolish the iniquitous CAP. One or more national governments will always block such a proposal. But delegates to a Convention could recommend abolition, and a majority of Europe people might support it. Above all, a European Constitutional Convention is a democratic way of deciding Europe's future. Inter-Governmental Conferences are not.

Germany's history under the Second and Third Reichs should have scarred the Germans for ever with the consequences of espousing national protectionism, rival economic nationalism and the centralisation of power in a unitary state. Germany must turn to advantage its gruesome past in order to save Europe from a gruesome future. The profound irony of Kohl's Fourth Reich is that it has the power to teach Europe a lesson in democracy. It has the ability to keep Europe open and free.

German Election Results 1919–94

Table A1 Weimar Election Results, 1919–32

	19 Jan 1919	6 Jun 1920	4 May 1924	7 Dec 1924	20 May 1928	14 Sep 1930	31 Jul 1932	6 Nov 1932
Electorate (m)	36.8	35.9	38.4	39	41.2	43	44.2	44.4
Turnout (%)	82.7	79.1	77.4	78.8	75.6	82	84	80.6
Votes %*								
Anti-Weimar								
Nazis	–	–	6.6	3	2.6	18.3	37.4	33.1
Nationalists	10.3	15.1	19.5	20.5	14.2	7	5.9	8.8
Communists	–	2.1	12.6	9	10.6	14.3	14.6	16.9
	10.3	17.2	38.7	32.5	27.4	39.6	57.9	58.8
Pro-Weimar								
Peoples' Party	4.4	14	9.2	10.1	8.7	4.5	1.2	1.9
Centre	19.7	17.9	15.6	17.3	15.1	14.8	15.9	15.0
Democrats	18.6	8.3	5.7	6.3	3.8	3.6	1	1
Socialists	37.9	21.6	20.5	26	29.8	24.5	21.6	20.4
Ind. Socialists	7.8	17.9	0.8	–	–	–	–	–
	88.4	79.7	51.8	59.7	57.4	47.4	39.7	38.3

Seats*

Anti-Weimar

Nazis	–	–	32	14	12	107	230	196
Nationalists	44	71	95	103	73	41	37	52
Communists		4	62	45	54	77	89	100
	44	75	189	162	139	225	356	348

Pro-Weimar

Peoples' Party	19	65	45	51	45	30	7	11
Centre	91	85	81	88	78	87	98	90
Democrats	75	39	28	32	25	20	4	2
Socialists	165	102	100	131	153	143	133	121
Ind. Socialists	22	84	0	–	–	–	–	–
	372	375	254	302	301	280	242	224

Total seats	*421*	*459*	*472*	*493*	*491*	*577*	*608*	*584*
No. for a majority	211	230	237	237	246	289	305	293
Pro-Weimar *less* Antis	328	300	65	140	162	55	–114	–124

* Excludes independents and smaller parties.

Table A2 Federal Republic Election Results, 1949–94

Date	Total seats	CDU	CSU	SPD	FDP	Main parties	Minor parties		
							No.	Seats	% seats
14 Aug 49	402	115	24	131	52	322	8	80	20
6 Sep 53	487	191	52	151	48	442	3	45	9
15 Sep 57	497	215	55	169	41	480	1	17	3
17 Sep 61	499	192	50	190	67	499	0	0	0
19 Sep 65	496	196	49	202	49	496	0	0	0
28 Sep 69	496	193	49	224	30	496	0	0	0
19 Nov 72	496	177	48	230	41	496	0	0	0

Table A2 Federal Republic Election Results, 1949–94–*continued*

Date	Total seats	CDU	CSU	SPD	FDP	Main parties	Minor parties No.	Seats	% seats
3 Oct 76	496	190	53	214	39	496	0	0	0
5 Oct 80	497	174	52	218	53	497	0	0	0
6 Mar 83	498	191	53	193	34	471	1	27	5
25 Jan 87	497	174	49	186	46	455	1	42	8
Post-unification: 2 Dec 90									
Old Länder	507	195	51	200	60	506	1	1	0
New Länder	127	61	0	30	16	107	2	20	16
Berlin	28	12	0	9	3	24	2	4	14
Total	662	268	51	239	79	637	2	25	4
16 Oct 94	672	244	50	252	47	593	2	79	12

The Costs of Unification
(as seen at the time)

The following assessment by the author of the situation on the eve of unification was published in the Business Section of *The Sunday Times* (29 April 1990).

'To bring East German living standards up to West German levels requires a huge investment and a dramatic rise in East German productivity, which is about one-third of West Germany's. East Germany's houses, roads, railways, phones, factories, power stations, machines and equipment, and its stocks of consumer durables such as cars and washing machines, are insufficient, inefficient, aged, dangerous and dirty. The West German net capital stock, excluding consumer durables, amounts to around DM 160,000 a head. To re-equip the 17 m East Germans to the same level would cost DM 2,700 billion, or more than one year's West German GNP. Not all their industry was worthless (*sic*), though, so the cost will be less, and it will be spread over many years. But it still must be large. Halved, and spread over a decade, it equals 6% a year of West German GNP.

'German economic and monetary union poses a problem of gaps. The gap in output and productivity can be closed only slowly. But the gap in living standards must be closed quickly if mass migration is to be stopped. Then, however, a third gap will be created, between East German output and income, which must be filled by West Germany money (*see chart*). The terms for monetary union determine the size of the second and third gaps. If too mean, migration will continue. If generous enough to stop migration, the cost to the west may be excessive. The Bonn government has proposed that, for most purposes, one Ostmark be exchanged for one D-mark. Savings above OM 4,000 a head will, however, be converted at a rate of two for one, as will state-owned companies' debts to the state-owned banks. According to Karl Otto Pöhl, president of the politically-independent Bundesbank, this is "a generous offer which reaches the limit of what is still just tenable from an economic point of view". Against this, the East German premier, Lothar de Maizière, reckons that 500,000 East Germans would have headed west in the next six months if the deal had been any less generous.

Closing the Gap

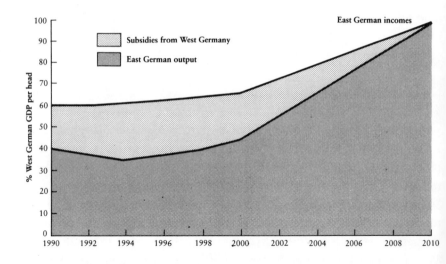

'If East Germany were a closed economy, the conversion of Ostmarks to D-Marks would have made no difference to anything. East German income would continue to equal East German output. The problem arises because goods and services can be freely bought and sold between east and west. The pattern of prices on each side is very different. Food, clothes, electricity and rents are exceedingly cheap in East Germany; manufactured goods are very dear (*see table*). Following economic and monetary union, these differences must largely disappear.

'At one Ostmark for one D-Mark, East German wages will be 60% of West German ones. East German pensions are to be raised to 70% of

The East/West Price Gap

	East Germany OM	West Germany DM	Implied exchange rate OM per DM 1
Tram ticket, one way	0.20	2.07	0.10
Rye bread, 1 kg	0.52	3.17	0.16
Potatoes, 5 kg	0.85	4.94	0.17
Monthly rent, 2-roomed flat	75	411	0.18
Electricity, 1 kWh	0.08	0.42	0.19
Pair of toddler's shoes	18.50	60.60	0.31
Beef, 1 kg	9.80	17.19	0.57
Washing machine	2300	981	2.34
Refrigerator	1425	559	2.55
Colour TV	4900	1,539	3.18
Coffee, 1 kg	70	17.86	3.92

East German wages. Wages are to remain unchanged, although East German subsidies, which make food, clothing, energy and rents cheap, are to be withdrawn. While this will make East Germans worse off, cheap manufactured goods from the west will compensate them. The West Germans reckon the gap in living standards will be sufficiently narrow to reduce migration substantially.

'The problem is East German industry. With wages at 60% of the West German level and productivity 30%, it cannot compete. If it keeps its prices at pre-unification levels, it won't sell much and will go bust, causing heavy unemployment. If it lowers prices to West German levels, it will incur losses on everything it makes – and will also go bust. So the West Germans must subsidise either unprofitable East German industries or unemployed East German workers. Industry produces three-quarters of East German GNP. Industrial output is some OM 260 billion, but worth only DM 100 billion at West German prices. It would thus cost around DM 160 billion to bail out all East German manufacturers. Unemployment benefit is OM 9,000 a year in East Germany. It would therefore cost DM 32 billion to support all its 3.6 m industrial workers on the dole. But as their incomes would then fall to a quarter of the West German level this would not work. Raising benefits to 100% of East German wages, roughly equal to West German benefits, would cost DM 80 billion. These numbers are upper and lower limits – not all East German industry is equally inefficient. But they show that the cost of bridging the East German income–output gap is between DM 80 billion and DM 160 billion. In addition to subsidies, the Bonn government must finance the rebuilding of East German infrastructure. Industry can be rebuilt by the private sector, but unless productivity is improved rapidly, this will be a slow process. So the income–output gap could remain large for a long time.

'The real resources for economic and monetary union must come initially from higher West German output and lower domestic spending on other things, or from abroad through a lower balance-of-payments surplus. Growth could be pushed 1% higher in the short term, worth DM 23 billion. There are at present no plans to raise West German taxes, although Pöhl said this cannot be ruled out. If they are, any cut in domestic spending must come from inflation or dearer credit. The Bundesbank will opt for the latter. But the main impact will be on the D-Mark and on foreigners. The DM 100 billion current account surplus could become a deficit by the end of next year [1991].'

Britain's ERM Entry
(as seen at the time)

The following article by the author was published in *The Sunday Times* on 14 October 1990 following sterling's entry into the European Exchange Rate Mechanism. It shows that one did not have to be a genius to see that the result of pegging the pound to the D-Mark immediately after German unification was bound to be disastrous.

'Wrong time, wrong rate, wrong reason
It's done. We're in. But Margaret Thatcher may rue the day she withdrew her veto on the Exchange Rate Mechanism. John Major has pegged sterling to the D-Mark at the wrong time, at the wrong rate and for the wrong reasons.

'We joined on 8 October to shield sterling from downward pressure when increasing evidence of recession indicated interest rates had to be cut to avoid deflationary overkill. But Major has pegged at a manifestly overvalued rate, repeating Winston Churchill's 1925 mistake when he put the pound back on to gold. An economy on the brink of recession, simultaneously running a current-account deficit of more than 3% of gross domestic produce, either cannot sell what it can make because its prices are too high, or cannot make what it could sell because there are no profits from investing in capacity. Were this not so, any decline in domestic demand would be offset by rising exports and import substitution. Unfortunately, while this shows Britain is uncompetitive at sterling's current exchange rate, it does not follow that it could be made competitive by a move to a lower one.

'The rigidity of British real wages in response to any price rises means that the advantage initially gained from a lower pound is eroded by additional inflation. However, if real wages are so inflexible that no competitive gain can be made, any policy designed to bring down inflation by putting up prices must also fail. The government cannot both claim higher interest rates, increased local taxes or public-service charges, which raise the cost of living, nonetheless cut inflation, and at the same time reject a lower pound on the ground that it will not work. Both work, but not as well as we would like.

'But Major's greatest mistake was his timing. Britain has boarded the D-Mark bus without finding out where it is going. Conditions in Germany today closely resemble those in America in the early 1980s, during President Reagan's supply-side tax cuts. The cost of bailing out East Germany should rise to about DM 150 billion (£50 billion) next year, equal to 6% of the combined German gross national product. Part of this will be met, after the general election on 2 December, by higher taxes and cuts in public spending. Even so, German budgetary policy has become exceptionally inflationary. The independent Bundesbank, will, of course, prevent this massive fiscal stimulus from feeding into higher prices. It will keep German monetary policy hugely restrictive.

'The combination of dear money and easy budgets drove the dollar sky-high between 1982 and 1985. The D-Mark is similarly set to soar, particularly as growing recession in America puts downward pressure on American interest rates. That is why the dollar daily hits new lows against the D-Mark. All other ERM members will suffer. None can match German budgetary profligacy. France, Spain, Italy, Belgium and the Netherlands are struggling to cut budget deficits. All must apply deflationary fiscal policies. Yet to avoid devaluation against the D-Mark, east must also match Germany's austere monetary policy. Already growth in continental Europe has slowed. Unemployment, still 9% in France, 10% in Italy and 16% in Spain, is set to rise again.

'The ERM proved a fine fair-weather system in the 1980s. Inflation and growth rates converged because unemployment rates diverged. But enduring continued high unemployment while German unemployment falls is one thing. Suffering rising unemployment as German unemployment climbs is another. So the ERM now faces the test of foul weather during a recession. The betting is not on whether someone will devalue against the D-Mark but on who will be first and when. Overvalued sterling is in the running. Half our trade is outside Europe. For every 1% by which the D-Mark drags the pound up against non-ERM currencies, sterling's effective exchange rates climbs 0.5%.

'Dealing with a current account deficit with an over-valued currency is bad enough. Dealing with one at an increasing competitive disadvantage is awful. Like all other European countries that have taken a ride on the D-Mark bus, Britain will have to pursue more deflationary policies than necessary. This may have been Major's aim. Inflation will not come down unless unemployment goes up. A period of very slow growth, or outright recession, was inevitable. By joining the ERM, he has forced the Government to accept this. By spring the issue will not be how far and how fast British interest rates can safely fall, but whether sterling can avoid devaluation without interest rates rising.

'Economically, this might not be so inconvenient. The Treasury is clearly losing its battle to limit public spending in 1991 to £192 billion. The total looks set to exceed £200 billion. There is no way this excess spending can be financed out of higher taxes in a tough election-year budget. The golden scenario of ERM entry was billed to deliver a pre-election "boomlet". Unless sterling is devalued, it is more likely to produce a "slumplet". But for a government that has nailed the pound to a D-Mark cross as proof of its determination to defeat inflation, yet has found no way of doing so other than by increasing unemployment, this should come as no surprise.'

How the European Union Works

First, consider its name. Originally it was called the European Economic Community or EEC, but often simply referred to as the Common Market. The Single Market agreement in 1986 changed the name to the European Community, or EC, to signify its broader scope. Finally, under the Maastricht Treaty the name was changed again to the European Union, or EU.

There are four main European institutions: the Council, the Commission, the Parliament and the Court of Justice. A fifth body, the unelected Economic & Social Committee, formally represents interest groups (the European equivalent of Britain's old 'Neddy' or National Economic Development Council). It has to be consulted and issues opinions and reports, but has virtually no importance or influence.

The European Council is composed of the heads of government of member countries, foreign ministers and two Commission representatives. It is the EU's most powerful institution, but it is not all-powerful. It cannot initiate legislation. The presidency of the European Council is held in turn by national heads of government for periods of six months each. The German Chancellor, Helmut Kohl, was president in the second half of 1994 and the French President took over on 1 January 1995. The President's task is to set the agenda and to broker agreements bilaterally. The Council generally meets twice a year in the capital city of its president. About every five years there are major conferences to determine the way the EU should evolve. The 1985 intergovernmental conference, IGC as it is called, agreed the terms for the Single Market and the 1991 IGC agreed the Maastricht Treaty. The next IGC, due in 1996, will decide whether the EU, or some of its members, will move swiftly to monetary union and a single currency. It will also have to tackle the problems of enlargement.

Beneath the European Council is the Council of Ministers, which brings together departmental ministers, such as for agriculture, trade, foreign affairs etc., according to the issue under consideration. The Council of Ministers covers all aspects of European affairs. It is chaired by the relevant minister from the country holding the presidency. The most important group is called ECOFIN, being composed of economics and finance ministers from member countries. Poor Norman Lamont was ECOFIN chairman in September 1992 when sterling was booted out of the ERM. Like the European Council, the Council of Ministers can only respond to initiatives from the European Commission.

The European Commission is the executive branch of the EU and consists of a president (currently Jacques Santer, who replaced Jacques Delors in January 1995) and twenty commissioners appointed by national governments. The President is chosen by the European Council and requires unanimous support. In 1994 Kohl and Mitterrand tried to railroad other countries into appointing the Belgian Prime Minister, Jean-Luc Dehaene, to succeed Delors, by announcing their support for him in advance. But Britain's John Major vetoed his appointment. An emergency meeting had to be called. It took place in Brussels in July and agreed upon Santer, the former Luxemburg premier. The Commission is the guardian of the EU's treaties and has the power to act against governments who break the rules. It alone proposes new European laws, and it administers existing ones. It is responsible for the single market, the common agricultural policy, trade and competition policies, and it handles the EU budget which hands out cash for regional and social development projects, R&D and overseas aid. But two-thirds of Europe's budgetary expenditure is on agricultural subsidies under the CAP.

European laws originate as proposals by the Commission. They go to the Council of Ministers for consideration. The Council passes European laws either by weighted majority voting or unanimously (the method depends on their subject). Within defined limits, where responsibility has been transferred to Brussels, European laws become the national law of member countries, being superior to and overriding any existing national laws. Council meetings are secret and so is voting. British newspapers have been putting pressure on Brussels to open up, but with limited success. In 1994 the British Government was forced to reveal that of 233 Single Market decisions taken by the Council since 1988, 142 were unanimous and 91 by weighted or qualified majority over the opposition of one or more countries. It has proved impossible to find out which decisions were made by majority voting or who was on which side. Thus laws affecting all Europeans are made in secret in a manner which befits a dictatorship rather than mature democracies. But national politicians, jealous of their power, like it that way.

The European Parliament was originally a talking shop made up of 78 part-timers seconded from national parliaments, but since 1979 has been directly elected every five years. The most recent elections were held in June 1994 to a 567-seat house. The Parliament's powers were strengthened by both the 1986 Single Europe Act and the Maastricht Treaty. Originally the Assembly, as it was called until 1986, had no power except to sack the entire Commission by a vote of censure passed by a two-thirds majority. Now it can veto the passage of the European budget. It can also veto laws passed by the Council of Ministers. Its veto can only be overthrown by a unanimous vote. This veto was first used on 1 March 1995 when a directive covering patenting of genetically altered organisms was rejected. The Parliament approves the appointment of the President of the European Commission (which it reluctantly did for Jacques Santer) and can veto membership application. In 1994 it agreed to let Austria, Finland, Norway and Sweden join the EU. All four made membership conditional on approval by national referenda. Austria, Finland and Sweden voted to join and did so on 1 January 1995. In Norway the vote was lost (as it was in the early 1970s when Britain joined).

Votes are allocated to countries according to their size. Before the recent enlargement, Germany, France, Italy and Britain had 10 votes each; Spain had 8; Greece, Belgium, the Netherlands and Portugal had 5 each; Denmark and Ireland had 3 and Luxemburg 2. That made a total of 76. A veto required 23 votes, meaning two large countries plus one small one. When the EU was enlarged on 1 January 1995, Austria and Sweden got 4 votes and Finland 3 votes each. The number needed for a blocking vote rose to 27 out of 87. European law stipulates which issues require unanimity and which can be passed by a qualified majority vote.

The European Court of Justice sits in Luxemburg and is not to be confused with the European Court of Human Rights in Strasburg. It is composed of 17 judges appointed for six years by each member country. It is the guardian of the Rome Treaty and the highest court in the EU. The Commission, the European Parliament, Governments and individuals can appeal to the Court where Europe's laws appear to be being flouted or require clarification. The Court has been deeply involved on issues concerning pension rights, affecting companies throughout Europe. It recently decided that, since 1976, under European law part-time employees had had the same membership rights in occupational schemes as full-time employees. Many companies, who are under no obligation to offer occupational pension schemes to their employees, had not included part-timers. As a result of the Court's decision, they can now make back-dated claims to be included. Where schemes were non-contributory, the cost will be born entirely by the company. Where schemes are contributory, the claimant will have to pay up his or her back-dated contributions to acquire pension rights. The cost in money and time in unravelling all back claims could be horrendous.

Index